The Life
CHEVALIER JACKSON

AN AUTOBIOGRAPHY

New York
THE MACMILLAN COMPANY
1938

Set up and printed. Published May, 1938.
Reprinted June, 1938.

SET UP BY BROWN BROTHERS LINOTYPERS
PRINTED IN THE UNITED STATES OF AMERICA
BY THE FERRIS PRINTING COMPANY

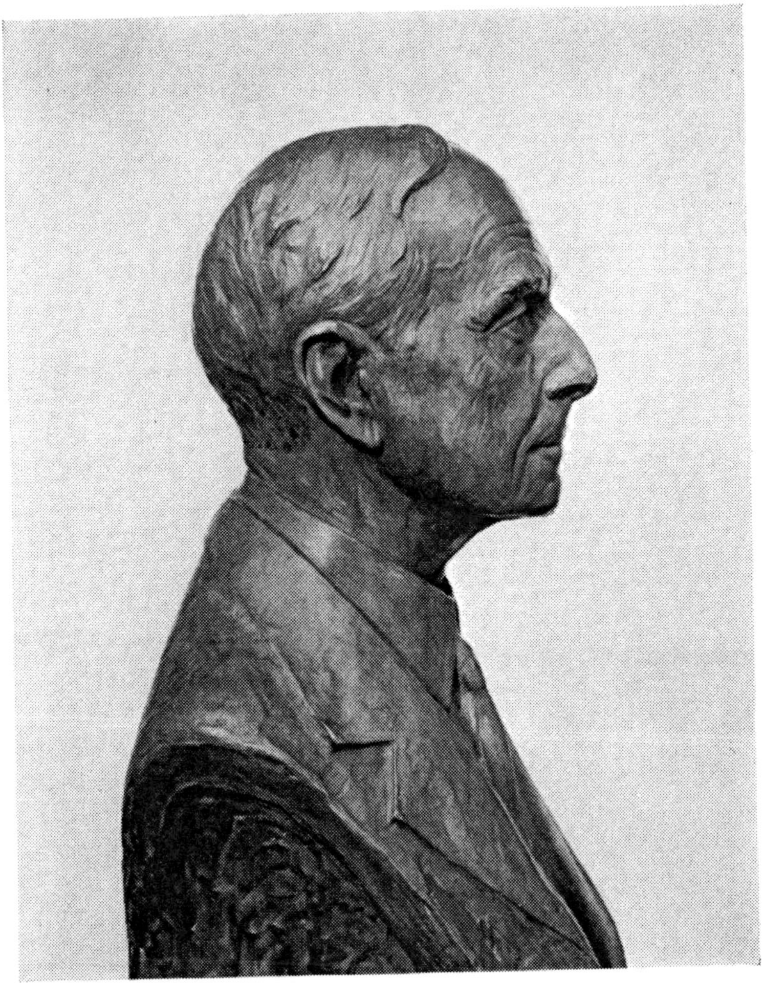

Bust by Luigi Maraffi, presented to Chevalier Jackson by a group of his pupils and colleagues, in 1937.

TO

MY WIFE

AND

SISTER JO

PREFACE

THAT ANYONE might be interested in the events of my life did not occur to me until there came from high-school students, editors, endless numbers of newspaper writers and other sources requests for biographical data. Then came inquiries from book writers and, finally, book publishers. The advent of the last two groups seemed to indicate the possibility of readers, and the task was undertaken. The author disavows any thought of presenting an example to be followed.

Chevalier Jackson

CONTENTS

CONTENTS

The Life of
CHEVALIER JACKSON

CHAPTER I

A CHILD IS BORN

(1865)

"LITTLE RUNT, ISN'T HE?" teasingly said his livestock-raising, Lancaster County father.

"Well, he's well baked, anyhow—look at his finger nails," indignantly retorted his bread-making, Knickerbocker grandmother, as she went to the scales.

"There, now, just a shade under eight pounds. Umph, runt! He's perfect. And he's punctual; not a day early or a day late."

This little episode occurred on a dark, dreary November day in 1865, the year that ended the Civil War, in the then black, gloomy, dirty city of Pittsburgh. The place was a conventional three-story brick building on Fourth Avenue where the classic columns and pediment of the Union Trust Company now symbolize financial solidity.

The outstanding feature of his babyhood was activity. His father said, "He squirms like a maggot." His French grandfather's comment was, "Il ne se repose jamais." In later life his restfully disposed brother said, "Chev will neither rest nor let anybody else rest." After many years, a book reviewer in the *British Medical Journal* referred to the seventy-one-year-old author as "the indefatigable Chevalier Jackson." His mother said that, as a baby, he wakened at four in the morning and commenced to crow and play and was then ready to begin the day. This habit of early waking and morning activity persisted throughout life. When he reached walking age his mother would dress him when he wakened and send him downstairs where Bridget would give him his simple breakfast of bread, rich milk and brown sugar.

But he did not burn the candle at both ends. He would fall asleep at the five o'clock supper table or soon after leaving it. Paternal care guarded his mounting the stairway to bed lest he fall asleep on the way. More than once he toppled over backward into his father's ready hands. When five years of age he was one of Queen Elizabeth's pages at a masked ball. After the grand entrée Good Queen Bess buckled up her long train and went on with the dance. The forgotten page stood up against the wall and very promptly slid down in a heap as he went to sleep.

Most of the foregoing is secondhand information gleaned in later years from family sources.

From early childhood I always had daily duties. I was allotted certain chores for which I alone was responsible: in winter to carry wood and coal for a certain room. Before I was physically able to do this I had certain vases to be kept filled with twisted paper lighters. The latter was good training for nimbleness of fingers.

CHAPTER II

BOYHOOD

(1870–1879)

MANY PHASES of my boyhood days seem very different from those of the average boy, and it seems certain that most of these phases had important bearings on after life. The phases referred to extended over a number of years, and the various yearly groups overlapped in such a way that any attempt at sequential chronology would be confusing, inadequate, space-wasting, and at best inevitably inaccurate. These phases will be considered under a topical arrangement, and the overlapping chronologic periods will be indicated as accurately as may be possible.

As a boy I had no intimate friends and few companions. I seemed always so filled with incentive to do some particular thing that I had no time for mere play; dancing, tennis, baseball and football had no more attraction in my later youth than "hide and seek" and "pussy-wants-a-corner" had in my childhood. I seemed unsociable because these things did not interest me enough to overcome an innate urge to make things, to create something, ornamental or useful or both. I began working with wood and sharp tools at four years of age. Thereafter I was never without a workshop; later it was called a laboratory, but it was always a place for constructive work.

A standing joke at our home was a regular page in the *American Agriculturist* devoted to the subject of "The Long Winter Evenings." The climax came when the title was changed to "The Interminable Winter Evenings." In those days the average family library consisted of two volumes, the Old and the New Testament. A page or so from each was read, with benefit; but there remained much time that hung heavily. No motion pictures, no radio, no daily papers in rural communities, no daily-mail showers of gratuitous printed matter. Magazines were few, rarely more than the farmers' monthly just mentioned. In our family it was different. Father was deeply absorbed in his books by Darwin, Tyndall, Huxley, and other scientists; Mother was busy with her books on housekeeping and medical science; the three brothers were occupied with first their lessons, then their books on science for the young by Jacob Abbott, drawing, writing of letters. The time passed so quickly that nine o'clock, the hour to get ready for bed, arrived lamentably soon. My evening was usually spent in drawing, sketching or designing something to be made in the shop the next afternoon. Information on the best wood for the purpose was always obtainable from Father, who knew all the woods in general use. Sorrento and inlaid work called for copying of designs from layouts. The winter evenings were entirely too short. As Christmas time approached they became utterly inadequate and had to be lengthened to nine-thirty. There were brackets, clock cases, wall pockets, bread boards, picture frames, and no end of similar things to be cut out of thin wood with the jig-saw or to be turned out of heavier wood on the lathe, for sale. I acquired quite a reputation for making unsplittable gumwood peg tops with tool-steel points from discarded, temper-drawn saw files; I had plenty of orders at six cents each as the gift season approached. To call winter evenings long was obviously absurd. Social affairs did not enter the program. This was not because we were unsociable; but social affairs would have interfered with the things we wanted to do. The family had endless resources for self-entertainment because every member of it was interested in numerous things. I often said I should like a job as lighthouse tender where the supply boat came only once every three months; I thought that possibly thus I might have enough uninterrupted time to get something done. This attitude seems to have persisted throughout my life. From the cradle to threescore and ten I have been a slave to an innate and insatiable urge to make things,

AT THREE YEARS OF AGE 1868

(Frame turned out of dogwood in later boyhood)

HOME OF
FLORENCE
NIGHTINGALE

From an old print that hung over my crib. It is associated with my earliest recollections of Mother's stories of angels.

Circa 1863

to achieve; though never for the mere glory; the achievement itself was the objective and the source of temporary satisfaction. The satisfaction was ephemeral because each achievement was quickly followed by another slave-driving urge to finish another task.

The advent of the high-wheel bicycle naturally created a boyish longing. The parental budgetary limits did not warrant the relatively enormous expenditure, so for four years the wish was unsatisfied. Finally manufacturing production reached the point where the *American Agriculturist* could offer a bicycle for a hundred annual subscriptions. Soliciting was commenced at once; Allegheny and Washington counties were scoured to find one hundred farmers willing to part with a dollar and a half for a journal. Many scorned "book-farmin'." After a year's weary effort the entire field was worked over and only fifty-one subscribers were obtainable. The names and money had been turned in as received and the subscribers were getting their respective copies of the magazine. The matter of the completely exhausted territory was explained by letter to Orange Judd the publisher, and he offered to supply a cheaper bicycle to compensate for the fifty-one subscriptions. When the bicycle came it was found to have wooden wheels and no ball bearings. It was heavy; driving it on the level was hard work for a frail boy like me, and climbing the slightest grade was impossible. Lacking all the mechanical features that diminish resistance to propulsion, it was a bitter disappointment. But two months later winter weather ended bicycling, and a light sled was built in the little home workshop. It required less effort mounting hills and was speedier and safer descending. The latter philosophic conclusion was confirmed when the bicycle was finally stolen and the thief's leg was broken in a tyro's collision.

In my memory the tearfulness of my childhood and boyhood hangs like a pall over everything. All of my contacts with life seemed to have one or more tearful phases. Looking backward, now, from the impartial, analytic viewpoint of later life, I do not see that I had more than my share of the usually recognized causes for sorrow; but some of the tears were justified, and all the troubles were very real to me then. For one thing, I was woefully out of harmony with my surroundings in the farming and coal-mining community in which a large part of my boyhood was spent. One of the most frequent causes of grief arose from an unusual degree of hypersensitiveness to the suffering of human beings or animals. Other boys could look on, enjoy looking on, and seek opportunities to look on, at bloody cockfights, dog fights, boy fights, man fights, and all similar contests. I always ran away crying and hid until it was over, in case such things came my way unexpectedly; I never sought them.

Among the coal miners cockfighting was a regular summer evening and winter Sunday amusement in which the boys as well as men participated. The hand-digging of bituminous coal required sharply pointed and properly tempered, tool-steel picks. The skilled toolmakers required for this were constantly behindhand in filling their numerous orders for cockspurs. These were needle-sharp, slender-pointed deadly weapons fastened on over the natural spur on the inside of the cock's legs near the feet. The only protest against their use was that they made the cockfights too brief; a longer but none the less fatal battle was claimed by some to yield a greater sum total of sport! A pair of cockspurs and a supply of whisky were necessities to the coal miner whether his children had food or not. I never saw a cockfight, and my refusal of invitations degraded me in the estimation of the coal miners' boys. "Chicken-hearted crybaby" is what they called me. There was no doubt about the crying, but I could not understand the term "chicken-hearted," meaning cowardice, inasmuch as the battling was being done by what we in the United States call chickens. Domestic fowls have anatomically small hearts but the opprobrious term referred to behavior. In addition to the arranged cockfights there were many impromptu battles.

Just as the bloodthirsty modern dictator maintains his supremacy by murdering all potential rivals, just so the barnyard male bird kills or tries to kill possible competitors. As nearly everyone had some sort of flock of poultry, such impromptu battles were numerous. All the near-by boys would rush to form part of the circle of spectators surrounding the battling birds. I would always run away. On one well remembered occasion I started in to chase the belligerents and break up the fight, but before reaching them I was seized by the collar, shaken, kicked, and flung onto the manure heap with the admonition: "Spoil a bit o' sport, will ye? Now git out o' hyur, ye crybaby, ur I'll break every bone in yer damn' lil body."

And so it was with dog fights. They were of two classes: the regularly scheduled bull-terrier fights arranged on a challenge basis, and those by accidental encounter. The bull terriers were bred by the miners from stock originally brought by them or their parents from England, Wales, Scotland, or Ireland. The impromptu fights were usually between dogs of mixed lineage, of which it was said, "Them ain't no fightin' dogs, nohow." Although mongrels were sneered at as unworthy of challenge, the chance-encounter fights always drew an interested crowd the size of which depended on the number of men and boys near by. Woe to the owner who dared spoil the sport (!) by attempting to stop the fight to save his pet dog. Possibly the combating dogs would not bite him, but the onlookers would beat him into unconsciousness if necessary to stop his intermeddling. Galling jeers pursued the owner if his dog was of non-combative type and ran away. This was a life-saving measure. The bull terriers always fought to the death. I never saw a dog fight because I always ran away as fast as tear-filled eyes would let me. I once saw a miner, obviously after a fight was over and the crowd dispersed, drag out and bury a dead and horribly mutilated bull terrier with the comment: "That's the bes' t'ing kin hap'n ter a dawg what can't noways hol' his own. Betters thur breed."

Among my recollections of dogs are those of childish play with

"Billy," a white bull terrier that as a puppy had been given to me by the widow of miner. Notwithstanding the combative instinct he doubtless inherited, and no matter how rough the play became, he was always gentle with me. One day he was missing. The next day when Father came home he lifted out of his buggy Billie's limp, tooth-marked, blood-streaked, dead body. Evidently a miner had stolen him for a fight, then turned him loose. Father had found him on the roadside, dying, headed toward home.

It was much the same with boys fighting. The rule of action among the miners and pit boys was: "Hands off. Let 'em fight it out thursel's." Boys and men formed a circle, enjoyed the fight, and encouraged the belligerents. "That wuz a good un," "Hit 'im ag'in," "Give him one in da jaw" are memories of shouts heard on different occasions as I ran away terrified, to get beyond seeing and hearing distance. Only once did I fail to run away. On an errand for Mother one day I came upon two boys younger than myself, streaked with blood from the nose of one, both covered with the mud in which they were rolling over and over. With tears in my eyes I begged them to stop. To my amazement they both pounced upon me, bore me down to the ground, and rubbed my nose, ears, and eyes full of mud; then left with the sneering comment, "Now yuh got somethin' to cry about." As in the impromptu cockfight I learned the well-known fact that the way of the peacemaker is parallel to that of the transgressor.

Prize fighting ranked high among the coal miners; as is natural, considering they were of British birth or descent. No fatherly pride could exceed that of the miner whose son developed prowess in fisticuffs. Regularly scheduled fights were great events; relative merits of contestants were discussed often so intensively as to give rise to quarrels and even unscheduled fights. If money or valuables were unavailable for wager, agreement for the loser to undergo public torture, such as walking a mile on hands and knees, was substituted. The torture was always hugely enjoyed by a hilarious crowd. Both the prize fight and the torture were horrors that I could avoid. Fights resulting from banter, quarrels, and drinking were almost daily occurrences. The combatants were always surrounded by an interested crowd that brooked no peacemaking interference. There were no policemen; if there had been, they would not have interfered. When a quarrel started or when anything indicated an approaching fight, I always burst into tears and made my escape to a place out of sight and hearing. Other boys struggled to get to the front where they could see the fight, and were disappointed if it did not develop bloody proportions. I could not understand why an inferiority rating should be assigned to the boy who had not seen giant Davy Welsh end a fight by breaking the arm (collar bone) of his adversary. To this day the huge audiences attending prize fights are a mystery to me. I am utterly unable to understand how thousands and thousands of people of intelligence and, in other ways, of humane sympathies can voluntarily look on a prize fight. To fight is atavistic, but to enjoy looking on at a fight is not. Man is the only animal known to manifest pleasure in a fight between two of his kind. In this he is more brutal than all brute creation.

But the greatest of all causes of sorrow of my tearful boyhood was cruelty to horses. My sufferings were so great and so frequent I would deem them almost morbid were it not for the fact that the reality of the cruelty was corroborated by my father, who had a diploma in veterinary medicine and had spent much of his life raising and working with horses. Moreover he had at every opportunity interceded to stop the cruelty.

I never had a horse of my very own until it became necessary as a means of getting about as a physician. In boyhood it never occurred to me that I was in any way entitled to a horse of my own. Horses were required for work in connection with the summer hotel and its two especially attractive features, the fresh vegetable garden and the small herd of milch cows. Additionally, a saddle horse and one for light driving were required to accommodate the patrons. Some patrons had horses of their own, and a few of these were boarded over winter. Out of season it was part of my duties to give these animals exercise, and I became perfectly at home in the saddle. I discovered horses could be taught.

Our home was on the edge of one of the bituminous coal districts a few miles west of Pittsburgh. Coal was mined by hand, hauled to the loading platforms by small pit mules. Thence it was hauled by four-horse teams drawing huge two-ton wagons to the fringe of iron mills whose flame-belching stacks gave to Pittsburgh the nickname of "Hell with the lid off." Those four-horse teams filled me with admiration when they came fresh from the stock farm; they were a pitiful sight a year or two later when wrecked by the cruelties inflicted upon them. The horses were taught nothing, except the near-side leader of the four-horse team. Perhaps it should be explained that the front pair of horses were called leaders, the rear pair wheel-horses. "Near side" meant left side. The near-side leader was the one reined; his rein was a single line bridled so as to pull equally on both sides of his mouth at once. He was taught not to stop but to go to the left when there was a long steady pull on the line; to go to the right when there was a succession of jerks. The crude shouts of "Gee!" and "Haw!" usually but not necessarily accompanied the signals on the single rein. A jockey stick (which was usually an iron bar running from the near-side leader's collar to the off-side leader's bit) pushed or pulled the off-side leader whichever way the near-sider went. The wheel horses followed the lead of the leaders. The near-side leader stopped at the word "Whoa," and the other three horses soon learned to stop also. Thus with the aid of a single line, the four-horse team was guided by the teamster who rode in a huge black saddle on the near-side wheel horse, the single line in his left hand, the whip in his right.

It was one of the proudest days of my life when, as a boy of ten years, I was allowed to sit in the saddle and steer those four powerful but gentle animals on the homeward journey with the lumbering, empty coal wagon. The teamster lay on the wagon floor in a drunken stupor.

I remember thinking then what a remarkable thing it was that the leader should know the difference between right and left, and I have never ceased to wonder at and admire him for his possession of this faculty. Few other animals have it at all, and none to the same degree.

All of the foregoing refers to the pleasurable phases of my fondness for horses. The sum total of all pleasure was more than counterbalanced by the daily observation of the then prevalent cruelties to horses. Apart from gross cruelties inflicted in so many instances, practically all work horses were jerked, beaten, and battered into doing what they would have done willingly if taught what was required of them. This cruel ignorance was at its worst in the then Wild West. Young horses were never taught anything. They were herded like cattle on the range with no knowledge of halter, rein, or bridle until three years of age. They were then lassoed, thrown, bridled and saddled with the cinch-girth that, with its mechanism like a compound pulley, compressed the chest almost to the point of suffocation. Before an admiring crowd a heavy horseman, thrilled with delusions of heroism, leaped into the saddle. The animal was ridden until he fell in a heap, limp and exhausted. He was then called "broken"—a not inappropriate term. Thereafter there was usually a sullen obedience to rein, whip and spur, notwithstanding an ulcerated back from the misfit saddle. Father often said the cruel, suffocating compression of the chest by the cinch-girth was a large factor in the development of the bucking trait in the bronco. The huge cruel spurs and the practice of "breaking" were contributory.

In western Pennsylvania cruelty took other forms. The colt was hand-raised, ran beside his working mother, and in general was not badly treated until sold off his home farm and into the hands of the teamster, who in those days was almost always an ignorant, high-tempered, brutal, drinking wielder of the black-snake whip. The criteria of excellence in a teamster were based not upon his efficiency in getting a smooth coördinate pull from all four horses at once, but upon the accuracy with which he could cut into any desired tendermost spot of a horse's anatomy with the lash, the loudness with which he could crack his whip and roar his commands, and especially the amount of whisky he could drink and still retain his seat in the saddle on the wheel horse. His brutal nature enabled him to get a recondite joy out of his conception of heroism in conquering defenseless horses trace-chained to heavy wagons; and joys arose from wreaking cruel vengeance for supposed misdeeds. To him a spavined horse was a joke. He knew not and, knowing, would have cared not, that every spavin, every lump and exostosis that seemed to him so comical in the wretched, down-and-out, old, crippled horse was a record of an injury caused by a violent leap against a heavy load under the lash. Taverns were numerous along the roads; at each was a watering trough for the horses and a bar for the teamster. His weapon, the blacksnake whip, always in his hand or under his arm, was six feet long, of solid leather, tapering from the two-inch-thick, lead-loaded handle out to the finger-thick, hide-cutting part—beyond which was the cracker. The reason for the lead in the handle was that the long flexible lash could not be wielded efficiently on the near-side wheel horse, on whose back the teamster rode in a huge black saddle. After lashing each of the other three horses in turn he hit the saddle horse between the ears with the lead-loaded butt of the whip as with a blackjack. Nearly all wheel horses developed poll evil, an abscess at the base of the skull between the ears. The unworthy successor of the blacksnake whip is still sold under the gruesome name of "mule skinner."

One of the greatest cruelties was the mired wagon. The terrible picture of it is burnt into my memory, like the red-hot branding iron that seared the Western horse. The rising generation, bowling along the hard highways of today, built with the enormous proceeds of automobile taxation, has no conception of the road conditions during the earlier half of my life. In the coal-hauling regions of western Pennsylvania, as in many other sections of our country, the so-called roads were mere mud tracks; and, except in summer, the mud was deep. The limestone clay made a thick, tough mud into which the loaded wagon would sink and become fixed. It was difficult for horses even to pull out their feet. Hitched to the immovable wagon and sunken to their bellies in the mud, they were cruelly beaten and flogged with the blacksnake whip wielded by the powerful arm of the usually half-drunken driver until their backs were crisscrossed with welts from which blood streamed down into the mud.

In that day most people who were otherwise kindly did not seem to realize the cruelty. Father did, and many times he went to the rescue. The greatest tact was necessary in such situations. If the teamster were irritated he would become stubborn and combative, and would later wreak vengeance on his horses. Father's remedy, when in going along the highway he came upon a stalled wagon, was to unload, pull out with wagon empty, and then load up; and he nearly always could get the work-shirking teamster to do this. My prestige as a physician, after I acquired that distinction, enabled me to do the same thing; but in my boyhood days I had no prestige. On many occasions I begged the brutal teamsters to try Father's remedy for their mired wagons. All I ever got was dire threats. One vivid memory may be cited. A huge, burly, half-drunken negro was in the saddle lashing a team of four beautiful, well built, young horses hitched to a hopelessly sunken, heavily loaded coal wagon. Bellowing like a bull and roaring curses, he was lashing his bleeding team *seriatim* and beating the leader over the head with the butt. At each savage onslaught the hit horse would plunge into his collar, which meant one-horse effort instead of slow steady teamwork by all four leaning into their collars at once, as they would have done with a good careful, sober teamster handling them. Even so there would have been no hope of these powerful horses, up to their bellies in mud, pulling out the loaded wagon, sunken axle-deep. The uproar had attracted a crowd. Crying so that I could hardly see through the streaming tears, I pleaded with the savage brute to unload on a platform of fence rails. "We will all help unload," I shouted, expecting coöperation from the crowd. The negro glared at me through his bleary eyes, shook his bloody blacksnake at me, and shouted, "Hey, you damned skinny little houn' crybaby, 'f yuh don' shet up an' git ta hell out o' here I'll cutcha in two." The threat was emphasized by the loud crack of his blacksnake in my general direction. The crowd started to carry split rails from the roadside stake-and-rider fence; but to my horror they were used to make a narrow platform beside each horse; and on each platform a man with a hickory coal-pick handle took his place so that all four horses could be beaten synchronously in addition to the *seriatim* lashings of the teamster. Realizing the futility of my efforts, sick and faint with the horror of it all, I started to run for home. The first hill was steep, but before I fell exhausted I managed to get over the ridge out of hearing of the horrid uproar of the shouting, cursing, beating, and lashing. After a few moments' rest I ran the remaining distance home. Almost breathless, I managed to tell Father there was a coal wagon stuck in the mud on the other side of the hill. I could not go with him back to that horrible place. I ran to the haymow and hid until I could stop the hiccoughing, sobbing, and crying. For weeks that scene of horror came back upon me so suddenly and overwhelmingly that, repeatedly, I burst out crying. Hundreds of times in later life the memory of it has rushed back with a vividness that has marred many a moment. Even as I write today, notwithstanding the fact that the horses are dead, the teamster is dead, all the men of the crowd have probably passed away, that horrid memory lingers. And the sequel afforded little solace. Father reported finding the scene as I had left it. His convincing suasion turned the crowd to unloading; the empty wagon was pulled out; the coal afterward was taken away in small part-loads. He said: "Those abused horses will have many painful, sleepless nights; and to the end of their days they will never be free from stiff, aching disease of the joints."

My young life was often saddened by similar horrors in the coal mining and hauling district on the edge of which I lived. I remember seeing a newly acquired little pit mule blinded with a sharp-pointed coal pick by the pit boss because of refusal to enter the black darkness of the pit mouth into which it was required to drag the pit cars. All of the mules in that pit were blind. The shocking cruelty haunted me for days; and long afterward I shuddered at even the mention of the coal pit.

The tearfulness and terror of my childhood seem to have been concerned with the cruelty and my helplessness to stop it, rather than with the gruesomeness of the sights. This is inference from incidents like those of baby Murphy and Tommy Walsh. Late one afternoon when I was about nine or ten years old Mother sent me to buy some eggs from the wife of teamster Murphy. The stock on hand not being sufficient, Mrs. Murphy sent Micky and me to the haymow to search for more. As soon as we entered the stable we saw the baby dead in the stall near the hind feet of one of the horses, evidently trampled to death. His skull was burst, crushed flat; brains and blood were oozing out. It was a gruesome sight, but I did not shed a tear nor run away. Speaking to the horse, I went into the stall and dragged the baby out. Micky, terrified at his negligence in watching the toddling child, had run to get his mother; she met me halfway as I was carrying the heavy burden toward the house. She seized the body and ran shrieking through the doorway. Micky and I followed. She asked me to go for the priest and the doctor; she sent Micky to the haymow to waken the father. "Asleep in the haymow" meant, of course, that he was drunk. When I got back with the doctor the priest was already in the house and Micky was at the stable door watching as his father with a bloody blacksnake whip lashed the trembling, quivering, crouching horse tied up in the stall. Tearless up to this time, I burst out crying and ran till I got out of earshot of the lashes, the curses, and the struggles in the stall. Then I hurried home to see if Father were there, for I knew he would go and stop the senseless cruelty.

Another tragedy bearing on the character of the tearfulness of childhood was that of Tommy Walsh. One June morning, going for strawberries for the hotel, I saw teamster Walsh coming down the hill. The dry summer road was good, and the loaded wagon was pushing the team rather hard. It was Walsh's habit to make his team pull downhill as well as up by use of the brake. At the foot of the hill I saw him stop his team, dismount from his wheel horse, hook his blacksnake whip by its leather loop over the hames and walk quickly back to where Tommy was standing at his post beside the side-brake lever. Then he slapped Tommy first on one side of the face and then on the other with his big dirty opened hands. Tommy shrieked at the first blow and fell at the second. What happened after that, I never knew because I burst out crying and ran away. That afternoon on another trip to the market garden I saw the same team and wagon just coming over the hilltop. The jolting, springless wagon was well held back from the horses by the heavy braking of Tommy, this time standing on the side-brake lever. The alternate catching and slipping friction of the dry, shrieking, shoe-sole-lined, wooden brake-blocks on the iron-tired wheels caused the lever to jump and jerk up and down, bouncing Tommy, who supplemented his precarious foothold by holding on to the top edge of the wagon bed. Whether a lump of coal toppling over on his hands caused him to loosen his grip, or whether the jolting shook him loose was never known; but I saw him fall in front of the rear wagon wheel, which passed over him. I waved and yelled "Whoa" at teamster Walsh; he roared "Whoa," and his team stopped; the wheel horses backed strongly on the pushing unbraked wagon. Walsh bore down heavily on the side brake and hooked it with its chain. I hurried to Tommy and found him lifeless. His neck and face were crushed, and his eyes were squeezed out of their sockets. I felt for his pulse, as Mother and Father had taught me, but there was no pulsation. I supported his mangled, bloody head as his father carried the limp and lifeless body to the roadside. Walsh methodically moved his team to the other side of the road, unhooked his wheel horse, stripped off the collar, hames, and harness, and said: "Here, Bub. Gallop fast as yuh kin, 'n' git Doc Walker. I'll stan' by here till he comes." He gave me a lift into the saddle by my left foot; and sticking my feet into the strap above the stirrups, I started. The trot of the heavy work horse was rough, but his lumbering gallop was not bad. On the return journey Doctor Walker overtook me in his buggy, and we arrived together at the scene of the accident. Walsh had evidently visited the near-by tavern in the meantime. Quite a crowd had gathered, and it included the Coroner. Tommy's dead body was lifted into a proffered light spring wagon, and his maudlin father was helped into a place beside him. A teamster rehitched the wheel horse and took charge of the coal wagon. The Coroner notified us all to be at the inquest the next morning. I climbed onto the seat of the spring wagon, and we started for the Walsh cottage. The father was in an alcoholic stupor when we got there. To my dying day I shall never forget the piercing, agonizing shriek of the poor mother as she lifted the handkerchief I had laid over Tommy's ghastly, mangled face.

Up to that time I had not shed a tear; there had been no fight, no struggle, no cruelty, no suffering. The boy had been killed before my eyes, but the death was obviously instantaneous and painless. But the anguish of that shrieking, sobbing, moaning mother, and her infliction, the helpless besotted father, were too much for me. I cried and sobbed all the way home; and even today, sixty-two years later, I gulp when I think of that wretched woman.

I do not recall ever having shed a tear because of danger threatening myself.

As the only eyewitness I was called upon to testify at the inquest the next day, though because of my age I was not sworn. The Coroner did not ask me about my having seen Tommy punished apparently for inefficient braking by bearing down on the side-brake lever while walking alongside, instead of standing on it; and I did not feel called upon to volunteer the information.

It cannot be truthfully said that all teamsters were always cruel; but I heard one of the least brutal say, "I don' whip my hosses, 'ceptin' when they needs it; then they gits it good an' propah." I noticed they always "got it" when he was angry or drunk.

In all the cruelties the sight of which made my childhood tearful I never saw a woman or girl participate, either actively or as an onlooker. Coarse and uneducated as were the miners' wives and daughters, they always seemed to deprecate cruelty to man or beast. Undoubtedly the interest in the sportive type of cruelty and in the "manly art of self-defense" (!) on the part of men and boys was a matter of false education; but the women and girls were exposed to the same vicious propaganda. Though the immature mind did not arrive at conclusions by logic, I now realize that the facts borne in upon me in boyhood went a long way to strengthen my inborn conception that women and girls are better than men and boys.

Our home was twenty-five miles from oil-producing territory. When I was about twelve years old a "wildcatter," as prospecting drillers were called, agreed to put down a test well free of cost to Father, on the basis of an agreement that Father would get one-eighth interest in the oil if any were found.

After some weeks of drilling operations the driller sent word the tools were lost down the well. When Father and I arrived at the derrick Father asked if the tools could not be recovered.

"'Tain't possible, Mr. Jackson—'tain't possible, I tell ye. She's down more'n fifteen hunnerd feet; 'n' the bottom fi' hunnerd feet is plugged full o' rope; ol' rotten, wet, sand-soaked rope rammed down like er wad in a gun. Nippin' tools ain't no good. 'Tain't no use wastin' time tryin' to git that out. Better start a new hole some'eres near; not too near, though, er the two holes ull pull theirsel's together. Leastways that cussed ol' hole ull pull the new hole over inter it afore ye git down fi' hunnerd feet. Ther ain't nothin' meaner'n a cantankerous ol' drillin' wot's gone wrong. She's allus bewitched. Hell-bent on spoilin' any nigh drillin'." And the old oil driller gave vent to his feelings about mean wells by ejecting a mouthful of tobacco juice across the shed into the matted hair of his sleeping dog. "Good for fleas," he said, parenthetically.

Two things intrigued me as I listened to the report Father got about the calamity that had befallen the prospective oil well on which hope of getting out of debt depended. The verdict "impossible" started me thinking hard. With the powerful pull of the rope that I had watched hundreds of times drawing up the half-ton of drilling tools, power seemed plentiful; it was only a question of attaching a new rope to the plug of rope. But this plug of old rope was nearly a thousand feet from the surface down in a six-inch hole drilled in the rock and lined part way with iron casing. The drilling tools in common use consisted of a drill bit somewhat like a gigantic cold chisel. This was incessantly hammered into the rock, and rotation of the bit gave an approach to roundness to the hole. The hammering mechanism was quite simple. It consisted of a loose-link jar resulting from the coupling together of two long bars of steel by long eyes forged in the joining ends. To the lower end of the lower bar the chisel-like bit was attached with a taper screw threading. In drilling the rock strata the tools alternately were raised and dropped a few feet by the rope attached to the walking beam. The heavy bit and steel rod dropped with heavy impact; then the upper rod dropped the length of the loose-link joint and struck a heavy blow on the lower rod and its integral bit. This loose-link jar hammer appealed to my budding mechanical genius as a means of driving a harpoon into that plug of old rope; but my mechanical instinct reasoned that a single pair of barbs like a harpoon would pull out, so I sketched a long harpoon bit of triangular cross-section with barbs staggered around the distal three-fourths of its twelve-foot length. This was to be screwed into the lower rod of the jar mechanism in place of the drill bit. " 'Tain't a bad idee," said the old driller as he anointed the dog with a dose of flea exterminator. I was sent with my sketch to the huge forge in

Pittsburgh where oil drilling tools were then made. "Idea's all right," said the toolmaker, "but ye can't make no sech tool." This impulsive preliminary opinion was revised when a nicely carved wooden model was presented. The harpoon was made, attached to the jar tools, lowered into the hole on a good new rope, hammered down with the jar until all the barbs had been buried in the plug of old rope. Then a barrel of oil was put down the hole. At the first upward pull the stretch was taken out of the new rope; and then the plug began to move upward. The enthusiasm engendered by the appearance above ground of the harpoon firmly embedded in the proximal end of the old rope resulted in extermination of probably all the fleas.

The monetary results were nil. The well was a "duster." The multi-barbed harpoon became a standard fishing tool; but no patents were applied for, and no recompense accrued to the inventor. This first foreign body case was thus typical of hundreds of subsequent, technically very successful bronchoscopic cases.

The statement of the old oil-driller that a drilled well would draw in the tools of a well drilled near by aroused in my tow-covered head not doubt, nor ridicule, nor prompt dismissal as unworthy of credence. On the contrary it aroused what must have been an instinctive, inborn incentive for research. Inquiry among drillers brought abundant evidence based on numerous well authenticated incidents in which a well drilled into the rock near a previously drilled well after some hundreds of feet penetration through the strata would drift into the old well. Shop work had taught me, as every carpenter knows, that a hole bored in wood close to another hole would lead to a merger by the giving way of the thin partition between the new hole and the old; but research showed the wells with the supposed affinity for each other were not close enough together, at the start, for such an effect. Lowering a toy lantern into a drilled well showed that the lantern soon went out of sight because the axis of the well was neither straight nor plumb. Investigations and precise measure-

Decorating china helped to balance the collegiate budget

1883–4–5

"THE OLD SHOE"

Ohio River Hills

(OIL AND PALETTE KNIFE)

1912

ments of the marks of quarry drilling on huge stones showed that deviation from the vertical did not always continue to follow the primary deviation, and that secondary deviations resulted sometimes in a more or less spiral course as the drilling proceeded downward. The spiral course explained the mystery. The well swung round and round in a constantly widening circle as it progressed downward, as a vine growing upward seeks a support, until the bore of the old well was within the diametric sweep of the spiral—when it was, of course, entered. The value of research was demonstrated; and never forgotten.

"Can't be done, missus," said the old gardener when Mother asked him to remove the pushed-in cork from an old olive-oil bottle. "It is such a nice bottle for making a little vinegar from that glass of spoiled currant jelly, but the oil in the cork would spoil it all. They said the rope plug couldn't be taken out of the oil well. I shall ask Chev about this cork problem." Again the intrigue of the impossible. It was a proud moment when I fished out the cork in a few minutes with a wire loop. This was my second foreign body case.

Play, as the term is usually understood, entered little if at all into my boyhood activities. What time was free of duty was taken up with making things. It was more pleasure for me to make a sled than to coast on it, except as incidental travel on an errand or to and from school. It seems that little time was ever available for mere play; but in boyhood days some degree of skill was acquired in a few of the recreative sports, especially those that could be done single-hand. Potentially crippling sports like football and baseball were never learned; and the lack of crippled fingers was a great help in the later, delicate manipulations of bronchoscopy that required a gentle touch.

Father and Mother believed every boy should learn to swim as part of his education: there was no thought of recreation in it. Practice in Chartiers Creek developed me into a good swimmer, though frail physique made for little endurance.

Skating was learned in childhood on a near-by pond. One of my few relatives gave me his old skates. Being statistically inclined I recorded falls; they were fifty-nine during the first hour. The statistics on roller skating showed fewer casualties, seventeen in the first hour. The falls on the ice were eliminated by practice, but the physical endurance for speedy or fancy skating was lacking as well as the money to buy the good skates required. On the best skating days the surface of the ice was softened by the sun before all the chores were done. The roller skates were given to me because it was impossible to skate on them: they were an early model with rubber wheels and stuck to the floor. By substituting hard dogwood rollers turned out on the lathe the skates were rendered practical. After seventeen falls I got control of the skates and executed prodigious curves on the smooth, empty hayloft floor. The original owner was fascinated, took back the skates, and paid me fifteen cents for rendering them workable. My pleasure in the roller-skating episode was threefold: the enjoyment of turning out the dogwood rollers; the intrigue of the impossible; the acquisition of fifteen cents that enabled me to buy a beautiful piece of white holly wood required to finish a job of jig-saw work for which I had a customer impatiently waiting.

My first boat was a miniature scow, a coat cut according to available cloth. There were no funds for the purchase of suitable materials. Scraps of lumber left from building a shed were mostly too short; but when pieced and lapped together they resulted in an amount of wood that would float. From the roofing of the shed enough coal tar was left to make the little scow water-tight. It was a proud moment when the *Fanny* was launched, and the successful crossing of a near-by half-acre pond was a grand adventure proving seaworthiness. My joy was of short duration. The shortening days of autumn left little daylight for boating after school work and chores, and the little boat was hauled out for the winter. A quarry teamster who obviously had no soul commandeered it to feed oats to his team; it was just long enough for both horses to feed at once without unhitching. But, alas! the horses suffered from dietary deficiency. Lacking bulk diet, they gnawed notches in the sides of the boat that reduced the already too low freeboard below the water line. It was a cruel blow to me, but the worst was yet to come. When approaching spring aroused thoughts of boating, bitter tears were shed at the sight of the wreck of the *Fanny* in the mire of the sty serving as a hog trough.

A few years later, as a reward for saving some valuable papers in a planing-mill fire, I received a bundle of "1/2 x 3 door battens." Sixteen feet in length, of beautiful, clear white pine, they enabled me to build a very light canoe. The material was ideal for the purpose, but the neat fitting necessitated care. Though I utilized every moment left after school, and after chores were done, making the drawings, laying off, making molds, fitting ribs and planking, a whole winter was required to finish the canoe. As a Christmas present Mother gave me a small can of varnish and a brush. It was a beautiful job; at least it seems so to me in the retrospect. Mother's name, Katharine, was carefully lettered on the side, near the stem.

The pleasures of the single paddle were marred by my lack of endurance. A sailing canoe required only agility. Mother clipped out of a paper an illustration and description of a sailing canoe. The lugsails, main and mizzen, were not hard to make and rig, and Mother had enough unbleached muslin and clothesline to spare; but suitable straight, clear white pine pieces for masts, yards, and booms were hopelessly beyond my financial resources. Penny by penny, a fund was accumulated from sales of jig-saw work, peg tops, and other products, supplemented by birthday and Christmas gifts, by special request on a cash basis. The contributions of Mother and Father are vividly remembered because of the amount, fifty cents, a huge sum in those days. The day after Christmas the precious materials were obtained and carried home, two at a time. In the spring the *Katharine* was launched again—this time rigged as a miniature lugger. After a few duckings I became satisfactorily expert at handling a sailing canoe.

The light, frail, beautiful, but ill-fated *Katharine* was totally wrecked by a piratical gang of drunken, Sunday bathing coal miners.

CHAPTER III

SCHOOL LIFE

(1869–1877)

MY EARLIEST RECOLLECTIONS are of hours in school. Supplementing memory with later learned facts, I may say that at four years of age I was sent to Miss Ward's Catholic School on Diamond Street almost over the Pan Handle Railroad tunnel which followed part way the old canal, in Pittsburgh. It was not a parochial school, and most of the children were not Catholic. Miss Ward was a kindly lady, devoutly religious. She took great interest in me as her youngest pupil, and I soon became the show pupil to be called upon to perform when visitors came; as much perhaps because of tender age and diminutive size as for any great attainments. Prayers were said twice every day. At first, responses though fervid were ill timed, but the simple routine was soon acquired; and a visiting priest was amazed and pleased at the recitation from a "child's catechism." Sisters of the various Orders were delighted. It seems probable that the foundation was laid here for three characteristics manifested through life: respect for teachers, respect for women, and respect for the Catholic Church, although I was never a Catholic. Miss Ward and the Sisters always seemed to be angels to my childish imagination. At six years of age my parents moved into the country, and I never saw Miss Ward again. Father told me afterward that she came often with tears in her eyes to make inquiries. It was the last of my happy school days.

When the family moved to Idlewood in 1871, the nearest school was the old Greentree Township public school, located nearly two miles away. It was a picturesque old building, part log, with frame addition and roofed with hand-made shingles.

The children were almost all from neighboring small farms and miners' shacks, and all were poor. Most of them had enough plain food of the farm-raised kind. With the exception of a few who lived very close by, all carried luncheon. A fair average sample was "the feed trough" of Dave Holmes. It consisted of a box made of shingles with a short, bail-like handle of cord. It held usually two slices of bread of huge area, without butter, plastered with very dark apple butter. Dave did not like the crust, and so he used to eat his way into the soft part until his cheeks were decorated with smears of brown apple butter from the horseshoe-shaped crust that reached both ears. For dessert he had occasionally a cold buckwheat cake rolled up in molasses—a sticky mess. The other boys preferred for dessert a dust-covered, smoke-begrimed sliver of dried apple from a festoon that hung from the ceiling joists of most farmhouses in those days when preservation of food by sterilization was unknown. The boy whom all envied was Jake Slushman, the son of a tavern keeper on the Washington Pike, a highway between Pittsburgh and "Little Washington"—the diminutive distinguishing Washington, Pennsylvania, from Washington, D.C. Jake had all the luxuries. Sandwiches of rye bread with daily varied ham, pork, lamb, and beef for a mid-layer *de résistance*. His various kinds of pie—cherry, blackberry, elderberry, and so on—used to make our mouths water. The dark juice, running down from each corner of his mouth, dripped to make a stain on his shirt. The sympathetic flow from our mouth-corners was stainless. Frequently Jake had an orange, a high-priced luxury in those days of slow transportation. To this day there are memories of the acute pain that struck me in the angles of the jaw when looking on at Jake Slushman's sucking of an orange through a small hole made in the end after rolling. My luncheon consisted of bread and butter. The bread was the home-baked kind made in huge loaves from the gray flour that all the old buhrstone mills made. The slices were cross-cut in smaller squares so as to go into the pint-sized pail. A raw apple carried in the pocket was the usual dessert. The luncheon was sufficient when

I had it; but often I went hungry all day because the luncheon was destroyed and the apple confiscated by the tormenting group hereinafter mentioned.

Even when I was allowed to have the luncheon, eating it was spoiled by sympathy for Jim and Mary Kelly: they often had nothing to eat. They lived in a little stone house that I passed every day. The father was a coal miner. I often stopped at the entrance to the little country mine to see him come out with his handcart full of coal assisted by two large, lean, hungry, harnessed draft dogs. He and his dogs earned about a dollar a day, which in those days of high purchasing power of the dollar was good wages. The great trouble was that, every pay day, Kelly went first to the tavern. He never thought of going home until put out penniless and so drunk it was difficult for him to reach home. Once I found him breathing but unconscious in the roadside ditch with his two half-starved dogs standing guard, one licking his face. I had decided to leave him under guard of his dogs while I went for help when I saw a farm wagon approaching. The farmer and his son lifted Kelly into the wagon, and I climbed in. When we arrived at the little stone cabin we found Mrs. Kelly in tears.

"He'll bate me whin he wakes; I've nary a cint o' money to gi' him for more whusky. The few cints I made the wake, washin', I did gi' for some taters for the childer."

The contrast between the starved children of the man who drank and the luxuriously filled lunch basket of the son of the man who sold the drink made a deep impression on my childish mind. It has often been revived by parallel circumstances. The same contrast is to be seen today. It was much less in evidence during the days of prohibition. Pity for hungry Jim and Mary Kelly led me to beg for them, from Dave Holmes, the horseshoe-shaped crusts from which he had eaten the soft inside. We were all three blissfully ignorant of septic mouths and contagion. The elder Kelly died of alcoholism. Jimmy followed in the drunken footsteps of his father. He killed his widowed mother with a pick handle because she did not have a dime to give him to buy more drink. The whole tragedy made a profound impression upon me and alone would have made a total abstainer even if I had not had later thousands of instances to show that alcohol as a beverage is the greatest curse that has ever befallen the human race.

One day, coming home from school, I heard a shot, and a moment later I saw a rabbit come hobbling along toward me with one forefoot and one hind leg dangling. His pace became slower and slower, and as we reached each other he fell over on his side. I sat down on the ground and picked him up. He was quivering and twitching all over. He seemed to look up at me reproachfully, then became limp, and all was still. I spoke to him and stroked and stroked his soft fur in a childish effort to bring him back to life. I tried to stand him up on his mangled legs; he was limp as a rag. Realizing he was dead, I burst out crying, because of my helplessness. I had learned a fundamental biologic fact, that I have never since forgotten: Death is an irreversible process. All my professional life I have had ever before me the dread that the patient would cross the line beyond which I should be powerless to help him.

Every school has its little store where pupils go to spend their pennies. A penny was a rare thing with any of us, but we had the little store; it was operated by one William Heaps. Possession of the cent justifying an excursion to "Billy Heaps's" was a rare event with me and was possible only by the sale of a hundred paper lamplighters or other product. A penny would buy three slender sticks of licorice root, but I had no opportunity to chew them. They were confiscated by overgrown pupils, and I was chased. Torture of some kind would have been inflicted had I not escaped into the old abandoned cemetery adjoining Mr. Heaps' tiny establishment. The cemetery was filled with a dense growth of cherry trees that admitted very little daylight. My conception was that the trees grew from sprouting of cherry stones swallowed before death; it was customary to swallow the pits in eating cherries. Anyway the trees in growth had tumbled the tombstones over at various topsy-turvy angles, and there were some old bones in dark corners. It was a gruesome place, but I did not mind it; my pursuers did, and I escaped that time. I tried once subsequently to obtain some licorice root, but overgrown pupils deprived me of it; so Billy Heaps lost the trade of an unimportant customer, whose potential transactions aggregated about four or five cents a year. Going out of the schoolroom at recess became shortly afterward altogether too precarious, and was given up.

It seems strange that, in the latter half of the nineteenth century, the life of a schoolboy could be a nightmare of persecution and torment, yet such was the case with me. There was no persecution by teachers: I never had any trouble with them. In a letter to a parent who recently complained to me that her boy was the victim of a teacher who had a grudge against him, I wrote:

> In all my life I have never known a teacher to be unjust to a pupil. I do not say there never was such a thing, but I do say that I never saw it. Teachers have a hard life and suffer much, with so many sides from which criticism and even attacks may come—the pupils, parents, other teachers, the principal, boards of directors, politicians. Among all of these groups are some who are lying in wait for ammunition to use against the teacher. Like the militarists of Prussia who claimed all Europe had a grudge against Germany, the bad boy in school claims the teacher is always picking on him. I would advise you, before making any official complaint, to get unbiased evidence from some source, such as the girl pupils in the same room, as to your boy's behavior.

The persecution, torment, and abuse in my case came from a group of older pupils and was the result of peculiar circumstances that do not exist today in the same community, nor, probably, elsewhere in this country. Modern psychology fully explains everything, but let us consider first the bare facts in the case: we can theorize afterward.

The best opportunity was on the way home alone from school. Almost always I was waylaid, tormented, and tortured. Physical torture was cunningly planned so as to leave no telltale marks. A favorite torture was to hold me by the feet, first suspending me and then swinging me round and round with head at the periphery of the circle until I would cry because of pain and fall with vertigo when released. Another torture was to choke me with both hands around the neck until unconsciousness approached. Many times I felt I should never get home alive. A favorite torture was to say, "Now we are going to kill you." Sometimes it would be, "You'll never see your mother again."

One day my little dog Dan got away from home and found his way to school. He was waiting at the school door and was bounding and romping with joy when I emerged. We had not gone far on the road home when we met Big Bill Drake, one of the overgrown boys, setting muskrat traps along Whiskey Run. Bill grasped the little dog by the collar and, choking him into submission, took him away across the fields. The dog was never seen again. Bill tauntingly said, "I'll get a quarter for this silky black hide." Bitter tears were shed on the way home, but facing bitterly cold northwest winds caused such additional flow of water from my eyes that my grief was not noticed and the mysterious disappearance of the little black dog was unexplained. I never think of him without a pang of sorrow.

Boys at Greentree School often brought their sleds with them, not only for coasting during recess but also for use as a vehicle. The country being very hilly, the roads were up and down most of the way; with a sled the downs could be swiftly coasted, and the uphill climbs were little, if any, harder unless it was heavy. After many evenings of painstaking work I finished a sled that was light enough for a frail little boy to drag up the hills and yet strong enough to stand the coasting down. At last the sled was varnished. Proudly it was shown to my always appreciative father. Mother supplied a strong white cord for traction. One winter day conditions on the roads were good for a trial trip on the way to and from school. The new sled ran well and was light and easy to drag. On arrival at school it attracted great attention as it stood up against the wall of the coal shed among the heavy, rough, cumbrous sleds built of unsuitable materials, with poor tools, by overgrown boys from farms and coal mines. To avoid my tormentors, as usual, I did not go out at recess. When after school I went to get the sled it was missing. Prolonged search located it as a bundle of splintered wood tied with its cord that Mother had given me. It was on the woodpile, and under the cord was a dirty piece of paper with the crudely printed words, "KINDLIN WUD."

On the road to school in the morning the tormentors were less often encountered, but when they were the abuse took a form that would not leave traces to attract the teacher's attention. At this time of day and during school hours the little tin luncheon bucket was often the means of torment. Some days it was confiscated, later turning up empty in the coat room. At times sand, at other times coal ashes, sprinkled on the buttered inside and concealed by putting the slices together again, rendered inedible the contents of the returned tin pail. Or, by use of a rotten egg, the bread was made nauseating. Hunger to the point of faintness became my usual afternoon condition. Even the raw apple in my pocket was stolen. One day the pail was tied to a dog's tail, the contents spilled in the mud, and the container lost. Another day the bucket was tied to a stick and held under the rear wheel of a passing farm wagon in such a way that it crushed the top rim flat shut. The painful, fruitless efforts to get my little hand into the crimped top and extricate some morsels of bread caused great merriment. Particular delight was taken in the ringing of the bell calling all pupils to work before I had time to get any bread out. On the way home mechanical ingenuity enabled me, ravenously hungry, to pry apart the bent-in top with a woodman's iron edge momentarily borrowed from a rail-splitting farmer; but then it became evident that the tormentors had first sprinkled the sandwiches with earth. This was a curious parallel to hundreds of happenings in the bronchoscopic work of later life, in that the reward for the solution of a difficult mechanical problem was the satisfaction of achievement, nothing with which to satisfy hunger.

Another form of morning torture was to take off my cowhide boots, fill them with snow, and throw them over the fence into a snow-covered field. By the time they were recovered, emptied of wet, icy slush, and put on, my feet were nearly frozen; and they remained cold and wet in school all day. Fortunately no toes had to be amputated, but chilblains made many a night miserable. Nobody in those days, in that community, regarded chilblains seriously; hot salted vinegar was supposed to be curative.

One day there was to be an exhibition of school work. For a number of evenings, in spite of eyes bleary with an acute conjunctivitis, I painfully and carefully prepared some drawings. Before the start in the morning Mother put them between clean flat sheets of tissue paper in the large-paged geography. When almost in sight of school I met two of the overgrown pupils. The geography book was opened, the drawings were rubbed with dirty wet hands and utterly ruined. Miss Moore, the teacher, said: "Why, Chev, I am surprised that you did not bring some drawings, I must mark it against you."

The foregoing are not isolated instances, simply examples of frequent happenings. Ordeals varied. Snow was often packed down inside my clothing. "Now we'll show the great Barnum sword swallower." And a long icicle was passed down inside collar and undershirt; I was usually held till the icicle broke up or melted. Dipping me into the watering trough, suspension over the precipice of the quarry or mine cave-in, were never-to-be forgotten ordeals. One day I collapsed on the floor on entering home. As I recovered consciousness I heard Mother say: "He ran home too fast. He is a frail child."

One day the school was dismissed at noon because the plaster fell off the ceiling, an accident demanding immediate repairs. Elated with the thought of getting all my home chores done long before dark, and especially with the thought of a few hours' work in my little shop before supper, as we then called the evening meal, I was hurrying homeward when suddenly I was seized from behind by powerful unseen hands; my cap was pulled down over my eyes, blindfolding me. Another pair of hands seized me, tied my hands and feet together behind my back, and I was carried off. By the cool, damp, peculiar odor of the air I realized I was being carried into a coal pit. There were a number of pit mouths: some were in use, others were for drainage, still others had been abandoned; they were here and there along the way, a little back from the edge of the road. It seemed like a long time in the mine before I was dropped in a puddle of cold water. I heard footsteps hurrying away; then all was silent, except for the drip, drip, drip of water. Not a word had been said by my captors at any time. The cap slipped off my eyes, but I could see nothing in the absolute darkness. My feet and hands had not been tied tightly; the slimy mud enabled me after a time to slip out first one hand, then the other. Taking the boots off enabled me to slip off the loops on my ankles along with the boots and stockings. Then I felt my eyes; they seemed all right, but I could not see anything. Fumbling in the dark, I separated the cold wet stockings from the loops of cord and put them on; then emptied the boots of water and put them on. I was soaking-wet and shivering with the cold; my fingers were numb. Getting on my feet, I bumped my head against the slate. This showed that I must be in one of the worked-out "rooms" of the mine where the coal ribs and props had been taken out to let the room cave in. I knew I could walk upright in the working part of a mine, because I had gone in once with Father and a surveyor. I felt sure that if I groped along touching one wall I could come into the main entry and see daylight. But there must have been a labyrinth of worked-out rooms. Turning corner after corner, I got to no entry with a gleam of daylight nor any passage where I could stand erect. Many times the headroom grew less and less—by which it was evident I was going wrong, because my captors must have had headroom to walk so briskly when carrying me. No sound of voices or picks or of barking draft dogs came to my ears. All was silent except the dripping water. I realized I was lost in old abandoned workings. But I kept on and on groping with the hope of seeing the daylight of the pit mouth. The footing was bad; loose slate piles alternated with pools of cold mine water and slimy, slippery mud. Often I stumbled or slipped and fell. I was getting very tired. More and more often I sat on a slate pile to rest and listen. Becoming weaker and weaker, chilled and shivering, I kept on until after a hard fall I was so tired that even the slate pile seemed restful. Whether I fainted from exhaustion or fell asleep, and for how long I was unconscious, I never knew. I felt something cold on my face; then hot breath on my nose and a hot rough tongue licking my cheek. My hand touched leather on a woolly hide, and I knew it was a harnessed pit dog that was standing over me. Then I heard a faraway shout: "Come on hyur, Jack. Where be ye, anyways? Damn ye, come on, ye Jackanapes!" The cursing voice was getting farther and farther away, and then it faded out. I tried to cry out, but my voice was so weak I could scarcely hear it myself. Jack stopped licking my face and let a bark out of him, deafeningly close to my ear. Then the barking became almost incessant with a few licks in between. I tried to hold on to his harness, lest he get away; but my hands were so numb, and he was so excitedly moving about, that again and again I lost my hold. After what seemed a long time I heard shouting and cursing getting louder and louder. "God damn yer dirty hide, I'll lick hell outen ye—break every rib in yer body—if ye don't stop yer damn skunk huntin', stinkin' yersel' up so's nobody kin stan' workin' wi ye!"

But Jack stuck to his barking. The smoking cap lamp of a miner appeared in the distance. He was banging the walls with his pick handle as he crouched along, boding ill for Jack. The miner crawled into the low headroom over the slate pile, grasped Jack's harness, and dragged the dog out. There was a loud whack and a a howl. But, probably because there was not "room to swing a cat," * as the sailors say, Jack broke away from his flogger and got in beyond me, and increased his barking. "Ther baste must be goin' mad. Stay where ye are, 'n' be damned." The miner started away. I seemed dazed; I could see and hear but could not cry out loud enough to be heard.

Then, coming back and crawling in again, the miner saw me.

* Meaning, not height enough between decks to wield a cat-o'-nine-tails efficiently.

"Holy, howlin', jumpin' ——! What ye got here, Jack?"

It was huge Welsh Davy, the champion prize fighter, and champion blasphemer of the whole mining district. Surprise, amazement, joy, rage, every emotion was always expressed by a volley of oaths, of which he had the largest vocabulary. More than once he had almost knocked me senseless by roaring curses at me.

The Welsh giant dragged me out over the slate, slung me under his arm as if I were an old rag, and soon we were out into the five-foot headroom of the main entry. Though dazed and semiconscious then, I have indelibly fixed in memory the vivid picture of the smoking lamp swinging to and fro on Davy's oily cap as he crouched and swung his huge frame along. Big, woolly, black Jack romped and galloped in, out, and around us, as he made the underground air ring with his joyous barks. He pawed Davy, but the consequent volley of fearful oaths did not lessen his joy. He licked my hands as my arms dangled limply and swayed about to giant Davy's great swinging, crouching stride.

"Fur lovva God an' the Howly Virgin, Davy, what do yez be bringin' me home? Well-if-it-ain't Shove Jackson. What yez been doin' tuh the bye?" said devout Catholic Biddy Welsh.

"Ain't been doin' nothin', Biddy," said her giant, irreligious, blasphemous, non-Catholic husband. "Jack found thuh brat in thuh ol' workin's, off th' ol' back entery, and wouldn't leave till I went back after um. Him's a good un, Jack is. Saint Bernd blood 'll tell. More sense'n some good-fer-nothin' brats ut don't know no better'n to go inter ol' workin's." Davy started for the tavern to get a drink before "washin' up."

"Hyur, ye baste, come back hyur! Git yez over tuh Pat Garrity's. He do be a-dyin'. Git thim two Sisters tuh come hyur. The praste uz just lift, an' they be tryin' tuh gi' a bit o' comfort tuh Mrs. Garrity, the poor sowl."

I tried to stand up but slumped on the floor.

"Oh, wurra, wurra! It's near dud, yez are, me dear bye."

Kind-hearted but powerful, Biddy Welsh picked me up and laid me on the wash bench with something soft under my head.

"A bit o' a sup o' tay ud help yez. Drink this now."

Then she washed my face and hands.

"Sure, ye must 'a' been wallerin' in pit mud—blacker'n a nayger in a tar barl. Yez ud skeer yer mither tuh death."

She pulled off my wet, black-mud-caked clothes, and put on me some nondescript garments; anyway, they were dry, and she had warmed them.

Then the Sisters arrived with their little black-covered one-horse wagon. Biddy picked me up as if I were a baby and laid me on the side-seat in the wagon, and the Sisters wrapped a blanket around me. They seemed so gentle. Their wide collars seemed so white and so clean. I felt so safe and comfortable. That is the last I remember.

What followed, I know well from Mother's oft-repeated description:

"The Sisters brought Chev home to me. He was a very ill boy for a long time. Doctor Walker said it was pneumonia." (That was then an all-inclusive name for many different diseases.) "He had a chill, followed by high fever." (How high was not known because clinical thermometers were not then in general use.) "When Chev has high fever he is always delirious. This time the delirium was worse than usual; he was incoherently muttering almost all the time. He would start up, crying, then would talk of angels, often saying, 'Angels like you, Mother.' Even when his fever was high he would say, 'I'm so cold, and it's so dark, so cold, so dark.' He would suddenly start up in bed with his eyes wide open, but apparently seeing nothing. Then he would weakly cry out: 'Jack, don't leave me. Oh, don't leave me here, Jack.' He would clutch and claw frantically in the air and then sink back exhausted and say: 'I'm so cold. It's so dark.' But dear old Doctor Walker brought him through all right."

Doctor Walker's version was: "Desperate case of pneumonia from cold and exposure in a weakened condition. For two weeks recovery seemed impossible. He always had a weak heart. It was his mother's good nursing that brought him through."

ALICE

(OIL)

1912

OCTOBER
Kilbuck Run
Ohio
River
Hills

(OIL AND PALETTE KNIFE)

1914

When I got better, dear old Biddy Welsh came with the Sisters to see me.

" 'Tis near dud yez wur, me bye."

"Yes, Mrs. Welsh; and it was Jack and your big Davy that saved me. How are they?"

"Oh, Jack be all right enough; wurrkin' lek a gude dog ivery day. But me Davy, though that be n't his real name, him wuz kilt entoirely. Sure, him wuz a Molly Maguire, the worst o' the lot. The p'lice wanted him back up in the hard-coal mount'ns, whur he come frum, fer killin' an' officer long ago. The Chief said, sez he, 'Bill,'—'n' that wuzzent his name, nayther—'Bill,' sez he, 'we've got yez now. Come 'long peacible-like. We're goin' tuh take yez back up.'

" 'Not aloive, yur not,' sez Davy, though that wuzzent his name, 'not aloive, yur not. Not by a damn sight.' An' they dudn't, nary a step. He didn't never carry no weepons, Davy didn't. 'Me two sledge hammers zall I needs,' he allus said, puttin' up his two fists. Them fists o' hisn wuz like cannon balls. He broke the jaw o' two officers, the neck o' t'other; he died. Two he putt tuh slape. But they killed him. It tuck ten officers tuh kill him, 'n' six tuh carry him away." There seemed to be a little touch of pride in poor old Biddy's voice and manner as she sighed and wiped away a tear.

" 'F on'y wuh cud 'a' putt a bit o' fear o' God into um."

Then the gentle Sisters came over to the bedside; each patted my hand softly, and one of them said soothingly:

"You will soon be well and strong again, Chev. And we will pray for you every day."

On the morning of the start back to school after I got well, Mother said:

"Chev, you must come straight home from school. You must not stop on the way to play with the boys."

"Why, Mother, I never did play with the boys. I always run as fast as I can for home, though since the day I dropped over I try to be careful, as you told me, not to run too fast."

"Well, Chev, I have never known you to tell me an untruth, and I believe you. But that day when it was past the time you should have been home I sent William to look for you. He found plasterers working, and they said school had been dismissed at noon. On the way home he met Stewt Cutler and three other large boys. They all said you were all playing together, and when you couldn't be found they thought you had run on home."

Here were four witnesses against me. Whether Mother doubted me or not, I never knew. There were tears in her eyes as I hurried away alone on the long tramp to school. She never mentioned the matter to me again.

The distance between home and Greentree School was over a mile. It could be shortened a little by cutting across through deserted fields and woodland. The roadside path was usually better footing, but the road was more often beset with tormentors. Sometimes a farmer would see something was going on and would ask questions. At once utterly false charges were trumped up: "He called me names," "He called me a liar," and the like. Only too often the farmer was the father of one of the overgrown boys and shared the attitude of this group. Little sympathy and no justice was to be expected from the men. Women school directors were then unknown; evolution from the cave man had not yet progressed that far.

Though it was a tragedy then, it seems now, sixty-odd years later, merely curious that such bullying could go on so long without interference by teachers, directors, parents, neighbors, or some one. Conditions, at least in that farming and mining community, were different then. Almost all of the group of overgrown boys were sons of members of the board of directors, and the fathers not only were illiterate themselves but failed to realize the lack of education that resulted from early years of absence of their sons from school. They demanded that their boys just entering school for the first time at ten or fifteen years of age be put right through at the top of the class. Politics were of the shirtsleeve variety; no teacher could hold a position after finding fault with a director's son. No teacher dared initiatively to take up the misconduct of any pupil off the school premises, even if rumors of such misconduct had come in. Once Miss Moore was given a furlough, and a masculine teacher was put in to establish discipline. The overgrown boys put him out without overcoat or hat and locked him out in the cold until time for dismissal. Then they went home; he came in, dismissed school, and resigned. Miss Moore was sent for in haste.

One day Miss Moore sent me with a note to one of the directors. The director was not at home. "Meppe you find him py Slushman's, a'ready, yet," his wife said. Sure enough, there he was, seated at a little table in the sour-smelling barroom, with a stein of beer before him. He was a huge man with a face like a red full moon. His mouth was entirely hidden by drapery: an enormous fringe like a baleen whale. The strainer was filled with beer bubbles. I bowed, hat in hand, gave the note to the director, and was about to leave when there was a peremptory order to "vait a minutt." Slowly and laboriously the uneducated director read the note, following along the lines with his big, dirty finger. Suddenly he jumped to his feet, a mountain of flesh. He roared: "Py Gott, my Chim is yust so goot ez you vas. Get to hell out o' here."

The raging, bleary, beer-soaked brute lunged at me as I started for the door; I was not quick enough to escape a cruel stunning slap from his huge open hand. I never knew what was in the note, but years afterward the memory of that cruel, stinging blow came back to me with a rush to mar my enjoyment of one of the greatest and most beautiful compositions in the whole world of art, "The Slaying of the Unpropitious Messengers" (Lecomte du Nouy, 1872).

At last came the day of deliverance, one of the happiest days of my life. Examinations had been passed. A "Good-bye Session," as it was then and there called, was a forenoon affair at the end of the school year, the last Friday in April (1877). Short, original "speeches" were to be delivered by members of the graduating class. For my subject I had selected "Snow," and had intended accompanying it with drawings of snowflakes to be made on the board while talking. From Father's books I had memorized forms of crystals in snowflakes, and with freezing fingers, during the winter, I had drawn a few forms as seen through Father's little French microscope, outdoors where the flakes would not melt on the glass slide. I had memorized my speech, and on the way to school I rehearsed it many times. I remember seeing the schoolhouse a considerable distance ahead; and then I remember an angel leaning over me and saying in a soft gentle voice, "What happened, Chev?"

"Doctor, he must be delirious; he's talking about angels."

Then I heard the gruff voice of good old Doctor Walker, in whose buggy I had often ridden, say, "That's queer."

The gentle voice asked, "What's queer?"

"Why, that lump on the back of his neck. He must 'a' fallen backward and over a fence rail to hit the hollow of the back of his neck."

"No, Doctor; he was lying, face downward, on the side of the road. He moaned as I washed the mud off his face."

It was the angelic voice of Fannie Sheddon. She and her newly-wed husband had carried me into their home and had called in the Doctor, who was visiting an ill neighbor.

"Anyway, he is all right now. I'll take him home in my buggy; I'd be going that way, anyhow," said the Doctor.

Again Fannie Sheddon bent over me and said, "What happened, Chev?"

"I don't know. What did happen, Miss Sheddon? Excuse me—Mrs.—"

That was sixty years ago.

It was never known what had happened.

One thing came into my mind then, and I have often recalled it since, though until now I have never mentioned it.

I had often seen Big Bill Drake stun, then kill, trapped rabbits by hitting them on the back of the neck close to the skull with the edge of his massive hand.

Looking backward on this period of my childhood, I always naturally drift into abstract analysis and an outside viewpoint calling for the third person.

Psychology affords a simple and wholly satisfactory explanation of the acts of the tormentors; but it does not give any equally satisfactory explanation of the behavior of the child.

Why did the boy take all this abuse from older schoolmates without complaint to father and mother? When he ached so that he could not sleep at night, why did he not tell his mother of the rough handling he had received from some one or more of the overgrown boys? When chilblains rendered sleep fitful, why did he not tell of the tortures of icy, slush-filled boots? Why did he not mention the days of hunger when robbed of the luncheon his mother had so carefully put into the little tin bucket? When he started up out of sound sleep, screaming, his mother thought it was nightmare; really it was a dreamy review of the tortures of the day; when fully awakened, he was glad to find himself safe at home in bed. Why did he not make a confidante of his good, kind mother? Why did he so often help abusive pupils with their lessons? Why was there no vindictiveness, no attempt at reprisals?

The child himself, now grown to old age, cannot give a fully satisfactory answer, and abstract psychologic studies at this late date do not help much.

There was, undoubtedly, a curious dogged determination to suffer in silence; it is a most peculiar and rare trait in a child. It probably was made up of a number of factors, not all of them known, then or now. Perhaps one was a curious idea of being "game." He was probably apprehensive lest he be called "tattle-tale," or "fraidy cat" or "quitter." Maybe there was a foolish pride in demonstrating that, in today's colloquial phraseology, he "could take it." Another and more practical factor was that obviously any attempt at resistance or retaliation not only would be futile but would result in greater torments, or even in death as his tormentors often threatened. There also seemed to be a sort of fatalism; an idea that all these cruelties he suffered were a part of his lot, rather than wrongs to be righted by fighting. In addition there seemed to be an inexplicable instinctive feeling that, as with the opossum and some other animals, the only escape was in nonresistance. In fact on a number of occasions he gave way to a feeling of approaching unconsciousness in the hope that alarm of his persecutors might bring cessation of brutal physical onslaught; and it did.

As to confiding in his mother there was always the dread that, if the truth were known, he would be taken out of school.

When we come to psychologic consideration of the torturers, everything is simply and easily explained.

Having started school early, at four years of age, and having been there almost continuously, the boy Chev was, in classes, far ahead of the farmer and coal-miner boys, who, having to work, had had relatively few days at school until grown up. Other factors served to exaggerate the contrast. The jeering, taunting, often physical abuse, of recess led him to remain in the schoolroom during the recess periods as a means of escape; also it afforded opportunity to warm wet, cold feet. The natural way of putting in the time was preparation of the lessons for the day. This eliminated largely the necessity for advance home studies, thus leaving more time for the mechanical work that by preference occupied time at home. But the consequences at school were disastrous. The lessons freshly prepared, just in advance of recitations, naturally made high marks. "Teacher's pet" was the usual appellation. Miss Moore, an excellent teacher, naturally wished to make a good showing; when a director or other parent came in, Chev was called upon to recite, draw on the board, go through a spelling test, or otherwise perform. But it is easy to realize the feelings of inferiority (commonly called jealousy, envy, and enmity) naturally engendered in boys twice the size and twice the age, who, if called upon, could only humiliate themselves, their teacher, and their parents by poor performances of exercises in the primer. It was not generally realized that they did not lack intelligence—simply they had not been at school; some had entered school at ten or twelve years of age unable to read or write. The physical difference heightened the contrast. Naturally undersized, frail, and lacking vigorous outdoor life, Chev appeared younger than his years. A powerful, seventeen-year-old, almost six-foot youth, relegated to the background of a "Go as I go ox" primer performance by a child apparently half his age reciting poems of Longfellow, naturally developed what psychologists now know as an inferiority complex. One feature of such a complex is that it is usually vented by a powerful defense mechanism. This mechanism in these overgrown boys naturally took the form of a demonstration of physical superiority. Hence the physical torture. "The teacher's pet" had a pitiable life out of school hours. The destruction of the sled and of the drawings was a quite typical demonstration of the defense mechanism of the inferiority complex.

When we come to analyze the effect exerted upon his future life by the school days at Greentree, a few things are clear; but in considering other things we enter the field of speculative psychology that has no limit, no rules, no end; a field in which every psychologist wanders around loose.

Unquestionably the prolonged torture had a profound influence throughout life; but probably there existed basic temperamental factors in the dogged determination to remain silent and nonresistant under torture. Certain it is that all subsequent trials and tribulations seemed as nothing by comparison.

I am certain that I have not been, at any later time, tormented, tortured, or pursued in the way I was at Greentree School. In fact, all my later life was a happy one marred only by grief at the death of my father and mother. These matters will be referred to on a future page in connection with personal traits.

CHAPTER IV

HOTEL LIFE

(1874–1882)

THIS EXPERIENCE EXTENDING over a period of eight or nine years, though in the three summer months only, exerted a powerful influence on my whole life. It seems well therefore to consider it topically, though, chronologically, it has long overlaps.

When impending bankruptcy, due to a trusted employee's embezzlement, threatened Father with unpaid debts, he converted our old home at Idlewood into a summer hotel. It was a family hostelry without a bar. Pittsburgh was submerged under a pall of black smoke and a falling, all-covering black mantle of soot. The well-to-do iron and steel manufacturers were learning to take vacations and Sunday outings; week ends were unknown, and London bankers had not yet started the practice of Saturday half holidays. The people who could afford it saw the advisability of getting their puny, sun-starved children to the country. Cresson Springs, promoted by the Pennsylvania Railroad Company, was overflowing with summer patrons. Cresson Springs was a hundred miles away; we were only six—just beyond Pittsburgh's pall of smoke and fringe of iron mills and coal mines. The prospects were good, but it took money to convert a home into a hotel. A second mortgage was placed on the house and the twenty-four acres of woodland that had been Mother's heritage. She contributed a lot of Knickerbocker heirlooms toward furnishings, and cheap but decoratively painted cottage furniture was bought, in addition. Tempting offers for a bar concession were made by the liquor interests that even then dominated the retailing of alcoholic beverages; these offers were promptly rejected.

Until the summer hotel life was begun (when I was nine years old) I had a cultured home; but my only outside contacts were with the roughest of human beings—many of them criminals, potentially or actually, and almost all uncultured. Though many of them were honest, most of the men and boys were hard-headed, hard-fighting, hard-drinking, hard-swearing, swaggering, quarrelsome ruffians. Many of them, coming into the house, might spit tobacco juice on the carpet. The admired type was the man who "traveled on his muscle" and spent much of his money on fines in the police court and most of the rest in one of the taverns.

It can be imagined then what a revelation it was to me when the hotel filled for the summer with the families of clergymen, lawyers, judges, railway executives, iron manufacturers, and merchants. A few in the latter two groups were self-made men with little education or culture; but their sons and daughters were going to college or were in preparation therefor. Higher education was a matter of course. Every day and every evening there was a social function of some kind—picnics, riding and driving parties, dances, musicales, concerts, amateur theatricals, art studies. An art class was organized by the wife of Judge Kennedy; she complimented me on my drawings and asked me to join. I was relieved of work for a few hours a week to take part. I also had a few happy hours occasionally sketching with Mr. A. Bryan Wall. In all of the various activities that were suitable to my age I was invited to participate; but my duties at the hotel left practically no time. In the purely social affairs I would not have taken part anyway. Some of the activities, especially music, would have been intensely interesting to me if I had been free; but the greatest item of expense in operation of the hotel was the pay roll, and suitable help was difficult to get. Every member of our family worked sixteen or seventeen hours out of the twenty-four. He worked as long as he could stand or sit up and then went to bed with the feeling that he was not half done with the day's work. Not only was there the operation of the hotel proper, but there were the accessories essential to a summer family hotel—the stable, the dairy, and the vegetable garden. So far as possible, in the allotment of work, due consideration was given to my natural ability to rise early and disability for remaining awake at night. Exigencies often interfered with the early-to-bed part of the program. In fact one of the greatest hardships for me was the necessity to remain awake in the evening, unless the duty was active.

Tenpins was a popular pastime at the hotel. My participation in it was at the wrong end of the alley. Setting up the pins for the players to knock down was a lucrative job for boys, as pay was reckoned in those days. Often as much as twenty cents could be jingled in the pocket after a sweating summer evening in the sawdust pit at the end of the alley, setting up the heavy maple pins and stepping up lively onto the high shelf to escape the flying pins. That the shelf was not high enough is evident from the fact that one evening I was knocked off it senseless by a flying pin. At least that is what they told me when I recovered consciousness the next day. The doctor thought I had meningitis but revised his diagnosis to concussion after I recovered. I remember the headache as equal to that of my attack of smallpox. The two occasions were my only experiences with severe headache, for which I am duly grateful. It was three weeks before the doctor allowed me to set up pins again. Stooping over, he said, was not good after head injuries.

One of my emergency duties was every now and then to recruit a new staff of negro help, especially waiters, of whom four to six were needed. After dinner they would get very jolly, dance jigs, sing plantation songs, do impromptu minstrel acts. This was all very well and was greatly enjoyed by the guests. The trouble was that sometimes negroes visiting the help would join in, bringing whisky along. The hilarity was followed by combativeness, ending in a free fight and a walk-out of all hands. It was my duty to drum up recruits for replacement next day. I would go up Wylie Avenue and through its tributary alleys in Pittsburgh, make a round of the poolrooms, saloons, gambling rooms, dens of iniquity and vice where the negroes congregated when they got any pay envelopes. One of my discoveries of the psychology of the happy-go-lucky, floating negro population from which recruits for waiters were obtainable was that so long as any money remained in pocket an impenetrable armor of independence resisted all inducements.

"Work! You want me to work? Why, boy, you's crazy, you is. Crazier'n a bedbug. Listen dat"—jingling a few coins. "Listen dat, 'n' run along fin' some poor nigger wat's broke 'n' gotta work."

This good advice was followed until the required number was obtained, and I piloted my motley crew to the station and got them on the train. Promises to meet me at the station were of the piecrust variety and not dependable. To make sure of delivery of my recruits, I had to insist on their coming along with me.

Sometimes I arrived as a fight started, generally a drunken fight. Warned by the shouts, curses, and threats, I could usually escape without seeing anything. Once two colored men were pushed out through the swing doors of a saloon onto the sidewalk. Blood was squirting, and the combatants were slashing at each other with backed razors. I turned and ran away as hard as I could, with tears streaming from my eyes. Policemen, also on the run, met and passed me on their way to the fight. I little thought then that these razor cutthroat cases were to furnish me in later life with unique opportunities for the development of a system of laryngeal surgery.

It has been a wonder to me since, that dire disaster did not overtake me on these recruiting excursions into the negro slums of the Wylie Avenue district. Once I was knocked down, and all my expense money taken. I did not mind the six-mile walk home, but I did not want to arrive without the recruits for whom I had been sent. Finally I found three willing to walk. They were half starved, and my promise of all they could eat on arrival added largely to my powers of persuasion. Climbing the steep road up Coal Hill attenuated the courage of one to the point of dropping out. He had already faced backward for the return when I made his mouth water with the description of a big steaming plate of hot boiled beef, onions, and potatoes that was awaiting our arrival; plate to be refilled as often as he wanted. I had no misgivings as to ability to make good on this promise because my affinity for all things culinary had taught me that the old colored cook always had a huge pot of left-over plate scrapings on the back of the stove, and the odor therefrom was always appetizing, especially so to those who were not fastidiously disdainful of leavings. We all four arrived hungry and penniless and did ample justice to the scrap pot. I was a proud boy when my recruits, duly fed and well washed, were on duty in their white aprons in time to serve dinner. This pride in achievement in spite of difficulties, in principle the same but under circumstances varying from the heights of absurdity to the depths of pathos, seems to have pervaded my whole life. The degree of pleasure in achievement bore little or no relation to the commercial value of the particular achievement, but it always bore a close relation to the magnitude of the difficulties encountered. The pleasure was greatest when the difficulties were deemed insurmountable—the oft-recurring intrigue of the impossible.

After a few years of summer hotel experience, Father saw the necessity of piping spring water into the house, and of a better means of lighting than kerosene lamps. Electric lighting had not yet gone beyond a laboratory experimental stage. Coal gas was used in cities; natural gas was then considered too dangerous for household use, and service lines had not been laid. Father decided upon the installation of a gas generating plant for illumination. The process was to vaporize very volatile (88°) gasoline by blowing a gentle current of air, at exactly sixteen ounces pressure, up through the gasoline in the tank. The whole apparatus, in mechanical principles, was the same as the since commonly used apparatus for the insufflation of ether for anesthesia, except that water power was used for running the pressure generator. The parallel was curiously close when unconsciousness accidentally followed my breathing too much of the vapor. The water supply was from a great gushing spring on a neighboring hillside. The water was piped through the house as well as the gas. The extensive installation of pumps, pipes, valves, check valves, water and gas fixtures with no end of new tools, filled me with tremendous enthusiasm. For one four-months summer vacation I was a "cub," as plumber's apprentices were then called. The work was hard and heavy, ten hours a day; but I enjoyed every minute of it. Thereafter each summer it was my duty to maintain gas and water service. Under the precarious conditions this was a great responsibility for a boy. The spring water was pure but there were frequent obstructions of pipes by sand, gravel, rotten wood, leaves, grass, algae, worms, larvae, insects, crayfish, and the like. It was illogical, but it often seemed that the insects, worms, and crayfish waited for great social occasions at the hotel to occlude the small nozzle of the gas-generating water motor, putting the whole place in darkness. This meant an emergency call to go down into the depths of the pit to take the water motor apart and clean away the obstruction. It was necessary to work in the dark by sense of touch; flashlights were unknown and any other light, even a Davy's lantern, would have caused an explosive wreck. The fumes of the very volatile gasoline were so strong that I was a number of times hoisted up, unconscious, by the body-rope worn for the purpose; one of the times very nearly too late, they said. Even at that the plumbing job afforded me more pleasure than the gayeties that went on again after the light was restored to the dancing pavilion. Plumber's overalls, like operating clothes later, were more congenial to me than evening clothes. Moreover, at that time I had only the overalls; and they were extensively patched. Of the few other clothes in the wardrobe, none were such as to encourage appearance on the dancing floor even if I had so desired.

At a later period, while I was at medical college, natural gas was rendered serviceable for household use; the gas generator that under my struggling care had rendered good service was disconnected, and natural gas was turned into the hotel piping.

The contact with people of refinement was in sharp contrast to the atmosphere of Greentree School with its uncouth, overgrown sons of coal miners. The collegiate work of the older group of young folks at the hotel was an inspiration. I marveled at the use of language by the lawyers, judges, teachers, professors. All these contacts increased my ambition to get an education. I reëntered Greentree that autumn with a determination to get all the learning I could. Each summer thereafter I received the impetus that helped to carry me through the ordeals elsewhere mentioned. Stronger and stronger became the dread that I might be taken out of school and grow up ignorant like the miners' boys.

One of the important things in the hotel life was my experience with tubes and valves. This led to the later discovery that in the bronchial tubes there are vitally important pathologic mechanisms parallel to the stop valves, by-pass valves, and check valves fundamental to pipes, pumps, and plumbing. My whole life's work with the air and food passages seems curiously parallel in its fundamentals to those boyhood days as a plumber's cub.

Though the personal benefits to me from the hotel life were so many and so diversified as to be on the whole enormous and incalculable, yet commercially the summer hotel was not profitable. The season was too short, the house was really filled for only six or eight weeks. The expense of dairy, stable, and garden had to be carried through the entire year. Necessary repairs and improvements had to be financed. Father made some payments on his debts, but they were depressingly small. The interest was devouring the profits.

CHAPTER V

COMMUTING FOR AN EDUCATION

(1878–1882)

AFTER GRADUATING AT the Greentree Township public school, I passed satisfactory entrance examinations and began premedical education at the Western University of Pennsylvania, now the University of Pittsburgh. Residence in the country required a journey morning and evening of about an hour. The time spent on the train was sufficient to accomplish all the home work except the final copying of written exercises to be handed in at school. The habit of working in railroad cars thus acquired continued throughout life. (See page 102.)

Work at the Western University yielded high marks at first; but soon the classmates who cared little for drawing complained that their marks were dragged down by their inability to draw. Instead of working to improve their drawing they prevailed upon the faculty to omit drawing in calculating averages in scholastic work. Consequently the averages of pupils who did good drawing fell. The faculty did not seem to realize the usefulness of drawing nor the fact that anybody can learn to draw if he wants to do so. All cannot become great artistic draughtsmen; but the simple primary exercises of drawing in use in schools can be done well by any child who will earnestly try, provided, of course, the eyesight is good with refractive errors properly corrected.

Next to drawing my greatest interest in school work was in physiology, geography, Latin, Greek, English, and mathematics, about in the order given. History, telling about what the kings, dictators, rulers, and politicians did, was uninteresting. Except in physiology I did not regularly head the class as I had done at

Greentree School; but I managed always to keep above the average.

The Western University of Pennsylvania had no baseball team, no football eleven, no gymnastics. But if it had had these or any other athletic activities the attractions would not have been sufficient to prevent my getting home by the earliest possible train to do the chores early enough to leave some time for work in the shop, or at the designs preliminary thereto.

During this commuting period luncheon was carried in a tin pail. To understand the importance of the tin luncheon pail it is necessary to recall that waxed paper was practically unknown. Slices of bread in anything but tight-lidded tin containers dried out by noon. Luncheon baskets were satisfactory only when they had a pail inside. But soon after beginning to commute, I discovered that at any peanut stand two large pretzels could be purchased for a cent. With an apple carried from home two pretzels afforded an ample luncheon, provided one was not fastidious. The pretzels were grimy and decorated with many fingerprints—and, in warm weather, with many "fly specks," meaning excrement. After Mother saw the source of supply there were no more pretzel luncheons. The power of the fly and the food handler as distributors of disease was unknown to medical science in those days; but Mother and Grandmother were great sticklers for cleanliness in food. Thereafter I had a little basket with an apple and a tiny tin pail inside.

Tom Jones would not be bothered with basket or pail. He started out in the morning with both coat pockets bulging, a sizable sandwich, paper-wrapped, in each. Before arriving at school he would say: "Oh, I'm not going to carry these things around in my pockets all day! I'll eat 'em and carry 'em inside." So down they would go on top of a hearty breakfast. When he saw an amused smile he flared up and demanded: "I can't eat it more than once, can I? What's the difference?" The logic was good, but along about noontime there was a demand for a share of the slender supply in the tin pail and basket.

THE OLD MAN'S GARDEN

Ohio River Bank

(OIL)

1916

BROOKLINE BRIDGE (CHALK) 1920

The aristocrats of the noon half-hour were the Groetzinger brothers. They each had a daily allowance of ten cents; it was used to obtain a piece of pie and a saucer of ice cream in the not overclean "Ice Cream Parlor" around the corner—though why it was called a "parlor" was a mystery then, and so remains.

CHAPTER VI

ENTERING UPON THE STUDY OF MEDICINE

(1882)

THE CUSTOM OF THE TIME was to begin the study of medicine under a preceptor, the relationship being similar in many ways to an apprenticeship. The chief difference was that there was a terminal two or three years' collegiate work to obtain a diploma conferring the degree of Doctor of Medicine (M.D.). As in most other mutual arrangements the results depended largely on the personal equation. When both parties could and did fulfill their respective obligations there were advantages in the system. The pupil got in the various branches practical training that served as pegs on which to hang things. In preparing medicaments, he learned the physical properties of drugs, their appearance, taste, and odor along with their dosage and the conditions for which they were used. Helping in emergencies, at operations, at the setting of dislocations and fractures, made the work interesting and practical. Skill in the laboratory tests, chiefly urinalysis in those days, was quickly and practically acquired. The studious pupil eager for knowledge made ultimately an excellent practitioner; especially good when the preceptor was a good teacher. When the pupil was lazy and indifferent the results were poor; and if in addition the preceptor was neither a competent practitioner nor a good teacher the results were deplorable. In the case of Gilmore Foster and myself the results were ideal. Doctor Foster was a man of great knowledge and skill and was an excellent teacher: I was hungry for knowledge. At the end of a year, in the opinion of the preceptor, I was ready for collegiate work.

Then came the financial difficulties; notwithstanding the rigid economies that had been practiced, sufficient funds could not be gathered together to enter college. Father was almost bankrupt through embezzlements by employees. The home property had been mortgaged to pay the debts accruing from the defaults. Additional borrowings had been necessary to finance the hotel. This business had barely carried the interest charges and a few small payments on the debt. Mother was thrifty and a good manager, but her economies had been swept away by the foolish financial undertakings of her brothers. How to raise the money was a problem. To follow my artistic bent meant starvation. The solution of the problem came in an unexpected way.

Mother saw in a newspaper:

WANTED.—China and glass decorators; only skilled workmen need apply. Julius A. Burgun, Dinwiddie St., cor. Reed St.

Application was made immediately; I explained that, though lacking experience in work with colors that could be fired, I felt that I could do satisfactory work. The pay was by the piece. I was given two dozen glass lamp shades on which winter scenes were to be painted from copies given. These when fired turned out satisfactorily. Next, two dozen glass lamp stands were assigned for the painting of apple blossoms and butterflies. The designs were simple, and the results satisfactory. The study of oil painting with the art class, the sketching with A. Bryan Wall, drawing in school and out, had rendered this decorative art quite easy and simple. The wages then paid for such work were relatively high. Hand-painted glass shades and hand-painted china were very fashionable and commanded a high price. Skilled workmen were scarce. Mr. Burgun was a good trainer of decorators. Later a large decorating shop was built in Dithridge's Glass Works and Mr. Burgun and his decorators, including myself, were installed. I accumulated enough funds to justify entering medical college the following year (1884). Additionally, though I did not know it at the time, the art studies, the oil painting, and the practical work in decorating gave me skill with the brush that was to prove of inestimable value in after life. The facility in drawing in color enabled me to record what I saw through the bronchoscope and to reproduce it for medical illustrations. Had it not been for this training, many fundamental endoscopic, clinical observations would have been unrecorded and practically lost to medical science, because no illustrative artist could be had when the always unexpected views were seen through the bronchoscope; the cost would have been prohibitive; and moreover no such artist could see in the constantly shifting image in the tube what the bronchoscopist by long training had learned to see.

In October, 1884, with the earnings of the decorating shop in a money belt and a strong letter from my preceptor, Doctor Gilmore Foster, in my pocket, I went to Philadelphia, passed entrance examinations, and was enrolled as a student in Jefferson Medical College.

CHAPTER VII

COLLEGE LIFE

(1884–1885)

COLLEGE LIFE AS THE TERM is now usually understood, fraternities, dormitories, football, simply did not exist for me. Of the fund accumulated by work in decorating glass and china there remained after tuition was paid only sixty-three cents a day to meet all expenses for the entire collegiate year of six months. A meagerly furnished room in an attic was obtained at 925 Walnut Street for one dollar a week. An unlimited supply of anthracite coal in the cellar was available in consideration of the services of carrying it to the attic and to all the other eight rooms in the house. The four-flight climb as a "wind-developer" was a fairly good substitute for a football trainer's daily winter run in shorts.

An inborn fondness for cooking made it no hardship to prepare food on the flat-topped laundry stove with which the attic room was furnished. There was more than enough time for a quick cold sponge before the water boiled. A creamless cup of Arbuckle Ariosa coffee and the butterless butt of the previous day's French loaf at four-thirty in the morning started the day's work. Study filled every minute until nine. It then took brisk work to carry the morning supply of coal, shave, wash face and hands again, and get around the corner for the ten o'clock lecture. At noon an apple from home and two not overclean, much handled, costermonger's pretzels took but a few minutes from the two hours' work in the dissecting room that preceded the first afternoon lecture. The last lecture was over at six o'clock. While dinner was boiling, the evening coal was carried to the various rooms. The dinner consisted of vegetables boiled with a bone or sometimes a bit of meat for flavor; meat itself was naturally little desired. A lifelong bent for cooking, started under the tuition of Mother, made me a *chef de cuisine* in the art of flavoring. Delicious odors pervaded the attic and at times were sniffed by hungry roomers when the savory air-borne flavors permeated a floor or two below. Onions, flavoring mustard, bay leaf, thyme, sage, mace, cloves, and other spices blended inseparably in the aroma. Flavoring was cheap and a little went a long way. Moreover, the thickened gravy rendered butter (always expensive) unnecessary on the bread from the French bakery around the corner. The butt end of the loaf was held over for early breakfast. The vegetable elements in the boiled dinner were varied from time to time. Vegetables were absurdly cheap at the Farmers' Market on Market Street, where the Reading Railroad Station is now; but the variety was limited in winter. California and Florida were not then sources of supply; early spring lettuce from hotbeds, like tropical fruits, was utterly beyond the budgetary limits; a few oranges and lemons came along with the apples in the Christmas box from home. Cabbage and onions were about the only winter green foods; they were cheap, as were also potatoes, turnips, parsnips, carrots, dried beans and peas. Sauerkraut boiled with a pork bone by the open window was the usual Sunday dinner. The landlord's dog in the back yard got the bone when it would no longer yield a floating globule of fat. A keg of salt herrings from Holland cost seventy-three cents. When the box from home brought butter, a simple luxury was johnnycake. This was uneatably hard and very cheap ship's biscuit softened in boiling water and eaten hot with a little butter. The biscuit water and vegetable water formed a basic start for next day's soup. As an amateur provincial chef from Pittsburgh I was greatly intrigued by the (strange to me) Philadelphia pepper-pot soup. I soon learned to make it in delicious form, and because of the cheapness of its component parts it was a stand-by on the attic menu. Fried scrapple was another Philadelphia specialty that tickled the provincial palate without unbalancing the budget. Sliced apples browned in the fat that cooked out of the scrapple were a proper accompaniment, and the fat next day served to brown some previously boiled potatoes. The medical student occupying the third floor back used to visit often his home folks in Gloucester, New Jersey. In the spring the hauling of the net in the Delaware was to him an interesting procedure, and it resulted in the contribution of a shad to the attic larder in exchange for a copy of the notes on the missed Monday morning lecture. On one occasion the occupant of the third floor back brought in two reedbirds that were then plentiful on the marshy Delaware River shore. Pot-roasted, covered with some strips of bacon from home, they were delicious; but a bone lodged in the tonsil created great excitement when removed at the College Hospital, not so much because of the clinical features of the case as because of the mystery as to how a poor medical student could have come by such a gastronomic luxury as a reedbird. That was my last reedbird: not a matter of accident with the bone, nor of subsequent extinction of the bobolink. Love of wild songbirds spoiled my appetite for that kind of dish. In fact I came to care little for any kind of animal food. By reason of good cooking I fared well and was quite happy in the little attic room, after hard bumps on the head had trained me into instinctive localization of the ceiling limitations of the dormer window.

The only recreation during college life was a Sunday afternoon and evening walk along the Delaware water front. In those days sailing ships, mostly square-riggers, from all over the world could be found at the docks or anchored in the Delaware. Catboats and small sloops brought in produce and oysters from the Jersey shore; coasting schooners brought cargoes from Southern and West Indian ports. It was picturesque, ever changing, and always interesting. Often since, I have deemed myself fortunate not to have been shanghaied; but I never thought of it then. Possibly my undersize and frail physique did not appeal to short-handed shipmasters; it is more likely my total abstinence saved me, as I had many invitations from strangers, such as, "Have a drink"; "I say, 'ave a bit o' a sup o' hale"; "Matey, have a wee drop o' whusky wi' us"; "Say, whitey, we's got some ol' Jummaica in hyur—real stuff. C'mon in." Such invitations had some object; they were not flung around broadcast; acceptances would have been overwhelming in numbers.

Tuition is mentioned above. This is not an exact term under the conditions then existing. Each of the eight professors issued personally signed tickets for his lectures. It was considered in those more or less Latin days *infra dignitatem* to accept a salary. The college collected the money for all the eight tickets ("the professional jackpot," J. Chalmers Da Costa has since called it) and divided the net proceeds with the professors, who each signed a ticket for each student, a few after every lecture. Later, medical colleges collected a tuition and conducted the institutions on business principles; nothing was paid to the professors. It may be parenthetically added that, in the clinical branches, with the exception of a few endowed chairs, they are paid nothing today, in most medical colleges. It seems strange to the layman that the medical professorships should be so eagerly sought; they entail an enormous amount of work and little or no pay. The professorship may add to the incumbent's reputation, or the professor may bring renown to the college. Either way, it is attractively unbusinesslike. Pay for the grocer must come from private practice, if any. Sometimes a well rooted, middle-aged, famous professor may refuse an invitation to transplant himself without a guarantee that his income shall not be less than a certain sum, an agreement potent for trouble.

Professor Samuel W. Gross was doing his best to teach the then new methods of antiseptic surgery. William H. Pancoast, Professor of Anatomy, thought and taught that antisepsis was nothing more than mere cleanliness; otherwise he was one of the best surgeons who ever lived. He held his scalpel between his teeth while ligating blood vessels, prepared his bare hands only by washing, and dressed wounds with unsterilized zinc oxide ointment. On one vividly remembered occasion twenty students were each asked to feel in a fistula in a boy's neck to learn for all time the touch of diseased bone. They marched down single file and felt with finger "as is." Pancoast and his clinics were popular, but utterly at variance with the new surgical era that Gross was trying to inaugurate. A rift occurred in the faculty. Clinics were taken away from Pancoast. He resigned and later, with John Shoemaker, founded the Medico-Chirurgical College.

This episode marks the passing of the old surgical era of "laudable pus" and the advent of the great era of the aseptic surgery that has saved untold millions of lives.

Some of the "freshmen" in the class were over sixty years old. These men had already been practicing medicine many years but had never had a degree. The then recently passed legislation authorized issue of a license to practice either on oath of the applicant that he had already practiced medicine for at least ten years, or on presentation of a diploma. Any kind of diploma would do, if it were plate-printed or engrossed. The prothonotary's clerk did not know one from another, nor even, for sure, that there was such a college.

CHAPTER VIII

ADVENTURES OF A BOOK AGENT

(1885)

THE CURRICULUM of the medical college of those days consisted, as previously mentioned, of two winter courses of lectures and clinics, of six months each. There was no grading; both winters' lectures were the same. The course began the first of October and ended the last of March. At the end of my first winter's work I was very homesick. I had received a letter from Mother telling me of the awful struggle she and Father were having to make ends meet. They were trying to hold out without getting deeper into debt until the summer guests should arrive. Mother sent four dollars; all I had was five dollars—the proceeds of the sale to a wealthy medical student of a fine, dissected, dried and painted anatomical specimen I had made during the winter months in the dissecting room. The nine dollars would just barely pay my train fare home. I debated whether by walking home I could save anything, considering shoe leather, a little food en route and the expenses of shipment of my remnants of a wardrobe, my books, notes, specimens, and dissecting instruments that constituted my baggage—pitiably meager but, to me, priceless. I should have enjoyed the walk home over the mountains, a distance of about three hundred and fifty miles, by taking my time; but the heavy cost of express shipment turned the financial balance against the plan. I bought a ticket and was on the way back to my quarters to pack when I was attracted by a display of new medical books. I had no money to buy books; but I was on good terms with the manager of the publishing concern because my extolling the value of some of his new publications had brought a few students who were less enthusiastic readers but financially better able to purchase books. I was always cordially invited to look over the stock. This time the manager saw me looking in the window. He came out and asked me in. After I had congratulated him on one of his latest publications, he said, "Doctor"—it was always flattering to an undergraduate to be thus addressed—"wouldn't you have time to sell some books for us during vacation?"

The prospect of making a little money aroused my interest because we were really worse off than if we had had nothing and the awful burden of debt was depressing Father, Mother, and me. Father had written that the use of natural gas had so simplified plumbing requirements that they were easily taken care of by my younger brother, who had grown competent.

The manager knew my longing for books I could not buy. He offered me 50 per cent commission on sales—the commission to be paid in books of my selection, I to pay all expenses of travel. This prospect of new books in which I could revel was very alluring, but I had no money to enable me to carry on; and I told him so. He then proposed to give half the commission in books and pay me the other half in cash, out of which I was to pay my expenses; and he would advance me some money for a start. This looked attractive except for the starting out in debt: I had a horror of owing anybody anything, and knowledge of Father's troubles deepened my dread of debt. The kindly old manager reassured me with a promise of great leniency, and I was about to accept when he said, "Of course you know salesmen's territories are allotted, and so long as you are active we shall send no other man into your bailiwick."

This sounded fair enough, but immediately the importance of location became paramount; up to that moment I had a conception only of going wherever I might deem prospects best, and especially of being able to work my way home from town to town, selling a book here and there to physicians on the way. But the only territory offered was Massachusetts exclusive of Boston. This did not sound attractive, especially the exclusion of Boston, where presumably physicians' fees were often paid in money, eventually at least. The small-town and country practitioner took most of his pay in supplies, provisions and services; at least it was so in western Pennsylvania, and it seemed probable that in thrifty New England it would be more so. The manager finally agreed to add to the territory the part of Connecticut that lies east of the river of the same name.

My Knickerbocker grandmother had often indignantly repeated to me the wooden nutmeg episode and had told me often the Massachusetts people put a few shovelfuls of earth on the granite rock and raised thereon a few beans to supplement the salt codfish diet. Grandfather, who had lived in Dedham, Massachusetts, looked abused but did not question Grandmother's views. He said they were thrifty: Grandmother said many of them were skinflints, and unscrupulous at that.

"I fear you overrate my ability as a salesman. Do you think I could sell books to New Englanders?"

"Yes, medical books to physicians in New England. Doctors are always hungry for books."

I knew that, if they were as eager for books as I was, they would certainly buy.

The manager offered the services of his shipping department to box and ship my chattels home by freight.

I was very homesick. To go off into New England at that moment when, having done all duties, I was ready to start for home, was a bitter disappointment; but it was this very thing that influenced me to accept the offer. As soon as I found myself influenced in the decision by my purely personal, therefore selfish, feeling of homesickness I decided at once to make the effort to help the family and accumulate a little toward the expense of the next winter in college. I should be paying for badly needed books. I wrote home telling of the change of plans and hid my feeling under forced cheerfulness. I wrote gayly of reprisal for selling Grandmother's people those wooden nutmegs and enlarged upon the joy I should get out of reading the new sample books myself: trying them on the dog.

Fighting off the awful homesickness, I got a refund on the ticket for home. It seemed like cutting off home ties. It was with the utmost depression that I packed the few clothes I had into a handbag with toilet articles, not forgetting the little ditty bag, as the sailors call it, containing needles, thread, darning cotton, buttons, thimble, and scissors.

My salesman's outfit, given by the manager, included two complete books and a prospectus of six others, consisting of sample pages with a flatly pasted backbone cover of each to show actual size and appearance. The outfit was not heavy. Books were much lighter in weight then than now; the half-tone illustrations that require heavily coated book paper were then unknown. There was a book of order blanks not formidable in size as a book but appalling in the suggestion that signatures to all those blanks must be obtained before I could think of starting for home.

A man on the road selling books has endless opportunities to study life. If he be philosophic, he soon discovers that he must get used to all kinds of people. There are the good and the bad, the just and the unjust, the noble and the mean, the sincere and the tricky, the smooth and the uncouth, the polite and the rude. I certainly saw many examples of each kind.

Through all the trials, tribulations, rebuffs, and insults, one thing above all others kept up my courage. I knew the books were good, and they were new. Unquestionably there was not a single physician whose patients would not be potentially benefited by his purchase of the books. Discretion forbade expression, but the thought gave courage. When insults were unusually cutting I could always fall back upon the memory of my school days at Greentree; by contrast the worst that could be done to a lonely, homesick book agent was as nothing.

I did not mind being asked, politely or rudely, to get out. No one physically put me out; I went when it became obviously useless to remain. What worried me constantly was the financial situation. At various towns letters from home were awaiting me at the general delivery window. There was a forced cheerfulness about them, but between the lines the lack of improvement in money matters was evident. I could not help them, and I had been able after a month's work to send home only sixty dollars to put aside toward the collegiate expenses of the next winter. I had been frugal in expenditures to the point of impairing my health. A lookout during the daylight rounds located the cheapest possible lodgings for the night. Breakfast was usually an apple, a glass of milk, and, for a *pièce de résistance,* a cold, coarse, malodorous, stringy, codfish ball. The old, fishy, rancid, burnt fat imparted to the enduring cod fibers a lasting quality that entirely eliminated all need for noonday luncheon, which was always more or less perfunctory, anyway, with me. If the enduring codfish ball was unobtainable for breakfast, a glass of milk was taken at noon. The evening meal was a bowl of chowder or a boiled dinner—turnips and potatoes boiled with a bone; sometimes shreds of meat were traceable. In the shore towns fresh fish was cheap but was always ruined for palate and stomach by frying hard in old, strong salt-pork fat. Portions were always scanty, and I was often half-famished. At times, cold, lardy beans were welcome because of the length of time they would postpone hunger pains.

The great obstacle to profits in book sales was the time wasted; that is, wasted from a salesman's viewpoint. Much of this wasted time I rendered profitable by studying the books I was selling. It was necessary not only to catch the physician at home but to wait until he had seen all his waiting patients. Often, after I had waited two hours or more, he had to hurry out on an urgent call without seeing me—or he would say so. If I could catch his eye by the flashing of an attractive illustration in the book he might say, "Come back this evening, and I'll look at your books." Some men would say: "Leave the book. I'll look at it when I get time."

This of course I could not do because it would leave me short of samples for work in the meantime. The hardest work for me was in the evening. I was tired and sleepy, so sleepy I could hardly keep my eyes open. Studying the books made me more sleepy. To doze off in the doctor's office would have been degrading to me and ruinous as a business start.

At last I had covered my allotted territory. I ended at Gloucester, Massachusetts, with clothes threadbare, my only remaining shirt on my back. My shoe soles were worn through, there were holes in the toes. A piece cut out of each shoe tongue and inserted inside the respective toe holes, with a stitch each side for anchorage, prevented protrusion of darned socks. An insole cut from pasteboard fresh each day or two prevented wearing away of the socks at the holes worn through in the soles of the shoes. And always the shoes were cleaned and polished with the brush I carried in my bag. The tools in the ditty bag did good service in turning under frayed trousers. Not only socks were darned, but the seat of the trousers had several areas of basket weaving. Any skillful needlewoman would have pronounced it good work; there was no clumsy needlework to be ashamed of, but the shelter from public view given by the rather long coats then in fashion helped maintain an air of respectability. The worn-out and darned elbows were not so easily concealed; but hiding them was accomplished by keeping the palms turned forward. I always tried to appear fresh and clean, face, hands, and piccadilly collar of glistening celluloid washed often; and the pocket comb was used at every opportunity. But there is an end to all things—especially fabrics; and I was a shabby-genteel, threadbare, down-at-the-heel remnant of a book agent, gaunt and often weak from cutting too close on the food supply.

I had a good stock of books to my credit; all I should need to finish my collegiate work. I had repaid the advance given me by the manager of the publishing house, and I had sent the sixty dollars home for the college expense fund, but I did not have money enough to pay the carfare home. I should gladly have walked; but shoe leather was lacking, and a week's subsistence would be necessary. The most meager food for another day would see me penniless. I was homesick.

In the coastal towns I had always patronized by preference the little longshore nondescript eating places where sea food made subsistence possible at minimum cost. At these shacks I had heard many tales of great catches of fish, and good returns to the men on a basis of wage and share. Salted and dried codfish was standard food in New England and a staple export to the West Indies and South America. With due allowance for the amplification of sailormen's yarns and longshoremen's whisky-limbered tongues, there seemed to be a chance to make a little money and to get plenty of food, whatever it might be in quality, if I could get a berth on a fishing schooner. It required two months or longer to fill a schooner's hold with split, cleaned, and salted cod.

I had carried in my pocket always when away from home a stamped envelope addressed to my father for use in case of accident happening to me. I wrote on the blank page it contained that I had fulfilled my contract, and that if I could get a berth on a fishing schooner I would take it.

CHAPTER IX

COD FISHERMAN AND SEA COOK

(1885)

"I'M SHORT ONE HAND—could use two if I had 'em," fumed the captain on the wharf at Gloucester, " 'n' I otta be halfway to the Banks now." This was muttered partly to himself and partly to the decrepit, retired fishermen on the wharf.

"Could you give me a chance, sir?"

"Ye don't look like an able hand to me. Ever been to the Banks?"

"No, sir."

"Ever been to sea?"

"Yes, sir; but not on a schooner, sir."

"Well, what in the hell makes ye think ye'd be any good on a fishin' schooner?"

"I have sailed small boats, sir. I have never been seasick in my life. I can handle a dory; I can cook, and I can do what I am told, sir."

"Well, that is good as fur as it goes, but it don't go fur. 'Sides I have a cook."

Whether it was the determination to be off or the respectful attitude of the applicant is unknown—captains of fishing schooners are not "sirred" like big-ship masters and mates; anyway, the captain seemed to change his mind.

"Do ye drink?"

"No, sir."

"Thur ain't no rum on board an' thur ain't goin' to be none, seein' as I'm cap'n.

"Here, jump in the dory 'n' take me out to my ship. If ye can handle the dory, proper, I'll gi' ye ten dollar a month. If ye're good and willin', mebbe ye'll git a share; if ye ain't, ye won't. If ye're a lubber wi' the dory, I'll set ye ashore and I'll be off short-handed."

I was not set ashore.

On board I found nothing in the way of a slop chest; but from among the crew I managed to buy, on promise to pay, some clothes—twice too big for me, but heavy and warm withal.

The work was hard, but the life at sea was interesting. There were only two drawbacks: the odors and the open "gurry sores" on the wrists that came from the infection of the hair follicles by the putrefying material chafed in by the rubbing to and fro of the cuffs of the "oilers," as the waterproofs were called. Though the fish were packed in salt every evening as soon as cleaned, and the ship was washed down with endless buckets of sea water, the reeking odor of putrid fish was obtrusive everywhere, but particularly near the gurry butt and the liver butt. The present hygienic means of obtaining cod-liver oil were unknown. As the cod were cleaned, the livers were ripped out and thrown into the liver butt, where the oil was more or less tried out by the sun in summer. The process was completed ashore after the return of the schooner to port. Putrefaction entered largely into the process, so that the odors from the liver butt were all-pervading, no matter how hard or from whence the winds came. During summer calms the stench was so penetrating that it was a great relief to get out in the dories, a diluting distance away. There is no better established fact in medicine today than that cod-liver oil is one of the best remedies for certain diseases, and it is thought to be high in vitamin content; but one who has smelled the liver butt on a Gloucester fishing schooner of the older days wonders how anybody had the courage to take the oil, or make anyone else take it, the first time. Possibly it was the awful odor that made some practical joker advise it, or perhaps some serious-minded person was imbued with the once prevalent idea that to be efficient any medicine must be disagreeable: the more disagreeable, the more powerful for good. For example, it was one or other or both of these that led to the extensive use of skunk oil for "the rheumatiz" among the negro population in my boyhood. As the "rheumatiz" was really an arthritis from disease around the teeth the skunk oil was not as effective as rotten cod-liver oil for tuberculosis, rickets, and vitamin deficiency.

Cod fishing on the Grand Banks of Newfoundland at that time was carried on with a line trawl: a long line from which depended hooks attached with short lines spaced a few feet apart. As the hooks were baited the line was coiled down in a tub. The next day the tub was taken out in a dory and the line was strung out in the water. All was bottom fishing. Some time after the line was laid out the fisherman began to underrun the trawl—that is, pass the line over his boat, examining each hook, taking off whatever fish might have been caught on the hooks, and rebaiting the hooks as necessary. Sometimes the dories were quickly filled; at other times very few fish resulted from even a whole day's work. When this happened the anchor was hove short, the main sheet eased off, the jib backed. As soon as the schooner's head paid off, the jib was let draw, the anchor stowed, and the course was laid for other fishing grounds. If the course would bring the ship broad off wind and a good breeze was blowing, the ship was held close up until foresail and forestaysail were up. All sheets were gone over till all sails were in proper trim for the course. Often the riding sail was not taken in for weeks; in moving about the Banks it took the place of the mainsail, except in light airs. The mainsail was brought out later on for the race home. It was the captain's mysterious secret where we should try next. When the spot was reached the main sheet was hauled in flat and the helm put down. As the schooner was brought up into the wind, the jib was backed. Thus hove to, she would slowly come up to the wind and then fall off, up again and fall off. Backing and filling, there is a sidewise drift to leeward of a knot or two per hour. Current or "set" might increase or lessen the lateral drift. If the new spot gave no better luck than the first, the order soon came, "Ease off the main sheet." Then, "Let draw jib," and we were off again in quest of a better place to fish. Sometimes heaving to was done with close-hauled foresail and backed forestaysail; sometimes, with foresail only; usually, with riding sail (trysail) and jib. When good fishing was found, the anchor was let go and all sail lowered except the riding sail on the mainmast.

One day the cook became very ill; probably ptomaines rather than seasickness; he had apparently lost the sense of smell, anyway he did not know when food was rotten. No one wanted the cook's job; not so much because of the opprobrium of "sea cook" as because of the constant grumbling about the cooking common to ships and boarding houses; and, moreover, it was extra duty; the cook had to turn out for "All hands on deck" to shorten sail, get in the anchor, or other heavy or urgent jobs; and he always had to help in the evening cleaning of the day's catch of fish.

I volunteered as cook.

"I don't think much o' boy cooks, nor green hands in the galley," said the skipper, "but ye kin try if ye want to; on'y I won't be 'sponsible for what all hands may do to ye. I ain't particular about wittals, myself. I kin stand it if they kin."

Available materials did not look promising for good meals. Good cod and haddock were all salted down, only "sounds" and unmarketable fish were available. Fortunately there were left some bacon, potatoes, and a few onions. From these and some pounded-up ship biscuits a savory fish chowder was made in a clean sand-scoured kettle; and a big potful of it was devoured. That settled it: when the cook recovered, he had lost his job. He did not care much; he liked fishing better. The new cook was relieved of seamanship except when all hands were called, and even then it was more a matter of tailing on to a halliard or sheet for sake of ship's discipline. I was no heavy hauler. I could keep up with the average in eviscerating fish, which was for all hands the great and only detested drudgery. This, with good cooking, fair weather or foul, placed me in good standing with captain and crew throughout the two months on the Banks. What was most appreciated by the men was that, no matter what the weather, there was always something hot at meal time. The little schooner many times pitched and rolled and wallowed till it seemed she would never right herself. To stand up without holding on to something was impossible. But, never seasick in my life, I braced myself in the tiny galley and held one big, half-filled pot of chowder on the stove till the contents were cooked—not half raw, not scorched, but as the French cooks say, *au point*. Many a time it took that old stubborn, dogged determination to hang on come what might, of the school days at Greentree. It is a wonder how death by scalding was escaped. But there was always a quart of something hot for each man on board at meal time; and when he came to the galley for "mug up" there was good coffee to be had. Coffee was a very expensive and precious item of ship's stores: many of the schooners in the fishing fleet did not have any, though most of them had rum. But our captain would allow no liquor on board; he said coffee was cheaper and was better for the men and their work anyway. By cutting out rum and by cutting down on some other stores a liberal daily allowance of a cheap grade of coffee was available. The first coffee made by the new cook won over all hands. The great trouble theretofore had been that the coffee was mercilessly boiled; the old grounds were left in until the pot was too full to hold enough water; fish heads had been used to clarify (!) the mixture; the pot had never been cleaned; a thick, oily, evil-smelling coating lined its interior. When the three-gallon coffee pot was thoroughly scoured with sea water and sand, and a little fresh water boiled in it, old foul odors were eliminated. Then coffee was freshly made, in small quantities at a time, starting each time with a clean pot. It was not strong—no more coffee than before was required to make it—but it was fresh, aromatic, and hot. The men were delighted. The skipper was also; for the sake of ship's discipline he did not say so; he did not need to; he drank three pints of it at a time. In his enthusiasm he doubled my wage and promised a share. Usually the cook was the only paid hand. An early riser since babyhood, I found it easy to have fresh hot coffee ready when the morning watch came on deck tired and sleepy at four.

Though salt "horse" (beef) and salt pork were important for variety, the main stand-by was fish chowder. In fact this stew was introduced to New England by the Bank fishermen, who learned to make it from the fishermen coming to the Banks from France. The Frenchmen call it *chaudière,* referring to the caldron or pot. The Yankees corrupted the name to "chowder." Like most of our best dishes, chowder originated in France. If you want to start an argument, just mention this in the presence of a Bank fisherman.

It is born and bred in a "banker" that no good can come out of France. Norway, yes; Nova Scotia, perhaps; but France, "just naterly 'tain't possible."

Once an "old crate" of a leaky schooner came out of some Canadian port selling stores to the fishing fleet. I obtained authorization from the captain to make the amazing purchase of three bushels of onions, a barrel of potatoes, a can of black pepper, and ten pounds of prunes. With these additions to the stores all growling could be prevented. The onions, potatoes, and pepper made the daily chowder savory. An onion or two and a dash of black pepper in the pot went a long way toward overcoming the rancidity of the boiled salt pork and the boiled salt horse; the latter was very poor in quality, very salt, very old, and very leathery. The prunes rendered possible a plum dough ("duff" to sailors) every Sunday. It consisted of dough shortened with rendered salt-beef fat, seasoned with black pepper and boiled in sea water. Over a chunk of this dough, prune juice, with two or three prunes, was poured. It was a treat arousing great pleasures of anticipation, second only to the Sabbath rest from work. Sometimes we shifted to a new location on Sunday; but even so there was a chance to get shaved, and there was no day's catch of fish to clean.

One of the important reforms in the galley was to keep fishy odors and flavors out of food not fishy. This seems strange, almost incredible, but it is true. A fishing schooner reeks of rotten fish smellable five miles to leeward. It is true that fish fresh out of the water have no fishy odor; they smell like sea water. But the gurry butt, the rotting liver-oil butt, and the stinking old fish oil clinging to everything about the schooner would make one think the fisherman would not mind a fishy taste to anything. The truth is that when the men got something absolutely free from fishy taste or odor it seemed so entirely different that they were delighted with the change of diet.

The men were all glad to get ashore at Gloucester wharf. Most of them had relatives waiting to welcome them home; but every man took a moment to say "Good-bye, mate" to the young cook who was giving his galley a last scouring before going ashore. They were tough physically but not morally. The skipper's rule of no rum kept the worst men out. All drinking sailors are not toughs; but all tough sailor men are drunkards. Compared to Greentree School, a reeking fishing schooner out of Gloucester manned by eight rough men was paradise.

CHAPTER X

HOME AGAIN

(1885)

It was a happy day for me when I got home and turned in some money to add to the collegiate fund. The winter session at college followed by the adventures of a book agent and the sea-cook episode had made the longest absence from home in all my experience up to that time; but I had made good progress in my studies and had come out a little ahead otherwise.

Things were not prospering at home. The heavy load of interest-bearing indebtedness was devouring everything. Had there been no debts, a simple living would have been easily made from the summer hotel. There had been a falling off in the patronage at the hotel because the Pennsylvania Railroad, having abandoned Cresson Springs, was convincing everyone of the summer advantages of the seashore, especially Atlantic City.

A family consultation was held, and it was decided best that I resume work at the decorating shop until the opening of college on the 1st of October, in order to add to the collegiate fund. The decorating shop was shorthanded, and I was welcome. The hours were from seven in the morning till six in the evening: a half-hour at noon for luncheon; Saturday was a half-day. The pay was by the piece, but a full ten-hour day and a five-and-one-half-day week were required. I was permitted to work evenings and Saturday afternoon, so that I came close to a seventy-eight-hour week. This brought the collegiate fund up to the sum at which the last collegiate year could be finished if no emergency should arise to upset the budget based on the rigid economies of the first year.

The six months vacation (!) of 1885 was a busy period.

CHAPTER XI

LAST YEAR AT COLLEGE

(1885–1886)

THE SECOND AND LAST YEAR at college was quite like the first. I was delighted to find my attic awaiting me as tenant; the coal-carrying contract was renewed; by consuming every scrap and crumb of food, even to the water in which the eggs and the vegetables were boiled, I had enough to eat; the cooking was good and wholesome—delicious by contrast with codfish balls fried in old, rancid, burnt fat.

What pleased me most of all was that my hard-earned credit at the medical book publishers' enabled me to get the latest and best medical books: the credit was just barely enough. To these books more than to anything else I owed the breadth of my foundation in medical study. I came to know those books through and through. The college had no library; my preceptor's books were too old, even if I had had them in Philadelphia. My struggles as a threadbare, shabby-genteel book agent had not been in vain.

At last came the commencement day, the 2nd of April, 1886. The degree of *Medicinae Doctor* was to be conferred at the Academy of Music. As each candidate's name was called, he mounted the stairway to the stage amid the applause of the jubilant home folks who had come for the great occasion. When the name of Chevalier Jackson was called, I climbed the steps amid a silence that could be felt. Father and Mother had no travel money for the mere pleasure of attendance. The silence became so distressing that a kindly, pitying old lady feebly clapped her hands. Then everybody laughed.

A subscription dinner in celebration was given by the graduating class at the Natatorium on Broad Street. The temporary flooring over the old swimming tanks gave way and dropped the whole class into the tanks. Many were injured, and the accident made thrilling news. A telegram to quiet anticipated parental fears took nearly half of what I had saved by not going to the dinner.

ARRIVAL HOME FROM COLLEGE

(1886)

"I told ye so: he ain't changed none," said old Pat Kelly, the gardener. "Dutchy [Jacob Straub] kept a-sayin' ye'd arrive wi' a topper, a preacher coat, an' spats. But I knowed ye better'n that."

It was the custom of the time for the medical graduate to make a grand entry in his home town with full regalia: a silk hat, black frock suit, and whatever could be mustered in the way of hairy decoration on his face—sideburns if possible, mustache at least. "Success in medical practice is all bluff and whiskers anyway," said the cynical Doctor Albert Jones. Certainly a full beard and a bald head were assets. The smoothly shaven surgeon came later as a development of aseptic surgery. The boyish-looking twenty-year-old (I actually lacked six months of the legal requirement) Doctor of Medicine arrived home with the same short coat and cap he had worn away to college; under his arm was a diploma in the green tin, tubular box that was sold for a dollar by the college clerk, Joseph Leffman, the proceeds of the sale being one of the perquisites of clerkship.

CHAPTER XII

SPECIALIZING IN LARYNGOLOGY

(1886)

THE WORK OF Doctors J. Solis Cohen, Charles E. de M. Sajous, and Joseph Jurist had been interesting, and I had closely followed it at every opportunity during college years. There was no special chair, but there was a newly established dispensary for diseases of the nose and throat, and this I had regularly attended. Doctor J. Solis Cohen loaned, besides a copy of his own book, a complete set of all the writings of Sir Morell Mackenzie. These I read from cover to cover. The difficulties of laryngeal examination and especially the statement that it was impossible to see the larynx of some patients were very intriguing. The specialty of laryngology was decided upon, in consultation with my parents, within a month after my return home from college.

At that time the only recognized specialty was in diseases of the eye. The profession disapproved of the splitting up of practice into specialties. Notwithstanding at least one specialty was recognized by Hippocrates two thousand years before that time, specialists were still regarded as on the border line of quackery, even after the American Medical Association conceded the right to put on card and stationery the words "practice limited to." Doctor J. Solis Cohen had been expelled from membership in the Philadelphia Academy of Natural Sciences for "daring to specialize and be known as a specialist in diseases of the nose and throat," though he was, years afterward, reinstated.

CHAPTER XIII

TO EUROPE IN THE STEERAGE

(1886)

HAVING STUDIED EVERYTHING Sir Morell Mackenzie had written, I deemed a visit to his clinic in London essential. Funds seemed totally lacking, but by dint of parental sacrifices, much decoration of china and glass, and miserably small fees from a few patients a little money was accumulated. Then came a windfall in the form of fifty dollars advanced by an eccentric old bachelor who had known me when he was a guest at the summer hotel. He stipulated that I was to obtain the latest information on the best way of treating his chronic laryngeal ailment, and that I was to treat his larynx for the remainder of his life. He had, without improvement, tried many doctors and had taken much patent medicine. This contract brought the fund up to one hundred twenty-six dollars.

A passage was booked in the steerage of the *Leerdam,* a little, old twelve-hundred-ton steamship with fore-and-aft sailing rig for use when the wind was abeam or abaft the beam. Each steerage passenger was obliged to provide himself with a mattress, a coverlet, a tin plate, a tin cup, and knife, fork, and spoon. Nothing was specified as to sheets, soap, or toothbrush, nor would such specifications have been understood by the steerage passenger of that day. In the dim, frosty dawn of a dismal, hazy October morning a frail, serious young man might have been seen climbing up the gangplank, bending over with a mattress and coverlet on his back and a festoon of tinware strung from his neck, all just purchased by hard bargaining from a tricky vender on the dock. The "mattress" consisted of a flat calico bag with a little musty hay in it; the coverlet was a double layer of the same calico without the hay.

When I reached the steerage a surprise was in store for me. The so-called berths were two layers, upper and lower, of six troughs on each side of each narrow athwartship alleyway. The head of each trough was on the alley; the foot butted against the foot of a trough heading on the section of six troughs beyond. To enter his trough, the occupant must climb in the head end, about two feet wide. The troughs contained a little old, dried, clipped marsh hay crumbling into dust. This dust sifted down from the upper into the lower troughs when it was stirred around with the hand. The anticipation of this dust coming down in my eyes, as the occupant below, was not a pleasing prospect. It was a Dutch vessel, clean enough as to ship and crew, but, oh, those steerage passengers! They were not Dutch and obviously did not know the meaning of the word "cleanliness" in any language; they were unwashed, crawling with vermin, reeking with garlic, tobacco, and alcohol, and their clothes exuded the animal odors of prolonged, sweating wear. To have escaped by paying the difference on second-class accommodations would have meant curtailment of time at the longed-for European clinics. Again the dogged determination to endure. The first night out, everyone else was sick; the steerage was literally slimy with vomitus of a hundred filthy moaning passengers. A gale was blowing from east-northeast, so nearly dead ahead that no steadying sail could be set. The old *Leerdam,* of low freeboard and heavily loaded, wallowed like a log. She rolled and pitched her only open deck under solid water. All hatches were battened down. The only ventilation of the steerage was precarious, by funnel ventilators turned to windward. Forced-fan ventilation was unknown. The air was reeking with foul odors and stifling. The only light was from two bulkhead candle lanterns. It was an awful night.

The ship's doctor had his hands full. He was very seasick himself but was bravely staggering around, doing what he could to help poor wretches, especially the women and children who had the port side of the steerage. Exhausted with work, seasickness, and loss of sleep, he gladly accepted my help when shown the credentials; and, finding the services satisfactory, he soon obtained authorization from the captain to turn over the care of the entire steerage to me. This left him free to attend to the passengers aft. The wretched women steerage passengers were in little need of strictly medical care: what they needed most was spiritual support, especially assurance that the ship was not going to be lost at sea. Some wanted to die, but most were afraid of the hereafter. There then appeared upon the scene two Sisters of one of the Catholic Orders. Bravely they staggered around the reeking, slippery steerage of the rolling, pitching, wallowing ship. I instructed them in the sailorman's two fundamentals of physical safety in a rolling ship: "Never let go with one hand until you have a good hold with the other," and "One hand for the ship and one hand for yourself." It was a sight to be remembered, these two fearfully ill, ashy white Sisters ministering to the women and older children, doing what could be done, while the male steerage passengers were a sodden, dirty, useless lot rolling in vomitus and having no thought of anybody but themselves. Again thoughts of the superiority of women, and, during a short doze, visions of two white-faced angels.

At the end of the second day the gale blew itself out, hatches were opened, the hose was turned on, and the steerage deck cleaned out. The steerage passengers were supposed to clean their own sleeping troughs as well as themselves. They did neither.

The ship's doctor invited his assistant to partake of a bath. It consisted in wrapping myself in a sheet before daylight in the morning, going forward of the forecastle companionway on deck, and standing against a stream of sea water from the deck-scouring hose. The shock in October even there, in the Gulf Stream, was terrific, but the effect after putting on fresh, clean, louse-free clothing was delightful beyond all comparison before or since. It was not repeated because of quarantine restrictions. One of the men in the steerage became violently ill with headache and backache. Suspecting smallpox because of these symptoms associated with the absence of vaccination marks and the fact that smallpox was then occurring sporadically ashore, I promptly notified my chief. The man was isolated in the lazarette and I with him as attendant, doctor, orderly, nurse, on twenty-four-hour duty. But this was a great relief. The lazarette was clean and free from vermin, and the wretched sick man was soon rendered likewise. Washing facilities with fresh water were ample. I had had smallpox in boyhood, and had a pock mark on the nose and two antecedent vaccination scars. Though I was amply protected, additional vaccination was done as a precautionary measure; but it did not take. The only other patients in the lazarette were bedfast: a man with a broken leg and a paralytic. They were vaccinated and allowed to remain under my care. A hospital routine was established in the care of the three patients; and there was time left for rereading Morell Mackenzie's books.

Early one morning about eight days out of New York there was an unusual clattering of heavy boots on the deck overhead, and much yelling and cursing in Dutch. Shortly afterward the glass of the closed porthole of the lazarette was darkened by a flow of blood. The ship rolled the porthole under green sea water to leeward and washed off the blood, but on the next windward half-roll the flow of blood was repeated. Again it appeared, but soon the copious flow of pinkish water and the sound of the hose scouring overhead indicated the sailors were washing the deck. Naturally, disquieting thoughts of a fight were justified. The quantity of blood necessary to overflow the scuppers and come down over the ship's side and porthole would mean, if human, three or four men stabbed in the large blood-vessels of the neck. The mystery was solved when the steerage steward passed the evening meal wrapped in newspaper down through that same porthole, the rolling having lessened enough to permit opening the port for a moment. "You get little bit meat. We kill cow." It was then recalled that a cow was visible in a crate lashed to the fore hatch on boarding the ship in New York. There was no refrigeration, not even efficient ice boxes, on ships in those days. The only way to have fresh meat was to take on board a live animal to be butchered when about halfway over. The patients ate the little morsels of meat. That was the only time meat was served. Food consisted of plenty of good bread, oleomargarine cheese, and in the evening mashed potatoes mixed with purple cabbage; wholesome enough and not stinted in quantity as to the bread and cheese; this was abundantly stocked ahead in the lazarette as preparedness for a time when the sea would be so rough that the porthole would roll under solid water every now and then, and could not be opened. Moreover, the fathom or two of pilot's ladder overside, down which the steward came with the package of food, was too precarious a foothold at such a time. I washed the dishes; the newspapers in which food was handed in were thrown out the porthole into the sea. Nothing went back on deck. The door into the steerage from the lazarette was barred and sealed. The whole quarantine, though seemingly crude, was very efficient when carried out with Dutch thoroughness. In fact nothing could be safer for passengers and crew. The ship's doctor looked in at the porthole occasionally to find out if consultation was necessary. He reported no new cases of smallpox. He said the Sisters had offered their services to help me in quarantine, but he felt he needed their aid more than I did. Their hospital experience had enabled them to assist him in vaccinating everyone on board, passengers and crew. An ample stock of vaccine for the purpose was an obligatory part of a ship's medical stores in those days when smallpox was prevalent.

The smallpox patient in the lazarette made good progress. Though the headache and backache were severe, the disease ran rather a mild course. At the end of the voyage, seventeen days later, the rash was fading and the patient was convalescent. The other two patients in the lazarette had not acquired the disease. The ship was turned over to the authorities at quarantine. I was released after inspection of the old pock mark and vaccination scars, a good scouring with a fresh-water hose, and a thorough disinfection of baggage and clothing. In my pocket was an official letter of thanks from the captain and a letter of appreciation from the ship's doctor. The same evening I took a Channel boat to Hull, and thence made haste by train to London.

Arrival in London, the cradle of laryngology, marked an epoch. Unfortunately funds were so limited that my stay must be short. The most frugal living was imperative. Butterless bread by the loaf and the cheapest of cheese were the staples. Occasionally the great luxury of a huge bowl of poorly flavored but nutritious vegetable soup was added.

I made good use of my limited time in London. When funds got low I left for home. The voyage was uneventful. I reached Pittsburgh with one dollar and seventy-six cents remaining.

CHAPTER XIV

EARLY DAYS IN THE PRACTICE OF MEDICINE

(1887–1889)

THE PRACTICE OF MEDICINE differed somewhat in my early days from that of the average young physician in these days. Graduating at twenty years of age and returning from the visit to European clinics at twenty-two, I realized extreme youth was a factor to be reckoned with in getting started. Most people of that time were inclined to believe that the utmost in medical knowledge was contained in the shiny, bald skull to which was appended a long drop-curtain of gray, never-cut whiskers. The more shiny and expansive the bald area and the longer the drop-curtain, the greater the knowledge. The saving clause "other things being equal" was not applied. True, my personal appearance was youthful; but on the other hand, as Mother and Father said, there were many patients discouraged with failure to get results in their old chronic ailments from treatment by old established practitioners; and some of these patients would be glad to try treatment from the young practitioner fresh from the great medical centers, presumably filled with the latest knowledge. The correctness of the parental opinion was later abundantly proven.

Then came up for decision the matter of location. "Find a neighborhood where there is no other doctor," said many. "We do not think so," said Father and Mother Jackson. "People in search of a physician naturally go to streets where there are a number of physicians. Look at Harley Street in London. Besides, specialism is developing, and the specialist should be among specialists." Again Mother and Father showed their wisdom and foresight. The specialist streets in Pittsburgh then, before the days of office buildings, were Penn Avenue and Sixth Avenue. No vacancies were available on Penn Avenue. Partitioning of a just-vacated tailor's shop on Sixth Avenue made a satisfactory suite of two rooms. The location had the advantage of nearness to Doctor William H. Daly, who was a pioneer throat specialist in Pittsburgh; he was quoted in the literature. Doctor Daly traveled much. He employed a salaried assistant. Many patients did not like the assistant; this was unjustifiable as he was a well qualified man; but personal likes and dislikes in such matters are not reasonable. Some of the dissatisfied patients came to me. When Doctor Daly came back from travels, I sent those dissatisfied patients back to him and refused to see those who did not wish to do so. Those who were satisfied with the salaried assistant stuck to him. He opened consulting rooms across the street where Doctor Daly could see many of his old patients mount the steps for treatment by his former assistant. The result was that on departure for the next voyage Doctor Daly left the instructions: "Send patients to young Doctor Jackson if they cannot wait till I get home." Until his death by suicide, years later, he was always helpful to me. He subscribed for the leading medical magazines, and he had a copy of almost every laryngeal book published; these he generously loaned to me, and his aid in those lean years was invaluable.

In my first year of practice there was an event that called world-wide attention to the specialty of laryngology. The Crown Prince of Germany developed laryngeal trouble. Queen Victoria, whose daughter was his wife, the Crown Princess, knighted Doctor Morell Mackenzie and sent him to Berlin to care for the stricken Prince. Wise and well informed Queen Victoria knew of Morell Mackenzie's many years of work that had made him really the creator of the specialty of laryngology. Her excellent choice was perfectly satisfactory to the Crown Prince, later Emperor of Germany. Until his death over a year later by cancer of the larynx he retained perfect confidence in Sir Morell Mackenzie. This was a bitter pill for the proud and arrogant members of the medical profession of Germany to swallow. When Sir Morell Mackenzie first arrived he was bitterly opposed by Ernst von Bergmann, a Russian, who was professor of surgery at the University of Berlin. Stubbornly opposed to specialties in any form, he had not permitted even a German larynogologist, of whom there were a few, to examine the larynx of the Crown Prince. He published bitter personal attacks on Mackenzie. To the controversy were added politics and intrigue, local and international, personalities and recriminations that filled newspaper columns of the world for a year. One result of it all was the world-wide recognition of laryngology as a specialty. Undoubtedly, the international episode did more than any other one thing to enable a laryngologist to make a living without doing any general practice. Specialties in medicine, laryngology among others, would have come ultimately anyway, but those early years, precarious at best, would doubtless have been a period of starvation for me without the impetus alluded to above.

One incident helpful to me in inaugurating the specialty was the advent on Sixth Avenue of Doctor W. T. English, specializing in diseases of the chest. Such a specialty was not recognized among the physicians of those days, but it enabled Doctor English to divest himself of a heavy burden of general practice. Besides being a physician he was a widely known singer, with a powerful tenor voice of wonderful quality and clearness, and excellently controlled. I was so fortunate as to have had him as one of my first patients and was doubly fortunate in that the treatment I had learned on my visit to Sir Morell Mackenzie's clinic arrested an acute laryngitis promptly and in time to avoid the necessity for canceling a very important concert engagement. Acute laryngitis had been the bane of his musical career. He had not been having many attacks, but like almost everyone else he usually had two or three severe attacks of this acute infectious disease every winter. The trouble was that they had so often coincided with concert engagements that he hesitated to make fixed obligations. I frankly told him that, while I would do all I could, there was no certainty that the acute attacks could always be arrested. The second and third attacks yielded as promptly as the first. Doctor English was enthusiastic and referred a number of other singers and students of vocal music to me. Some could pay small fees, but many were struggling against poverty for a musical career; none among them was a high-salaried star. It was quite encouraging to have a few patients in the waiting room as harbingers of a success in what the profession then regarded as the experimental field of specialization in medicine. It was clear that I should not have to do any general practice. I had been told by older practitioners that some years of general practice were necessary before taking up a specialty. Others had advised me to make a lead on the specialty but to take all the family practice that came my way. This did not seem to me fair to the family physician; and I made it a rule rigidly to refuse to treat any patient for anything other than a throat ailment. I was often told by physicians and laymen: "You'll starve; there isn't enough special work to do, even if you get it all, which you won't." I did not think of it then, because I never could think in terms of business; but I soon found that my rigid refusal of all general work was an asset because it inspired confidence on the part of general practitioners, who were thus less hesitant in referring patients to me. I was enthusiastically fond of my special work and I was determined to succeed notwithstanding the infinite striving, privation, and poverty. Again the same old stubborn, grim determination to persist, come what might.

For a full understanding of my work in the early years of practice, some technical matters must be stated.

The operation of tonsillectomy, complete excision of the tonsil, had recently become recognized as one of the most important in surgery. Almost all children had diseased tonsils that were a menace to life and health. No operation in surgery yielded (and it is the same today) a higher percentage of satisfactory results, satisfactory alike to the surgeon and to the patient and his parents.

Pale, sickly, poisoned by the septic disease in the tonsils, these children were irritable and peevish; they had headaches, earaches, sore throats, laryngitis acute and chronic, and various slight ailments. These conditions kept them often out of school and made them dull pupils in the schoolroom.

Full recognition of these facts in that community had been brought about largely by my own efforts. Many of the older family physicians were hard to convince; but the clinical evidence of the results was irresistible. Talking with the teachers in the ward schools and studying the pupils' faces, I picked out the children with the typical, mouth-breathing, apathetic faces indicating diseased tonsils, including the nasopharyngeal tonsil, called adenoids. In almost every instance these children were the same individuals that the respective teachers designated as backward and even dull in their studies. I brought the matter to the attention of Professor H. I. Gourley, then general head of the public schools of Pittsburgh. He was not only a good executive but also a highly educated man. When I showed him the direct clinical evidence in the children affected he fully realized the need of remedy for the afflicted children; but he explained that officially he could do nothing because of the opposition that would inevitably be aroused if any official attempt to deal with the matter, even an examination, were to be attempted. He advised me to begin in my own ward.

This ward was the old "Bloody Third," so called because of the fierce political battles fought therein. The henchmen of the political boss, Chris Magee, stationed themselves at the approach to the polls, and, there being no such thing then as a secret ballot, the citizen who voted the wrong way (*i.e.* against the machine) shortly afterward arrived home with one or two black eyes and a bloody nose, or sometimes did not arrive at all, but was found in an alley, insensible. The attacks were reported as those of thugs: the direct political connection was suppressed as far as possible. If the citizen repeated the voting the wrong way his "best friend," acting only in an altruistic capacity, advised him as a matter of personal safety to move out of the Third Ward. Of course Chris

Magee did not himself order these bloody proceedings; but his ward heelers were held responsible for delivery of the vote for the machine candidate. No excuses of any kind were acceptable: "Deliver the vote, honestly if you can, but deliver it or make room for some other man who can," was the ultimatum. At the start of his political career many years before, Chris Magee, under the tutelage of his predecessor and father-in-law Tommy Steel, had borrowed from my father a horse and shabby buck wagon, with which in ragged frayed clothing to visit the millworkers and the poorest of the poor. As always, the vote getter professed a great interest in the always numerous poor.

I got Father to present me to Mr. Chris Magee, who had in the meantime risen to be the political boss of Pittsburgh and Allegheny County, though he held no public office. We were kindly received, and after I had presented the matter of the school children who were struggling under the handicap of diseased tonsils and adenoids, Mr. Magee comprehended the situation; but, as is natural to a man who is besieged all day long with self-seekers, he could not comprehend a purely disinterested attitude on my part. However, it was clear enough that he was correct in his viewpoint that nothing could be done officially. He could not, without arousing tremendous parental opposition, pass on the word to accept my offer to examine all of the Third Ward school pupils, a few at a time, free of charge. He advised that I see Doctor McKelvy, who was chairman of the Third Ward School Board, and try to work the matter out tactfully.

This advice of the practical politician was good; but Doctor McKelvy was a problem for me. He was afraid of losing votes, and moreover he honestly did not believe in taking out children's tonsils. He was horrified at the idea of doing anything officially; but our interview was very pleasant, and the matter was left open for mutual discussion.

Every now and then the poor parents would bring children to me for advice about "sore throat." Finding enormously hypertrophied and diseased tonsils, with dull expressionless faces, and constant mouth breathing, I would ask Doctor McKelvy to see the little patients and the diseased conditions before operation and again later after an appreciable effect of the operation was obtained. Then I would ask him to inquire, casually, on his regular visit to the school, about the particular pupils' scholastic record. The unbiased record showing striking improvement in almost every case convinced Doctor McKelvy. He still felt he could do nothing officially, but his prestige as a general practitioner enabled him to suggest to parents that the suffering children he then so quickly recognized be brought to me. Usually the suggestion met with an objection to the effect, "But, Doctor, we have no money to pay a specialist." As fully authorized by me, the good Doctor would say, "Oh, go to Doctor Chevalier Jackson! He won't charge you anything."

The old Bloody Third, with its hard-fighting, hard-drinking men swarming around the saloons (one of which was on every corner), had no end of families poverty-stricken because the weekly earnings of the father were spent for alcoholic beverages every Saturday night.

And thus it came about that hundreds of poor suffering little children in the old Bloody Third Ward were restored to health. The parents in adjacent wards learned of the good work, and before long I was overwhelmed with charity work. Occasionally a parent could and did pay a few dollars.

CHAPTER XV

DEATH OF MY FATHER

(1889)

On Christmas Day, 1889, my father died suddenly of heart disease at sixty years of age. This was my first great bereavement. Every Christmas Day since has been a sad one for me. In this calamity I had, however, two consolations. Father died painlessly, while sitting in his chair at home. The death was so sudden he had no time to worry over his affairs, as he would have done in a lingering illness. From the time of the embezzlements he had struggled on in the hope of some day paying debts contracted in his name by others who got the money. He insisted he had signed his name; the fact that it was affixed to blank notes in the hands of others was his fault, and innocent holders should not be allowed to suffer through his misplaced confidence.

My first impulse was to assume the debts and try to pay them off. The attorney, and Judge Hawkins of the Orphans Court, both advised closing the matter as an insolvent estate for the benefit of the creditors. The creditors agreed to this; they did not doubt my sincerity, but they said it would be beyond the power of any physician ever to pay off such a relatively enormous debt. Everything was sold. We were destitute and penniless except for what I could earn, and I was just three years out of medical school. I already was a busy man, but the work was almost all charity; probably if I had had more business ability I could have got ahead of the saloonkeeper, who always got first chance at the pay envelope. What little was left was needed by the poor mothers and their ill nourished children.

It may have been simply lack of business ability, but I could not bring myself to demand pay for services. Call it moral cowardice if you will, but I could not even ask a man for ten dollars after I had saved his life. My peculiar psychology seemed to get recompense enough from the achievement itself; I could not translate it into terms of dollars. Patients were unfamiliar with psychology; they just took it for granted that I did not need the money. Goaded by my increased responsibilities, I got as far as to name an amount when the patient or parent insisted upon payment. That the amount was too small was evidenced by the extremely profuse thanks, and occasionally by the referring physician upbraiding me for lack of good sense; by which, of course, he meant business sense. These instances were rare. Usually the referring physician in asking me to take over a case would frankly inform me of the poverty of the patient or his parents. No patient was ever refused, and the leniency of hospital executives was stretched to the limit to take in these poverty-stricken sufferers. One exasperated medical director said: "Doctor Jackson, don't you *ever* get a pay patient?"

Medical directors and hospital executives found that many of my patients could pay something, and they collected the something. This, of course, was right enough. The facilities for care of the worthy poor must be protected from overwhelming imposition. But the practical result all my life has been that the hospitals have always got more of the patient's money than I. The same condition has persisted to this day. A chronically afflicted patient, now coming in with a hundred dollars, usually pays me nothing. Though he is referred to me personally, all his money goes for hospital care, Roentgen-ray charges, special nurses. Sometimes I must lend him money to pay his fare home. Occasionally he forgets to reimburse me, not often. I have no fault to find with this, but hundreds of times in later days business men have told me I needed a guardian, or something to that effect. Be this as it may, the first dozen years or so of my medical life were spent in a struggle with privation and poverty, notwithstanding the fact that I was working, on the average, sixteen hours out of every twenty-four.

Parenthetically, simple justice requires that it be said that the foregoing remarks about what becomes of the patient's hundred dollars do not apply to hospitals under the direction of the Sisters of any of the Catholic Orders. Not one instance of that kind ever occurred to my knowledge in such institutions. Though I have been called in, hundreds of times, to do special work in Catholic hospitals, and have always had the utmost coöperation and have had every facility placed at my disposal regardless of expense, I have never been offered a staff position; why, I do not know. Not being on the staff, I have not had the opportunity to put in my own patients.

The reader is requested not to read into the statements of fact made in the foregoing paragraph and elsewhere in this book any implications of distinction or comparison. Appeals to Protestant or Jewish denominations happened to be rare, but they were never in vain.

CHAPTER XVI

DARK DAYS IN PITTSBURGH

(1890–1895)

LIKE A NIGHTMARE are my memories of this period. The Pittsburgh of those days was a dismal place. All winter long we lived as in a dark, cold, damp cellar. The sun was visible, on an average, four days in a winter month; and "visible" is a very proper word because one could look directly at it with the unprotected eye; it looked like a full moon. I once saw a transit of Venus as if through a smoked glass. Soot, grime, and black dirt covered everything, so that every time anything was touched the hands had to be washed. Every cleanly Pittsburgher learned not to touch his face. Many times daily he must "clean out the chimney crocks," which meant rotating his handkerchief-covered little finger in each soot-lined nostril in turn. The pockets bulged with the necessary supply of handkerchiefs. The contrast with my white-marble-step college days in the then anthracite-burning Philadelphia was strong. But it was not alone and directly that the dismal dirt was depressing. It greatly increased the fixed expenses. Artificial light was necessary all day long. Illuminating gas, manufactured from bituminous coal, was expensive; we were not allowed to use natural gas for lighting in the city. The constantly falling black soot and grime necessitated the constant service of a charwoman with soap, mop, and scrubbing brush. Laundry bills were large.

All these fixed expenses, along with those of rent and heating, made what was for me a large sum that constantly hung like a sword of Damocles over my head. As a result of Father's many years and death under a crushing load of debt, I lived in constant dread of owing anybody anything. No privation was too great if it would help to meet bills promptly when due. I felt that, if once allowed to start, debts would accumulate, and I should never get out from under the burden; they would ruin my life as they had ruined my father's later years. My mother had rented a home in the country; I would not bring her into the gloom and grime and dirt of the city. I had a folding, disappearing bed in the waiting room and a tiny kitchenette (though that word had not then been coined) curtained off in a corner of the consulting room. I lived from hand to mouth. Expenditures for clothing were limited to the least consistent with respectability. To make matters worse, fixed expenses were increasing. The rent was progressively raised. Telephone service and commercial electric light service became established in the city; they were necessities.

Professor Keen, many years later, said: "Chevalier Jackson's skill was acquired by a lifetime of work with the poor." This is true, but it is not the whole truth. Dr. Keen might have added, "He was poor himself and a poor business man besides."

Not only did I spend most of my none too abundant energy in the slums, alleys, and hospital wards of Pittsburgh, but a considerable part of what little income was derived from patients who could and would voluntarily pay something went to the instrument maker for special instruments and apparatus to help the poor children with supposedly incurable, difficult breathing or difficult swallowing. The methods were newly devised; the instruments, specially designed to overcome the particular problem in the particular case. Sometimes I made the instruments, myself; but many were required for the many little sufferers, and their needs were often so urgent that there was only time to make a rough model for the instrument maker, whom for years I paid myself. The parents could not pay; the hospitals in those days could not pay. I could not see the children die for want of an instrumental appliance. Often I worked in my little shop in the cellar till far into the night—a great hardship for me because of my early-rising habits—to work out some problem.

Hundreds of pathetic cases were encountered. One cold, dark, blackish-snowy morning a ragged woman came crying and screaming to the door on Sixth Avenue pleading for help. She said her drunken husband was beating her child to death. With no delusions as to inability as a policeman but with great faith in the power of persuasion of drunken parents, I made haste up Cherry Alley to the squalid room, where I found a girl lying on the floor breathing her last; but I noted, as the breathing ceased, the indrawing in the neck above the breastbone that indicates laryngeal obstruction. With the aid of a pocket case an emergency tracheotomy was done. This procedure consists of two cuts in the front of the neck. After the first one was made I was feeling for the trachea in the pool of flowing blood to make the second cut when I was jerked by the furiously drunken father. The mother and two of the onlookers pulled the savage brute away, and the second cut was made. The black-and-blue girl seemed lifeless, but after artificial respiration she began to breathe; her lips moved, and she began to cry. Tears rolled down her cheeks. She reached for my hand and tremblingly held it in terror as she saw her father cursing and struggling with her mother and the two neighbors. Then two officers came in and took the father away. Further examination showed that the child had been garroted by the father. The black-and-blue color of the face due to impending asphyxia disappeared when air was admitted through the tracheotomic opening in the windpipe; but on the skin later appeared the black, blue, and livid marks of cruel choking fingers.

When the child recovered sufficient airway to speak it was learned that she had met her father just as she was leaving the home to buy bread with the last money in the house, a dime the mother had given her. When she saw her drunken father approach she knew he would demand the dime. Thinking of her half-starved little brother and sister, she hid the dime in her mouth; but he saw her do this and, clutching her by the neck, dragged her into the house. That was the last she remembered.

OLD APPLE TREES (CHALK) 1925

(A SKETCH IN OIL)

One midnight I was aroused by a poor widowed mother wrapped in a ragged shawl. She said her only boy was choking to death with pneumonia. Thinking of the prevalent diphtheria I grasped an intubation case and accompanied the mother to the squalid bedroom. The child was ashy gray; his lips moved slightly, breathing was failing. A quickly inserted intubation tube soon changed the child's condition, and he dropped off to sleep.

A very unpleasant odor permeated the room. Search for the source revealed the partly decomposed body of a child wrapped in a ragged sheet under the bed. In a flood of tears the poor, half-distracted mother stated that a year previously her other two children had been taken to the "pesthouse," as municipal hospitals for contagious diseases were then called. She never saw the children again; both had died and were buried she knew not where. Recognizing diphtheria by the similarity of symptoms, she had concealed the illness of the last two children.

A little heart-to-heart talk, and my promise to go with the child in the ambulance, restored the mother's courage. Three weeks later it was a joyful day for the mother and me when I brought the happy little fellow back in my buggy to the humble home in the alley.

A mother brought her child with a quarter stuck in his throat. Both mother and child disclaimed knowledge of the cause of the many bruises on the boy's body. The little sufferer screamed when these bruises were touched. After the coin was removed, a message to the parents brought the father to the hospital to take the child home. He ungratefully demanded that the coin be returned to him. It was explained that all foreign bodies removed from the air and food passages were put into a scientific collection where they would be available for study by future physicians working on the problems of relieving little children. He left in a rage, taking the child with him. A few hours later the little fellow came back shrieking with pain. His sister, who accompanied him, said that his cut lip and broken arm were due to a brutal beating by his father for refusing to come back and beg for the removed coin. She said that the bruises we found on the first admission were from a beating by the father as punishment for swallowing the coin. The child was kept in the hospital for treatment of the broken arm. The sister was given a half-dollar as reimbursement for the retained scientific specimen and carfare home. She walked home to save the carfare, but the father confiscated the money and later appeared at the hospital, drunk, abusive, and threatening to kill "that Doctor Jackson who stole my quarter." In opposition to advice by those present I tried the soothing voice, before sanctioning the calling of the police. A gentle, kindly appeal to the man's better feelings soon persuaded him to leave peacefully.

Mentioning the soothing voice brings back many memories of an often used power of persuasion. The most desperately infuriated man seemed to yield to the calm, soothing voice of one obviously too frail to be considered as an antagonist. The mentally unbalanced, whose characteristic is suspicion, seemed to trust sincere efforts to relieve them of the pain or discomfort of the intercurrent illness for which I was called to treat them. The violently insane spending most of their lives in camisoles submitted quietly to whatever local treatment it was necessary to administer. Even in their deranged state of mind a simple straightforward manner and soothing voice seemed to convince them of sincerity.

This credit for sincerity has always seemed to me to be one of the important elements in whatever measure of success may have attended my career. In presentations at medical meetings, in dealings with patients or with fellow physicians, and in the miscellaneous contacts of a busy life, everyone everywhere seems to have given me credit for sincerity of purpose. I hope I have deserved it.

Sincerity is an asset.

One of the great honors showered upon me by my fellow countrymen was in the form of invitations to speak at medical

OLD SUNRISE MILLS

(CHALK)

1920

AFTERGLOW

Old
Sunrise
Mills

(CHALK)

1920

meetings. Travel to distant meetings has always been one of the greatest hardships of my medical career. For a physician, the total distance I have traveled is enormous. In the earlier years (1887 to 1912) the expense was a heavy drain on my limited income. After buying a round-trip ticket I often had too few dollars remaining to stay at the luxurious hotel at which such meetings were usually held, and had to go where lodging was cheapest. Breakfast consisted of coffee and rolls for ten cents at places where tips were unknown. Two pretzels and an apple were sufficient at noon, when any food was taken. Vegetable soup and bread was enough for dinner. On the train going, food was usually carried from home. For the return journey, fruit, rolls, and pretzels were bought before entering the train. It was not these living conditions that constituted the hardship; having no surfeit made these snacks taste good.

The great hardship in earlier years was in raising the money to go. Another hardship was in arranging to get away: at the last moment there nearly always seemed to be emergency ward calls that required work up to within a few minutes of train time; after the return there was always an accumulation of work. Another great hardship will be little understood by most people: it was, and still is, a sore trial for me to leave home. Like Tartarin, I seem to be a combination of Don Quixote and Sancho Panza in one personality. I have an irresistible desire to go out and accomplish utmost good in the world, but when the time comes to go I have an almost overwhelming wave of my natural love of home and family. I always go sadly; but return home gladly, at the earliest possible moment, and with feelings of the utmost satisfaction. Having had opportunities for clinical observations such as have fallen to the lot of few medical men, I always feel it my duty to humanity to pass on to the greatest possible number of physicians and students the fruits of this unique clinical experience. This feeling of duty has driven me from home thousands of times; driven me to accept perhaps too many invitations to speak in distant cities. Having accepted a place on a program I felt I had signed away my liberty for that day and the necessary travel days. It always has seemed to me that, when a man is on a program, it is his duty to be there, sick or well. Even during tuberculous attacks I attended meetings for which I had previously accepted invitations.

Perhaps few people will understand me when I say I never have traveled for pleasure. The feeling of homesickness would outweigh any possible enjoyment if pleasure were the only object. When, however, I was traveling as a matter of duty there were incidental pleasures.

First of all, there was the opportunity to write. Early in life, as mentioned in connection with commuting for an education, I formed the habit of writing in railroad trains; this habit has been continuous, and, the amount of travel being so great, I have done a large amount of medical writing on the road.

In addition, I have never lost my boyhood faculty of enjoying scenery. To look out of the window occasionally at the panorama of our great and vast country passing by is restful to the eyes, instructive and refreshing to the mind. To look out of the window all day long would be very fatiguing to the eyes because the extrinsic muscles would be jerking the eyeball to a new fixing point every fraction of a second. Occasionally something very attractive and sketchable would appear at the car window. A sketch would be made: sometimes with lecture chalks, sometimes with pen, sometimes pencil.

Sketching and writing were mostly done on the way home. On the going journey my thought was concentrated on the subject on hand for the meeting: the paper to be handed in for publication was given a final revision; the parts of the subject suitable for chalk and talk were noted.

No fault is to be found with him who spends half his daylight travel time in the dining car and the other half in the smoking, or as it is now called "lounge," car with back to the window. If that is his way of relaxing, well and good. I would not attempt to dissuade him. To me whose whole existence is under pressure to get through with life's work before life ends, the writing plan seems to help greatly, and arrival home is always with a feeling of achievement as well as of happiness at once more being home. This terminal phase of the trip has always been one of the chief pleasures of travel to medical meetings.

Undoubtedly taking part in medical meetings has been one of the largest factors in my accomplishment, be it much or little, for endoscopy, medical science, and humanity. Doubtless also it has been a large factor in building an international reputation and in an ultimately successful career.

When I hear an essayist read I cannot repress the wish that I were cozily at home in bed reading the essay myself and rereading the parts that might strike me as important. A read address has always seemed weak to me as a listener. I would rather hear a blundering talk if the thoughts are good. In my own work therefore I have never read an address from manuscript. The handing in of a paper was usually required, but it has always seemed that I could convey the ideas more forcibly and quickly by looking the audience collectively and individually in the eye while talking. In this way the audience feels it is getting the undivided attention of the speaker. When a manuscript is read, the audience unconsciously feels the division of attention. When a talker falters, the audience feels only that he is deciding on the best form of expression: when a reader stumbles over his own phrases, the impression is that he is not master of his subject, or that he wrote hastily, or even that he did not write the thing himself. It has been said that no one could memorize statistical tables. The answer is that, if the statistics are too long to memorize, they are too long to be read in full. Nothing so tires an audience as statistics. If they must be presented, the best plan is to summarize them and project them on a screen. A pointer will then fix the attention of the audience on the important features. The complete data should, of course, be made available in print later for those who want to study them.

It has always seemed to me that the best of all ways to convey an idea is with chalk. Not only does the speaker get a doubling of the receptive channels—the visual added to the auditory—but the progressive adding of each element to the structure of the drawing drives home, piece by piece, a thing not quickly or completely grasped as a whole from a previously prepared, complete drawing.

In teaching the medical student the primary requisite is to keep him awake; obviously you cannot teach anything to a sleeping man. Like the exhaust of the airplane the patter of words of a read paper is soporific. Chalk-talking arouses the drowsy. When a late-hour student seemed to be on the verge of succumbing, he could be brought back by speeding up the drawing or by changing to a correlated subject. For example, the sleepy student could not resist a chalk demonstration of tracheotomy, in which the patient, first shown as apparently dead of asphyxia, is changed by a few strokes to a smiling grateful patient, and is quoted as saying, "Thank you, Doctor Jackson."

CHAPTER XVII

DEVELOPMENT OF ESOPHAGOSCOPY

(1890–1899)

When I was in London I saw an impractical device designed by Morell Mackenzie in an effort visually to inspect the esophagus, one of the greatest needs of that day. After that time I had been working on the problem and had devised and carefully used tubular specula for this purpose. Finally in 1890 I had developed an esophagoscope worthy of the name. With it I had removed a tooth-plate from the esophagus of an adult, and with a smaller model a coin from the esophagus of a child. This was a great achievement. I exhibited the instruments and the specimens at the medical society's meeting. A shocking result followed. I had made a fearful blunder. In my haste to follow the custom of physicians, of reporting promptly anything they have developed that seems to be a contribution to the advancement of medical science, in order that others may test the value of the new thing and join in its further development, I had made a premature announcement. Worse still, I had failed to warn of the technical difficulties and pitfalls in the use of the new instrument. As a consequence disaster followed the use of duplicate instruments made from my model by an instrument maker. The esophagoscope was condemned. I was heartbroken. I felt that it was all my fault. In vain I tried to convince myself that making the instrument, modifying it, working along step by step in its use during a number of years had kept me from a full realization of the dangers that would arise from its use by the profession as something entirely new. I convicted myself of moral cowardice; through fear of accusations of egotism I had failed to warn of dangers that I must have known to be inherent in any instrument to be used for such a purpose in the anatomical region concerned. I was filled with remorse, and disconsolate beyond words. I told the instrument maker the instrument was not yet sufficiently perfected for general use and asked him not to sell any. I took the whole matter to the medical society meeting and explained the difficulties and dangers. The consensus of opinion was that the instrument was the hobby of an enthusiast, and that others had better let it alone. I was shocked and disappointed because I had thought I had added something to the science of surgery. It was little consolation that I did all the esophagoscopies the profession called upon me to do. I dared not write about the esophagoscope nor advocate in medical meetings its general use.

A few years later (1902) Doctor Max Einhorn made the excellent suggestion that a light carrier, then recently patented by a soulless mechanic for use on a cystoscope, be used on an esophagoscope. I adopted the suggestion; it greatly improved visibility and led to other improvements in the instrument and the technique of its use that rendered it practical.

All this is ancient history now, but I have never forgiven myself for my lack of courage and forethought.

Reference to my own work, only, is required by the subject of this book. If it were a history of esophagoscopy, the work of others, especially that of Doctor Harris P. Mosher, would be entitled to an important place.

The development of the esophagoscope brought me a long series of very sad cases, especially stricture of the esophagus from swallowing lye. These little children of the poor arrived usually in almost dying condition from food and water starvation. If they had not been without water for more than a week it was usually possible to save their lives. Some died on the way for want of water. One case will serve to illustrate.

A little girl seven years old, emaciated to a skeleton, arrived with the message she had not been able to swallow a drop of water for a week. She looked wistfully at a glass of water, then she tried to swallow some of it; she choked, coughed and all the water came back through the nose and mouth. The two Sisters of Mercy said they had found the child lying on the floor of a coal miner's shanty, where they had gone to see the mother who was dying of pneumonia. The father was lying on the floor in a drunken stupor. The little girl's ragged dirty clothing was soaking-wet. She was crying for water, and a little three-year-old brother was supplying it with a tin cup from a tin pail. But evidently the water had run out of her mouth and soaked her clothing because she could not swallow it. I put down the esophagoscope between her dry, parched lips and found a tight stricture of the esophagus (the passage from the mouth to the stomach). The scars had not completely closed the passage; in its narrowest part was a corklike plug of grayish material. I removed the plug with delicate forceps passed through the esophagoscope. After removal of the instrument the child was given a glass of water. She took a small sip expecting it to choke her and come back up. It went slowly down; she took another sip, and it went down. Then she gently moved aside the glass of water in the nurse's hand, took hold of my hand, and kissed it. She took more water and a glass of milk. The nurse put the child to bed, and coming back reported: "She dropped off to sleep. It will be a wonder if she lives: she is just skin and bones." She did live. When she got stronger the Sisters had her admitted to a Catholic orphanage and brought her in regularly for treatment. With the esophagoscope the stricture was dilated until at the end of two years she could swallow any kind of food in a perfectly normal way; and she grew well and strong.

No money could give satisfaction equal to that of such an achievement. That wan smile and kiss of the hand from the grateful child whose swallowing was restored after a week of water starvation meant more to me than any material remuneration; the memory of it now, over forty years later, still yields dividends of satisfaction. And associated with it are memories of hundreds of similar cases of children since brought back from the very edge of the grave. Not every life could be saved, but nearly all could be brought back if they had not reached the point where the dried-out tissues had lost their power to take up water.

The cause of the pitiable condition of these children was the swallowing of household lye. It was in every kitchen. It looked like sugar, and was mistaken for this by children. When a child put it into his mouth it burnt the esophagus; and when the ulcers following the burns healed, the contracting scars gradually closed the esophagus until even water would not go through. In the girl mentioned above, the scars had not quite completely closed the esophagus, but they had narrowed it to a tiny passage; this passage was occluded by the small piece of some substance, probably raw potato, the child had swallowed to appease her hunger when her mother was bedfast and dying.

In those days the containers had no poison label to warn mothers of the dangerous nature of lye; consequently it was carelessly left on the floor, most often in the kitchen cupboard right where the children could get it. Even worse than lye were the cleaners. These preparations were diluted lye; on their containers were such criminally misleading statements as, "Will not injure the skin or the most delicate fabric." But when these sugarlike lye-containing substances entered the esophagus of a child they burnt like a red-hot iron.

Obviously these lye burns were preventable accidents. Two things were to be done. A warning label must be put on the containers, and a nation-wide campaign of education must be inaugurated so that these caustic poisons would be kept out of the reach of children.

I went to the packers of lye-containing preparations. As business men they said in effect: "No such thing as a poison label can be put on my preparation unless it is put on every preparation in the market, because such a label would single out my preparation as dangerous and people would shun it in favor of unlabeled preparations. Even if all packers now in business agreed, there would be new concerns constantly bringing out unlabeled preparations. If you spent all your time at it, you could not keep up with the flood of new concerns." It was evident that it would be necessary to have a law that would be fair to all while protecting the children.

I was not one of those who think that passing a law is a remedy for every wrong; but no one questioned the necessity for the then existing law requiring the druggist to label carbolic acid "Poison," and it seemed to me illogical not to require the grocer to put a "Poison" label on caustic poisons—especially so because the druggists' poisons usually go on a high shelf in the medicine cupboard whereas the grocers' poisons if misbranded are likely to be put on the floor of the kitchen cupboard, in easy reach of children.

I then went to George von Bonhorst, who was closely associated with the political machine that then ruled Pennsylvania. He always accompanied Chris Magee on the frequent trips to Harrisburg, and although neither held office of any kind they were always present at legislative sessions. A speaker of the House of Representatives once opened a session by announcing, "A full quorum and Chris Magee being present, the House will please come to order." I had known George von Bonhorst since childhood. I explained to him the sad plight of the children whose mothers had had no warning that lye is a poison. He said: "Chev, I am sorry for the children, and I would like to help in your effort to help them; but I must tell you that you would have a long and expensive way to travel before you could get a bill like that through the State Legislature. In the first place you would have to get the backing of the heads of various powerful political groups. First and most powerful is the beer and liquor group: they dominate Pennsylvania politics. What legislative votes they cannot buy with cash, they can influence with a few complimentary cases of beer or whisky. They would not put it through for you, but nobody could if they opposed it. There are other groups. Then would come the lobbyists and the political hangers-on who make their living by bleeding everybody who wants a bill passed. Nothing but money and lots of it would get your bill up for consideration, let alone have it passed. Unless you have a wealthy philanthropist with loose purse strings to help you, don't attempt it. Sorry, Chev, but such is Pennsylvania politics today."

I was sick at heart. First of all, it seemed so sad to me that I could not help protect the children. Next was the humiliating thought of the utter depravity of the political rulers. That I must get the permission of liquor interests before I could do anything toward welfare legislation made me feel the utter degradation into which rule of my state had fallen. I had not lost my faith in human nature and felt that many legislators were humane men to whom I would not appeal in vain if I could get to them; but here I visualized "the long and expensive way to travel."

It was disheartening. I was willing to work hard, but I had no philanthropist to finance the undertaking. I made up my mind that the day would come when I could and would put through the legislation requiring the labeling of household lye. Meanwhile I would collect appealing and convincing evidence to show legislators when the time should come. I would collect photographs of the poisoned starving children, and the label of the lye container in each case.

Year after year I collected the clinical data. Again the old stubborn determination to hang on.

The discovery that the part of my esophagoscopic work concerned with foreign bodies, as well as lye strictures, in children was due to preventable accidents filled me with determination to devote a large part of my life to the prevention of these causes of needless suffering.

CHAPTER XVIII

DAYS IN BUGGY AND SADDLE

(1891–1903)

As MY REPUTATION as an operator, tracheotomist, and intubationist spread, I was called upon to get over so much territory that transportation at instant command became a necessity. The first half of my life was in the horse age, the latter half in the motor era. My fondness for horses brought pleasure and sorrow; more grief than gladness. I never have witnessed a horse race in my life, and always had a horror of the track, regarding it as a lame excuse for gambling. Race-track devotees care nothing for the horse that cannot win. I was fond of the horse as an intelligent animal and interesting companion. I never had a horse of my own until it became essential for professional purposes; and this came early in my professional career. The work of some specialists was chiefly in the "office," as the consulting room is usually called in this country. But my work was different. As special operator I was called upon to go to all the hospitals, but this was the lesser part of the trips required. Many operations that today are done in a hospital were formerly done in the homes of the patients. Nursing homes, so numerous in England, were unknown here. Only in case of desperately serious illness was the patient sent to a hospital; naturally, mortality was high; and in consequence many regarded the hospital as the last station on the way to the grave. Not only was I required to operate in the homes but, worse, the homes were scattered widely in the outlying districts of the city, in the near-by villages and surrounding country.

In summer a light buggy with a quick, nimble horse could get over many miles of the dirt roads. In winter better time could be made with a saddle horse along the narrow roadside out of the deep, tough, sticky, gripping mud.

In the buggy or on horseback, driving alone by moonlight and starlight was delightful. The voices of the night were broken only by the horse's footfalls. Nowadays, one cannot enjoy, even see, moonlight on a highway. All is obliterated in the piercing, painful glare of the headlights of innumerable swiftly approaching automobiles. The voices of the night are lost in the roar of the trucks and the rush of air displaced by catapulting motor cars.

In boyhood I had become perfectly at home in the saddle. The muscular habit of maintaining one's position in the saddle and coördinating one's movements with those of the horse, if properly acquired in childhood, becomes as natural as walking and remains through life. With me it was so much so that on long night calls in later years I could doze for miles in the saddle while the horse would unerringly follow the route home. Risk of failure to clear an encountered vehicle forbade dozing in the buggy. Whether I was in buggy or saddle, the horse was a faithful and interesting companion; it was a pleasure during these journeys to teach him some words, and within six months he was receptive to a vocabulary of about ten words. He could not talk back, but he understood and promptly obeyed requests in ordinary conversational voice using such words as right, left, slow, faster, stop, go, trot, rack, running walk, lope. Most people in those days attributed this to phenomenal intelligence in the particular horse; no credit was accorded the patience of the instructor. So it was with fire-engine horses: they were supposed to be an especially intelligent breed. No attention was given to the fact that the firemen, between fire calls, trained the horses in various duties, such as to leave their stalls when their halters were automatically released synchronously with the ringing of the alarm signal, and to take their respective places under the suspended harness promptly and without any lead or guidance. Any horse can be taught to do these and many still more remarkable things. Work horses, however, except the leader of a four-horse team, were taught nothing. Unfortunately the horrible cruelty that caused so many tearful days in my boyhood was still common along the highways in winter and early spring. My prestige as a physician, with my boyhood experience and knowledge of Father's methods, usually enabled me successfully to intercede and to stop the cruelty when I came upon it; but the horror of it all often utterly destroyed all the pleasure that might have accrued from a trip in buggy or saddle.

Cruelties to horses today are not so obvious, partly because of better highways, partly because the work horse is relegated to the remote districts; but chiefly because of the motor era. Those of us who loved the horse have reason to be grateful for his disappearance. Better for him never to be born than to go through the horrible cruelties that I witnessed in the bygone horse age.

CHAPTER XIX

MARRIAGE

(1899)

A PATIENT, JOSEPHINE W. WHITE, when coming for treatment brought her sister Alice and their mother with her. They were all charming people. I married Alice, and very soon found that her helpfulness and careful budgeting enabled both of us to live for less than I had spent alone.

Things had been going better in a financial way for a year or two, so that I felt justified in taking the step. We talked it over and concluded that, inasmuch as neither of us was burdened with social ambitions, we could get on very well. We were both fond of home and were perfectly contented with our little family circle. My wife did the cooking and also the household work with the exception of the scrubbing and the washing. She did the light ironing and the pressing of my clothes. Every morning I left home with a very proper professional appearance though with misgivings as to the amount of work my wife was doing. I was often remorseful when I compared her economy and good management with my carelessness in collections.

If only I could have developed a business sense in my professional work, it would not have been necessary for us to be so frugal at home for so many years.

CHAPTER XX

THE BEGINNINGS OF BRONCHOSCOPY

(1899)

LIKE EVERY OTHER epoch-making result of human endeavor, Bronchoscopy had its precursors.

Before the days of antitoxin, diphtheria was very prevalent and very virulent. It often attacked the larynx, and such cases were always fatal unless tracheotomy was done. Because of a reputation for skill in the rapid performance of this operation without anesthesia (contraindicated in diphtheria), I received calls, day and night, to perform it as an emergency procedure. It consists in cutting into the front of the neck and inserting a silver tube in the windpipe as a by-passage for air while the larynx is closed by disease, most often diphtheria. In those pre-antitoxin days laryngeal diphtheria had a mortality of about 70 per cent. If the child did not die of the diphtheria, he was usually doomed for life to wear the silver tube in his neck in order to breathe because his larynx was closed by the scar tissue that followed the self-limited diphtheritic disease. I acquired some reputation in the treatment of this form of strictured larynx so successfully that nasal and oral breathing could be resumed and the silver tube in the neck abandoned. This was a labor of love because all the patients were children. It seemed that diphtheria picked out the sweetest children for attack. Increased experience developed a new technique of tracheotomy that almost entirely prevented post-diphtheritic stricture of the larynx. O'Dwyer of New York had demonstrated that tracheotomy could be obviated in many cases by introducing through the mouth into the larynx a gold-lined, hard-rubber tube to be worn until the laryngeal diphtheria subsided: usually a matter of two weeks or less. This intubation of the larynx appealed strongly to me, and I took it up enthusiastically. Prior to the work of O'Dwyer, Horace Green of New York (about 1869) had demonstrated that a tube could be introduced through the mouth and larynx into the trachea. This method in modified form served me well. Some years after O'Dwyer's development of intubation for laryngeal diphtheria Killian demonstrated that a rigid, straight metallic tube could be inserted through the larynx or through a tracheotomic wound for the purpose of removing foreign bodies from the bronchi. The instruments and methods were rudimentary. The mortality was high; Fletcher Ingals estimated it at 25 per cent.

Having at that time worked for about a dozen years with esophagoscopy, and for five years with Kirstein's direct laryngoscopy, I took hold of bronchoscopy with enthusiasm. New ways made it not only safe but 98 per cent successful in foreign-body cases. The new technique proved it to be of utmost usefulness in harmlessly examining and treating the bronchi and lungs in disease. It was shown that bronchoscopy could be done through the mouth in a routine way, and that it could be thus performed with practically no mortality from the procedure considered apart from the condition for which it was used.

The construction of a practical bronchoscope, the development of a technique for its safe passage, and the proving of the harmlessness of its careful use were but initial steps. They were fundamental, of course, but to accomplish anything more than mere inspection hundreds of accessory instruments and technique for their respective uses must be developed; pitfalls and dangers in each new development must be eliminated. In all of this developmental work it was necessary to do almost every day things that had not been done before. To do untried things on a baby, so tender in his tissues, so helpless, so defenseless, was unthinkable. Some methodical plan must be developed and followed in testing each step of each procedure before using it on a baby. Baby cadavers could be used for the purely anatomical studies; but for the solution of mechanical problems—that is, the manipulation of foreign bodies so as to extricate them from the bronchi without injury to the tissues—work in living, moving bronchi was necessary. For this the dog was the recourse.

No one could have a greater fondness for dogs than I have, and it was a sore trial for me when in the prior development of esophagoscopy I did my first endoscopy on a dog. To my great relief I found that the dog could be perfectly narcotized so as to feel nothing, to know nothing, and yet come out of the narcosis unharmed, happy, and hungry. And there was always ready for him the wherewithal to satisfy his hunger. After devouring it he would drop off into a natural sleep as any dog does after a full meal. Moreover, the dog was not subjected to any procedure until after it had been fully tested and perfected by work with a bronchoscope down in a rubber tube so arranged as to simulate a bronchus. If the procedure was found practicable in the rubber-tube manikin it was next tested on the cadaver. If it proved satisfactory as to feasibility and safety, the test on the dog was undertaken. These two prior tests eliminated danger to the dog not only for his sake but for the more important reason that any bronchoscopic procedure to be justifiable must be workable entirely within the bronchial lumen without trauma to the normal walls. If any error were to be made, it was required to be on the safe side; anything potentially risky for the dog was by that very fact ruled out for use on the baby. In the many tests of mechanical problems of foreign body extraction not one dog died; nor was one injured. On the other hand incalculable thousands of babies' lives were, and will be, saved by the procedures developed.

The work involved in carrying out all of these preliminary details was tremendous. A procedure requiring only a few minutes to do on the patient required many days, sometimes even weeks, of preliminary work. If a planned procedure was unworkable in rubber tube, cadaver, and dog, obviously it would be unworkable on the child. Under such circumstances another method or methods had to be tried until the problem was solved. Being purely mechanical, the problem must be soluble, was the motto. And so it was proved to be by the more than 98 per cent of successes, on human beings, mostly children.

All of this system of working had been developed with the esophagoscope. It remained, however, to adapt methods to the anatomically and physiologically different passages. The esophagus is a soft, elastic, collapsed, baglike tube full of wrinkles and folds; the tracheobronchial tree stands open by reason of its rings of cartilage. The bronchi enlarge and elongate at each inspiration, diminish and shorten during expiration. The heart at each beat dinges in the bronchial wall or pushes the whole bronchial tube sidewise; the thumping is transmitted to the fingers holding the inserted bronchoscope. One gets the impression of being in the midst of the machinery of life itself. In a baby the obvious delicacy of life's constantly moving machinery is appalling. To work in such surroundings through a tube not much larger than a straw to manipulate a safety-pin, for example, is daunting to the utmost degree. Fully to comprehend this, it must be realized that "safety" of such pins applies only to location in clothing and even then only when closed. In the bronchi they are usually open, the sharp point is upward and being forced by the spring into the bronchial wall. Moreover that delicate wall is beset with catchy ridges.

Achievement, as usual with me, brought its pleasures. But with them came onerous feelings of obligation. It was obvious that all the bronchoscopy and esophagoscopy I could do in a lifetime, even if, as then seemed doubtful, I should live out the proverbial threescore and ten, would be as nothing compared to the results of the wide dissemination I felt sure could be accomplished by teaching every physician willing to learn. If the teaching could have been by talks and clinics, everything would have been quite simple; but practical work would be necessary in order to prepare the pupil for doing bronchoscopy. The anatomy and the dangers could be taught on the cadaver; but it was also necessary that the pupil have education of the eye and the fingers by bronchoscopic procedures in living, moving bronchi. Here was a problem. It was unthinkable to turn over to a tyro for practice in passing the bronchoscope a helpless little child obviously unable to give consent. But it was necessary that the pupil should have, not only practice in passing the bronchoscope, but practice in removing foreign bodies from living, moving bronchial tubes. To put foreign bodies into the bronchi of a living human being for practice was too atrocious for even a moment's consideration.

The solution of the problem was to use the dog. As in my developmental work, I had many qualms at first; but they were alleviated largely by the perfection of narcosis and the harmlessness of the tyros' procedures demonstrated after the first course given. All queasiness did not disappear until there arrived the happy day when Doctor McKee, the veterinarian of Houston, Texas, demonstrated that all the endoscopic contributions of the dog as a laboratory subject are accruing to the benefit of the dog as a patient.* Bronchoscopic courses were first given in Pittsburgh, then in Philadelphia, then in Paris. Invitations to give courses have been received from medical centers in different parts of the world, but the work and the absences involved have placed limitations. The invitations from London could have been accepted as on the way to or from Paris but for the British antivivisection laws. The facts that in our teaching we did not dissect the dog, that we only examined his natural passages, did not make any difference; nor did the fact that without harming or paining the dog we could teach and develop methods of saving untold thousands of human lives. The British antivivisection laws were not passed by scientists or physicians but by well-meaning, kindly persons. To the scientist uninterested in sport it seems strange that it should be legal, even admirable, to be first to arrive

* While I was reading proof on these pages there came the announcement of the safe removal of an accidentally inspirated needle from the bronchus of a seven-months-old dachshund at a veterinary hospital in Philadelphia.

on the scene of a bloody battle in which dogs are mutilated in tearing to pieces the hopelessly outnumbered fox; who, by the way, is also of the family Canidae. But, of course, two wrongs do not make a right; and the scientist may be biased.

I had occasion once to ask an antivivisectionist a hypothetical question:

"Suppose that your baby had a safety-pin in his bronchus and there were available only two physicians, who though otherwise equal differed in this way: One had never looked through a bronchoscope; the other had taken a course of instruction on bronchoscopy including many bronchoscopic safety-pin removals from the living, moving bronchi of a dog.

"Under such circumstances which physician would you choose?"

The reply was:

"But my baby does not happen to have a safety-pin in his bronchus. One should not assume conditions that do not exist."

I abandoned the discussion and gave the courses in Paris.

CHAPTER XXI

CALAMITY

(1911)

ONE DAY DOCTOR ENGLISH came in to have his larynx treated. As he was leaving, he stopped and said abruptly: "Jackson, I don't like that little occasional hacking cough of yours. I am going to examine your chest." He proceeded to do so. I had been getting up a little mucoid sputum and managed to get up a specimen for him.

It was a staggering blow to find I had pulmonary tuberculosis. I had been making good progress in building up a practice. I was just beginning to reap substantial rewards in a financial way from a reputation gained primarily by many years of privation and struggle in the treatment of the poor, worthy and unworthy. My wife could have help with her work. Our boy would be needing an investment in his education.

But the inevitable had to be faced. Plans must be made for survival of my little family and myself.

Dr. English was very kind and considerate. He said it was a mild attack, and it was discovered very early. There were as yet no bacilli in the sputum. He laid out a regimen for me that would attract little attention, and he thought if I would follow a diet and could manage to get twelve hours of rest in bed out of the twenty-four I should come through. The main feature of the diet was plenty of milk and meat: both of these I had not cared for, and doubtless the deficiency was a factor in vulnerability to the tuberculous infection.

The rule of twelve hours in bed out of the twenty-four was in itself no great hardship; there was plenty of work to be done in the four hours remaining after subtracting the eight hours' sleep: case records to be annotated, sketches of laryngeal and endoscopic views of pathologic tissues to be painted, reports to referring physicians to be written, letters to be answered. Correspondence had been a heavy burden for a number of years—all of it professional; I never had felt that I could spare time for either reading or writing letters other than medical.

All this work, even though done in bed, was not ideal in the treatment of tuberculosis; but it was a great solace to feel that I was losing no time, and that by doing this part of my daily routine in bed I was free during the other twelve hours to hold my clientele together. The fixed expenses were devouring a large portion of my income, and I was in constant dread of starting on the road to indebtedness and ruin that had made so many of the later years of my father's life so miserable.

But would this bed-working modification of the antituberculous regimen suffice to cure my attack of tuberculosis?

That was a depressing question that time alone could answer.

Lying in bed, I took a few moments now and then for philosophizing: material for this diversion was abundant. For example, there was the contrast between the old and the new era in Medicine: the transition had occurred in my own experience. As a boy I had gone to deliver a piece of Sorrento and inlaid work I had made to order for a lady ill with "consumption," as pulmonary tuberculosis was then generally called. I remembered her pale face, wan smile, and loose cough. The windows were closed with double sash. The doctor arrived while I was there. He put his hand to the window frame, and as I left I heard him say: "There is a draft coming in there. No wonder you caught cold. Those windows must be weather-stripped." The doctor had, in later years, become a convert to the open-air system of treatment of tuberculosis that marked the new era of medical science, and that called for windows with all sash removed as the next best thing to putting the patient outdoors. A sashless room on a dark, cold winter day in the grimy, dirty, smoky Pittsburgh of that time was not a cheerful place, but patients that would have died in airtight rooms got well. The open-air treatment in a sunny country environment would be still better; but the important thing was the passing of the old era with its fallacies of airtight rooms and "catching cold."

Response to the antituberculous regimen in my case was prompt, and at the end of six months Doctor English found the tuberculosis completely arrested. I was back on full duty. It was a happy day for me. Of course I had lost some patients, but I had not lost the support of any of the physicians who had been referring patients to me before my illness; on the whole I had been able to avoid the complete abandonment of work that would have been so disastrous.

One habit acquired during this attack of tuberculosis has never left me. It was due to two then recent epoch-making developments. The telephone system had been established in Pittsburgh; the bacillary cause of tuberculosis had been discovered. To protect others from tuberculous infection I covered the telephonic transmitter with a napkin at home and in the consulting room. For use elsewhere I carried freshly pressed, clean cheap cotton handkerchiefs. Time proved that the risk of dissemination of tuberculosis by the mouthpiece of the telephone is small; but that the risk of thus scattering acute respiratory infections is great. Anyway, the odor coming from any much used telephone transmitter is enough to render desirable as a matter of decent cleanliness the interposition of a fabric, and especially so as the best telephonic transmission of the voice requires placing the lips so close that an occasional touch is unavoidable. Moreover telephonic conversation with a Parisian colleague recently has shown that the protective fabric over the transmitter and receiver does not impair transmission. The efficiency of a cotton fabric as a barrier to infection is evident from the fact that no surgeon would think of operating without a mask over his mouth.

Two very busy years followed. Financial matters were again

reaching the stage where I need have no anxieties. Privation need no longer be a habit of life.

One evening at a medical meeting I had a copious and sudden hemorrhage. The salty taste of the mouthful of blood warned me in time to get out of the room before I was compelled to spit out the blood, so that no scene was created. The bleeding ceased before I arrived home. I went to bed, and next day called in Doctor John W. Boyce. I had developed a second attack of tuberculosis.

Again adversity had to be resolutely faced.

For a full understanding of the calamity it is necessary to recall the benefits of tonsillectomy and adenoidectomy obvious to family physicians and parents, referred to in Chapter XIV. These beneficial operations were the source of a major portion of the laryngologist's income. Having been largely instrumental in bringing these procedures into their deserved recognition, I was beginning to get quite a number of patients well able to pay proper fees. Bronchoscopy, esophagoscopy, and gastroscopy had, so far, brought me very little income—not enough to pay the most meager living expenses. The remunerative tonsil and adenoid operation involved anxieties, night trips for post-operative hemorrhage, sometimes an all-night stay in the hospital. (I and a few others had by this time established the procedure as a hospital operation.) Doctor Boyce was insistent that all of this night work and anxiety should be cut out. With it went the larger part of my remunerative work. To make ends meet out of income from direct laryngoscopy, bronchoscopy, esophagoscopy, gastroscopy, and the part of laryngeal work that pertained to cancer and benign growths was a problem. No one had ever before specialized in such a way. Could it be made to work? Unquestionably the specialties could be developed and a living made if I had good health; but to carry out the regimen of Doctor Boyce and at the same time make a living from the ultraspecialties was a problem.

Reviewing the work in the preceding years, I noted that, whereas the tonsil work was local, many of the patients requiring attention in the province of the other specialties were referred by physicians more or less distantly located. Appointments could therefore be arranged by telephone, telegraph, or letter. I had associated with me in the work at that time Dr. Ellen J. Patterson, competent to do anything I could do. It was planned that she should take care of all emergencies and arrange appointments for the part I was to do. This would give me the time for the antituberculous regimen of rest in bed out of doors. There were no restrictions on my writing in bed. This prospect was a great consolation, because there was a great demand for a book on bronchoscopy, esophagoscopy, and laryngeal surgery. I had a huge collection of notes on these subjects but had not had time to classify, analyze, and arrange the material in book form.

My wife had found, in response to a newspaper advertisement, a little place at the edge of the city on the Ohio River hills. Here a crude outdoor sleeping porch was built: an ideal place for a tuberculous patient.

CHAPTER XXII

HOME ON THE OHIO RIVER HILLS

(1911–1916)

"THE OLD SHOE," as we called it, was a little, old rambling farmhouse high on the river cliff, built of stone over a cellar quarried out of the outcropping strata of rock. Pittsburgh was only twenty minutes away by rail. Every moment was devoted to physical rest in bed out of doors while writing "Peroral Endoscopy and Laryngeal Surgery" from boxes of notes and case records. In the literary details invaluable aid was given by my wife and my sister Josephine White.

Those were happy days notwithstanding the restriction of activities imposed upon me by the rigid antituberculous regimen of Doctor John W. Boyce. Writing in bed was continuous from dawn till dinner. After the evening meal the sunset and the ever changing effects of fading daylight on the Ohio River hills were calm, peaceful, and conducive to a good night's rest. The family at this time consisted of my wife, her mother and sister (always Mother and Sister to me), and my son, Chevalier Lawrence. It was a happy little family, a beautiful life, with never a jar nor a harsh word.

At the end of the antituberculous regimen plus a year of less strict rules Doctor Boyce pronounced the tuberculosis arrested; my activities were unrestricted except that twelve hours out of the twenty-four must be devoted to rest in bed outdoors.

Tuberculosis was conquered for a second time; and the manuscript of "Peroral Endoscopy and Laryngeal Surgery" was in the publisher's hands.

Though the second attack of tuberculosis seemed at the time a dire disaster, it really was a blessing in disguise. It amputated the load of general throat surgery that was depriving me of the time and energy needed for the development of bronchoscopy, esophagoscopy, gastroscopy, and laryngeal surgery and, equally important, was depriving me of the time to put on record in textbook form the enormous and unique clinical experience in these new specialties. The time was ripe for such a book. It probably would not have been written for many years had it not been for the enforced limitation of clinical work. The world-wide recognition of bronchoscopy would have been long delayed. Most medical books are built up as improvements upon predecessors. Peroral endoscopy was a new branch of science. Many new and fundamentally different instruments had been devised; the new technique required new drawings and schematic illustrations; previously unseen endoscopic images of normal anatomy and pathologic changes required colored plates. The new science was not theoretic; it was based on facts; there was great need of presenting those facts; proper presentation required classification and analysis of the data collected in over twenty years' clinical experience. In the rush of clinical work full of life-saving emergencies, the notes were fragmentary and had to be supplemented by memory. Two things aided memory greatly: one was the wonderful power of sketching or drawing any object to fix anything in the mind; the other was the power of the sketch to recall correlated facts from the recesses of the memory, so to speak. For a long time the feeling of duty to humanity and the medical profession weighed heavily upon me because I felt that no one else could get full value out of those notes and records of original observations. Yet, with me as with all clinicians, urgent calls always relegated literary work to second place; disheartening interruptions threatened interminable delays. It can therefore be readily realized with what degree of enthusiasm I worked on the book.

When "Peroral Endoscopy" appeared it was well received, and the edition was soon sold out. All the reviews were laudatory, especially so in the recognition of the clinical facts recorded, the original schematic drawings illustrative of technique, and the color plates showing images revealed by the then new methods of examination. There came very gratifying offers for the right to translate into French, German, and Italian, and arrangements had been made for these when in 1914 all Europe was plunged into the World War. After the war it was felt that publication in French would be sufficient inasmuch as French comes nearer being universal than any other language. The French translation appeared in 1920.

"Peroral Endoscopy" was a massive presentation of classified facts with clinical evidence supporting the statements. After its publication there was a demand for an abstract in the form of a practical manual telling simply and dogmatically what to do and how to do it. This practical manual has gone through three editions in English and has been translated into Italian as well as French.

Aside from the particular subjects dealt with in "Peroral Endoscopy," it has come to be regarded as marking, if it did not help to create, a new era: that of direct inspection in the diagnosis of disease. Objective methods were limited to inspection of the tongue, from which no end of fallacious deductions were made. The attitude of physicians as shown by books, journals, and reports of medical meetings down to near the end of the last century is curious and would be unbelievable if documentary evidence were not so abundant. Deductive methods based on theory were the order of the day. Galen's writings and that great book, the Bible, were brought into discussions to disprove facts that were demonstrated before the eyes of the discussers. The use of newly developed specula was decried as a fussy pretense bordering on quackery. But history shows that direct inspection came as one of the developments of the new era. Among the first was the laryngeal mirror; then came rapidly many forms of specula, cystoscopes, ophthalmoscopes, otoscopes, endoscopes, proctoscopes, fluoroscopes, laryngoscopes, esophagoscopes, bronchoscopes, gastroscopes. At about the time of publication of "Peroral Endoscopy," or soon thereafter, direct inspection became the order of the day.

The prompt selling out of the entire edition of "Peroral Endoscopy" and the large steady sale of the abstract manual and translations would naturally lead to the conclusion that a steady income from royalties accrued to the author. The reverse was the case. This seems to render pertinent some comments on medical literature.

The public, accustomed to reading of royalties from "best sellers," has a vague idea of a substantial income accruing from authorship. It will be news to learn that, as a matter of fact, medical writing is a total loss except for any little reputation as an authority that may be acquired by the author. Medicine is constantly progressing. After the manuscript has gone to the publisher a case with new features is encountered. The medical author feels it urgent to insert in the proofs a report of the case, or to insert a sentence to include the newly observed fact, or to modify a statement. As stated in the preface to "Peroral Endoscopy," the writing of a busy clinician is done under stress of limited time and opportunity. He has not the time to rewrite sentences many times, as Macaulay did, in the search for better sentence structure. Better phraseology often comes to mind and errors in manuscript are detected in reading proofs. A charge is made for any sentence, period, or comma added or deleted in proofs; these printers' charges alone usually more than consume all royalties. Doubtless the medical book publishers are fully justified by the exigencies of business; but the fact remains that medical authorship does not yield direct reimbursement for paper and postage, to say nothing of secretarial expenses.

The fundamental purpose of medical literature is to record medical knowledge in a way that shall render such knowledge readily available for present and future generations. It is curious to note the widespread belief among the laity that physicians have precious, carefully guarded secrets in methods of cure. Even very intelligent people do not know and could not understand the fact that, as soon as a physician discovers anything, he immediately hurries to a medical meeting to publish his discovery for the use of the medical profession and for the good of humanity. The only benefit that can accrue to the discoverer is an addition to his reputation. The reputation may or may not ultimately materialize as an aid to the gaining of a livelihood. The claims of advertising quacks are largely responsible for the idea that physicians have secrets. The absurdity is, of course, apparent to anyone who looks at medical books and journals. It is universally recognized by the members of the medical profession that everything discovered must be put on record in medical literature for future generations to use, modify, or reject, as the discovery may merit. But the literature is not beyond criticism; far from it. It is cumbersome, verbose, iterative and reiterative, inaccessible. Many of the best things are buried under the titles of other things. But we are improving. As in every other human activity there is progress toward better things. The mass of knowledge we know as medical science is built of the activities of forgotten men. The structure is parallel in a figurative sense to the coral island that is built of the carcasses of obliterated lives. A medical investigator by a lifetime of work makes a discovery and publishes it. The medical writer afterward states the fact but omits the authority for it. The medical writer is quoted, the originator passes into oblivion. In medicine credit goes figuratively to Amerigo Vespucci, not to Christopher Columbus. But, after all, what difference does it make so long as medical science progresses?

One day while I was writing "Peroral Endoscopy" Doctor John Boyce came in and commented, "Making footprints in the sands of time?" I replied: "Exactly so; obliterated at the next tide. Anything of value I may write will be absorbed into medical literature to the credit of others. But that does not worry me in the least. It is our duty to help along a little if we can. It is utter folly to look, hope, or wish for any lasting credit for anything in medical literature; utter folly to pursue such an *ignis fatuus* as priority in anything medical or surgical."

The following letter is germane to this subject:

DEAR DOCTOR JACKSON:

Most things you have written served as quarries from which builders of articles obtained materials for new structures. I could recognize the stones you have carved, but others have attributed the handiwork to the quarrymen.

The following reply was sent:

Plagiarism of idea or phraseology is a form of imitation that is indeed the most sincere flattery. Nothing gives me greater pleasure because it means either the writer considers my work so good that he deems it worthy of himself, or my teaching has made such a profound impression on him that he really thinks he did it himself. In either case I have evidently done a good piece of work.

The ideals in medical writing as I see them are expressed in the following remarks:

"My inferences may be wrong but I hope some little importance may attach to the cases reported. Clinical facts always remain clinical facts, primary inferences are more often wrong than right. For example, when I was a fisherman out of Gloucester all British ships were called 'lime-juicers.' It had been discovered that lime juice would prevent scurvy, and the marine laws required that every ship, in order to get clearance papers for long voyages, must have on board so much lime juice per day, per man. Medical writers have given many different causes for scurvy and reasons for the efficiency of lime juice in its prophylaxis and treatment. The various opinions in turn have been rejected, but the clinical fact of efficiency remains today as stubborn a thing as it was a century ago."

The foregoing was in introduction to a lecture on "Bronchoscopy for Disease," that I gave before the Royal Society of Medicine in London. It illustrates views on the form I think medical writing fundamentally should take; namely, clear separation of clinical facts not only from opinions but from deductions.

In my own medical writing I never sat down and wrote out an

article from memory or from medical books or journals. The method was to write from material collected while doing clinical work. Sometimes an article or a chapter would present the materials collected during many years. It was habitual to jot down notes of cases, ideas, problems; to have photographs of specimens, prints of roentgenograms; to make sketches of lesions, mechanical problems, new instruments, material for illustrations, anything that might be useful. These materials were filed under subjects in boxlike, book-form files. Then when the time came for writing the article, or the chapter in a book, the clinical records referred to in the boxful of notes were obtained from the clinical files. This material, other than case records, was classified in envelopes or folders marked with subtitles and paragraph heads. All the material was put into a hand box and taken to where the writing was to be done; the outdoor bed, the big writing chair with wide desklike arms, the boat, the mill, the bird-feeding concrete veranda or whatever place might suit the weather or other conditions. Continuous writing was never done at a desk or table. Indoors it was always in the writing chair I had built myself in early life. A very soft pencil known as Eldorado 5B was a favorite. Yellow manila paper was used indoors; to lessen the glare, green-tinted print paper was used outdoors.

CHAPTER XXIII

A PROPHET HONORED IN HIS OWN COUNTRY

(1900–1916)

WITHOUT ARROGATING TO MYSELF any charismatic endowments and without for one moment questioning the general truth of the saying of Matthew (XIII, 57), I feel compelled to say that my experience was not an example.

Not often has it fallen to the lot of a pioneer to be so well appreciated and so highly honored by his contemporaries in the town of his birth. Appreciation is too often *post mortem*.

At about thirty-five years of age general recognition came to me as an authority on the larynx. It was a surprise to receive notice of election to the chair of Laryngology in the Western Pennsylvania Medical College, later absorbed by the University of Pittsburgh. The offer of a medical professorship in a medical school to a man aged thirty-five is rare today and was a thing unknown at that time. The custom was then, as it still is in Europe, to give professorial chairs only to men so old that they had few if any creative years left. The great honor carried with it additional expenses but no salary. The attached hospital position not only paid no salary but involved considerable expense for equipment and instruments; and, worst of all, was the impoverishing steady drain of the salary of an operating-room nurse. Not one cent toward any of these necessary expenses came from any hospital or collegiate source. Everything had to be financed out of a practice that was 95 per cent charity. No patient was ever refused treatment. Those were lean years. Notwithstanding sixteen or seventeen hours of professional duties it was only the thrift and hard work of my wife that enabled us to get enough food and clothing for ourselves and our child. For teaching purposes there were no charts, no models, nothing but a blackboard and chalk. By a very unusual degree of proficiency in the use of these, together with a large clientele of grateful charity patients who gladly coöperated by appearing as living examples of results there was built up an undergraduate and postgraduate teaching clinic that gradually became widely known.

The laryngologists of Pittsburgh referred to me all their patients requiring bronchoscopy, esophagoscopy, gastroscopy, and endolaryngeal surgery. This gave me an unusually extensive experience in the newer procedures and in the diagnosis and treatment of the diseases to which these procedures were applicable.

As elsewhere herein mentioned, I was elected to a position on the staff of fourteen hospitals in Pittsburgh, and I was called in as outside consultant in all the other hospitals. Some of these were so-called "closed" institutions; that is to say, only the members of the particular staff could be called on consultation. An exception to the rule was promptly made whenever a staff member desired my help in a special case. So far as I know, no other man ever received so much of this kind of courtesy, though I could name many who deserved it.

These honors concerned charity-ward patients. The increased hospital connections, however, brought a slowly increasing number of pay patients who could without hardship pay something for services, over and above the increasing hospital and Roentgen-ray and nursing charges. The expenses of my growing practice were increasing apace. The day had gone by when a physician's equipment consisted of a prescription blank and a table. My own requirements went far beyond those of the average physician of the new era. Instrumental equipment was a large expense, and it was continuous because of the constantly recurring necessity for replacement with improved models. Then there were sterilizers for instruments, utensils, dressings, and water. A microscope, incubator, chemical glassware, stands, and other laboratory equipment were needed. A typist as well as an attendant became necessary because of the increasingly heavy load of correspondence and manuscripts. First a horse and a buggy, then an automobile was indispensable if I was to get to the hospitals and the widely scattered consultations.

If I had been as good a manager as my wife, or if I had been a good business man, all of this steadily increasing "overhead," as it is now called, could easily have been taken care of and a good margin of profit maintained; but I simply could not think of patients in terms of dollars. As a result of carelessness in collections many long trips into the surrounding country with expenditure of energy, time, and money were a total loss financially, though usually successful surgically. The worst of it was the widespread misinterpretation to the effect that I did not need money. I am free to confess that this was one of my greatest faults. There is no excuse for it. I should have realized my shortcomings. I should have realized also the false impression that arose, and should have seen the propriety of stating that I was in constant need of money, and after the patient's recovery must be paid a proper fee, according to the patient's circumstances.

This need have in no way interfered with my taking gratuitous care of all poor that came my way. Nor, as I look at it now, would it have necessarily interfered with my greatest pleasure in all my work, that of achievement. Owing to a psychologic defect I could never mentally interpret achievement in terms of dollars. In many of these cases my predecessors had failed to do what I had done, or had regarded it as an impossibility; but even with this criterion of value I could not think of fee. If I had had sense enough to employ, as I did later in life, a financial secretary to think only of money matters, all of the heavy and increasing expenses could have been carried without keeping me impoverished, and without the slightest injustice or hardship to those who benefited by my work. Just and proper collections would have lessened my struggle for funds with which to defray the expenses of my charity work.

CHAPTER XXIV

BUILDING AN INTERNATIONAL REPUTATION

(1895–1925)

WITH NO SUCH OBJECTIVE in mind an international reputation was built during the intensely busy years from 1895 to 1925. In the retrospect it is curious, almost uncanny, to note how with utmost precision a young life was molded by a series of activities and studies, none useless, every one an essential part in the achievement of a career. No collegiate sponsor could have planned a curriculum for a definite goal in academic achievement better than "just happened" in my case of ultimate achievement of an international reputation as the creator of a special branch of surgery. I started with a foundation of activities that seemed remote from medical science, such as getting choked and beaten into unconsciousness; going weak and hungry all day because my luncheon was uneatable with ashes; jig sawing; wood turning; metal working; devising new means for removing lost tools from mile-deep oil wells; getting pushed-in corks from empty bottles; plumbing and gas-fitting; drawing winter trees; painting on china and glassware; selling medical books; learning knots and splices; competitive evisceration and decapitation of dead codfish.

With this inconceivably inappropriate training I started out to build, unintentionally, an international reputation for achieving the seemingly impossible in medical science.

To realize the importance of the then new field of bronchoscopy it is necessary only to recall that foreign bodies inspirated into the bronchi were ultimately fatal unless coughed up; and this happy result occurred in only about two patients in a hundred; the other ninety-eight died, some immediately, others after weeks, months, even years of suffering. The alternative was cutting out ribs and going in through the lung by an external surgical operation that in itself, in those days, resulted in death of the patient in 98 per cent of the cases. By bronchoscopy the foreign body could be removed through the mouth without the slightest risk or harm to the patient in almost all instances. A few examples may be cited.

A fourteen-year-old boy inspirated a scarf pin; it lodged in the right main bronchus. "He's a dead boy," said one of the greatest surgeons of the day. Other great surgeons said they could remove the pin but the operation, at the root of the lung, would probably result in death on the table. The mother prayed long and earnestly. Fortified by prayer, she dried her tears and went to Doctor Morris Leof of Philadelphia, pleading: "Save my boy, save him! In God's name I ask you to save him." Doctor Leof took the child to the late Professor J. Chalmers Da Costa, one of the greatest surgeons of all time. He said: "No, I will not operate on the boy. Take him out to Pittsburgh. Doctor Chevalier Jackson will take the pin out: and he will not hurt the boy, either." Events justified Da Costa's faith in the then new procedure of bronchoscopy. The other great surgeons had not yet heard of it. This dramatic case spread the knowledge of the possibilities of the method; but skepticism did not at once disappear.

A girl slowly dying of suppurative disease of the lung. Doctor Solomon Solis-Cohen, Doctor Tello J. D'Apery, and Doctor Willis F. Manges working together discovered that the cause was a price-tag fastener that the child had inspirated while at work in a stocking factory. Doctor D. Braden Kyle invited me to go to Philadelphia to remove the foreign body by bronchoscopy at the annual meeting of the American Laryngological Association. The novelty of the procedure attracted many celebrated physicians of the day. One great surgeon looked through the porthole in the operating-room door and passed on, remarking, "Damned nonsense." Less roughly expressed skepticism pervaded the audience. The case was technically one of great difficulty. The stage was set for failure, even disaster. Above all was the knowledge that the child's life hung by a thread. That day, as on hundreds of other occasions, I was grateful for "the clear eye and the steady hand that only total abstinence from alcohol and tobacco could give," as I expressed it years afterward in the acceptance of the Bok Award. I was a grateful, happy man when I went back to Pittsburgh and told my wife, sister, and our two mothers of the poor child whose life had been saved. Many similar demonstrations were made in different parts of the country before the tremendous life-saving possibilities of the new procedure were generally accepted. In all of this work there was no remuneration. Curiously, the patients were nearly all the children of the poor. Fully 95 per cent of my entire practice was charity. All of the expenses of special instruments and of travel were taken out of my slender income. Bills were always paid promptly, but subsistence for self, wife, and baby was often meager. Eventually bronchoscopy was generally accepted at its true value, and the children could be brought to the bronchoscopist, the traveling expenses being raised by contributions of charitably disposed friends and neighbors of the patient in the distant home town. Just why foreign body in the lung should be particularly an affection of the children of the poor has never been satisfactorily explained.

Children were sent in who presented problems that had proven veritable Gordian knots to others, often to many others. It was necessary patiently to work away on the problem until finally means of untying the knot were devised. It would seem that any fool can cut a knot with a sword or an ax; if Alexander had been really great he would have untied the knot.

The ordeals were often terrific. Many of the best surgeons are little bothered by the death of a patient; they are not heartless, and they take no unjustified risks of mortality. They are not fatalists. They are philosophers. Having done their best and being free of any inferiority complex, they feel no one else could have done better. But I could never get myself into this frame of mind; it would have been better for my precarious health if I could have done so. For days I would work intensively on a difficult problem; uppermost in my mind was the thought of the little child whose life depended on success. Failure did not mean immediate death; therefore no chances of fatal injury to the tissue should be taken. Means must be found to enable removal of the foreign body without risk. One false step, and all would be over. Death is an irreversible process. Take for example a little six-weeks-old baby with an open safety pin lodged point upward in his tender vitals. One inadvertent pull on that safety pin would have meant death. The small infantile passages imposed the size of a straw as the limit on the tube to be used. All instruments had to be tiny to pass through such a tube. Another and older child was sent from afar for the removal of a screw that had destroyed the function of one lung. If the screw should slip out of the grasp of the forceps during removal it would cork up the other lung. With both lungs out of function the heart would stop within two minutes. In these intervening one hundred twenty seconds the foreign body must be removed or the little child would die on the table. Hundreds of such cases occurred; the life of the bronchoscopist was made up of such ordeals. Loving little children, how could one stand the strain?

One thing helped greatly. I always had the utmost confidence in my eyes and fingers. I always felt I could instrumentally touch the tenderest tissues of the tiniest infant so gently that not the slightest harm would be done. There may be some measure of egotism in this; though there has been no end of substantiating objective evidence. Anyway the confidence, justified or not, was a sustaining influence throughout all the years of clinical work with suffering little children.

Perhaps the most important factor in the ability to stand the stress of the constantly recurring ordeals was a happy home life. Each evening I came home to a refuge where my wife not only refrained from tales of annoyance with harassing household help and tricky tradespeople but protected me from intrusions by those who had no idea that their visit could be otherwise than the bestowal of a favor. I never came home to find the house full of invited or uninvited guests for dinner. The evening meal was always a quiet, happy little family affair. Not once in all these years was I dragged out in the evening to attend a merely social function. Each evening I entered a sanctuary; each morning I left refilled with courage. When worried with the difficulties of saving some child's life, I would leave for the hospital with wifely parting words of cheer and of faith in my ability to succeed in apparently impossible tasks. To this more than to any other one thing I attribute success. I have often said that, if I had had to start out in the morning from a wrangling house of turmoil such as besets many men, I never could have survived the fearful ordeals of the developmental stages of bronchoscopy.

How did the ability to do the apparently impossible get to be known throughout the world? It was through medical channels. The satisfied physician who sent the patient told his confreres. Medical men who had encountered similar problems with fatal outcomes became interested. Children sent home to die after failure of older methods were brought in and cured by the new technique. Invitations came from medical societies all over the United States to present and discuss the methods used. Here entered the ability to draw and to describe the solutions of difficult problems. Medical magazines called for manuscript and drawings for reproduction. Then followed similar invitations from foreign societies, international medical magazines, and publishers. From all over the world came physicians, especially those who had experienced the difficulties; they came to the bronchoscopic clinic to compare notes and to see the new methods. Older men sent assistants to acquire the technique.

Thus the international reputation was acquired.

CHAPTER XXV

COMMUTING TO NEW YORK

(1915)

THE New York Post-Graduate Medical School and Hospital elected me Professor of Bronchoscopy and requested that a Department of Bronchoscopy be organized. The Board of Regents of the University of the State of New York, who then had the licensing power, granted, on "general reputation as an authority," and without examinations, the license to practice. Courses in bronchoscopy were given, and bronchoscopy was established as part of the curriculum in Otolaryngology. The chair was resigned (1917) as an essential part of curtailment of work necessitated by recrudescence of tuberculosis, the third attack.

CHAPTER XXVI

THE MOVE TO PHILADELPHIA

(1916)

LIFE AT THE OLD SHOE was perhaps the happiest period of the family existence. It was a sad day for all when the time came to move to Philadelphia. It was one of the great sacrifices we all made for bronchoscopy. Moving to Philadelphia would mean that I should see but rarely during her last years my widowed mother, then over eighty years of age. When I told her of the invitation to establish a bronchoscopic clinic in Philadelphia she said: "Chev, you must go; it is your duty to go; your father would want you to go. You and I amount to little; we shall both be dead in a few years; bronchoscopy will go on forever. Spread the life-saving work as long as you have the health and strength with which to do it. You must not falter now." Mother had for years followed the work of the Pittsburgh Bronchoscopic Clinic; she knew all about the sick children who came in ill nigh unto death; she knew that 98 per cent of them were saved. She died a few years later. I saw her but a few times. Each time she said: "Teach everything you know to everyone who will listen."

I myself felt it my duty to go, but the sacrifices to be made and the hardships to be borne by wife and family were appalling. I had accumulated no money. The Professorship of Laryngology at Jefferson Medical College offered great opportunities for the spread of the knowledge of the life-saving methods of bronchoscopy, but it paid no salary. To get bread and a little butter to put on it fees had to be collected from all patients who might be able to pay a little for services rendered. To "pull up stakes" and reëstablish myself at fifty-three years of age seemed injudicious, and especially so as my medical knowledge rendered impossible the ignoring of the fact that the additional load of teaching and of organizing a new clinic would probably reactivate my pulmonary tuberculosis; and it did. With one exception an entirely new personnel had to be selected and trained. Doctor Ellen J. Patterson, my able assistant for many years, could not leave Pittsburgh for family reasons. Miss Grace Ittel, my secretary, had recently passed away; and my very efficient assistant secretary, Miss Mildred Bird, for family reasons could not leave. Miss Margaret Dice, the instrument nurse, postponed her wedding day for a year, in order to train in new nurses and help organize the first bronchoscopic clinic in Philadelphia. Without her to shoulder the extra executive burden it is probable that my resistance would have been lowered below the threshold of recovery from the third attack of tuberculosis.

It soon became evident that I had made one miscalculation. It had seemed to me certain that moving to another city must surely lessen the load of clinical work so that I should have more time to lie in bed and write. In this I was mistaken. The clinical load was greatly increased.

My reception in Philadelphia surprised me then, and I still marvel at it. I was not unaware of having, as Professor Keen said, "revolutionized a whole department of Surgery"; but I was altogether unprepared to find a total absence of professional envy and jealousy among laryngologists whose field was necessarily being invaded. It was with utmost sincerity that Doctor J. Solis-Cohen, then dean of the laryngologists, said on a public occasion: "I know I voice the sentiment of every laryngologist in Philadelphia when I say we heartily welcome and adopt our colleague from Pittsburgh." Never once in twenty years has there been a remark or an incident that would raise a question as to the truth of Doctor Solis-Cohen's words. My reception by the medical profession of Philadelphia brought vividly to my mind that I had left no enemies nor even rivals glad to get rid of me in Pittsburgh. This is very remarkable when we consider the bitter feuds so common among rival professional men, especially medical men, in those days. No one has ever advanced any convincing explanation of the exceptional attitude. I told Professor Hare it was the atmosphere of the City of Brotherly Love; but he said the atmosphere has been here a long time and no one ever did it before.

CHAPTER XXVII

PONT READING

(1917–1918)

FOR THE FIRST TWO YEARS of work in Philadelphia my home was near Ardmore in the suburban country. Pont Reading was the name of the quaint old house, more or less dilapidated and long vacant but associated with many traditions. It was here that I weathered the third storm of tuberculosis. Outdoor conditions were established by windows never closed. Every moment not required at the hospital was spent in bed at Pont Reading. Writing and painting of endoscopic views again became continuous from dawn till dinner time except for interruption of trips to the hospital for duties connected with the clinic and the Medical Advisory Board of the State of Pennsylvania. A year of a rather strict antituberculous regimen resulted in an arrest of the third attack.

CHAPTER XXVIII

OLD SUNRISE MILLS

(1919–1937)

TWO YEARS AFTER MOVING to Philadelphia my wife discovered an old gristmill and sawmill with water right about thirty-five miles from Philadelphia. The buildings were dilapidated, and property was cheap in that locality; so the mill property was within limits fixed by funds available. As means permitted the little dam was rebuilt and sufficient repairs were made to restore the gristmill to running order. The sawmill was never repaired lest someone cut down a live tree to saw up. The quaint old wooden cog wheels in the gristmill turned once again to grind grain and cob feed for neighboring dairy farmers. This brought in enough money to complete the restoration of the old mill. A small generator was belted up, and for ten years the old farmhouse was never without electric light. At the end of ten years commercial lighting wires came along the highway and their current was substituted for the home circuit; but the service was not so good because thunderstorms damaged the commercial lines and put the house into darkness on the average three or four times every summer. The old mill generating and storage plant was then used to construct and operate an electric boat on the mill pool. Though an anachronism on the old mill pond it had the advantage of silence. With it one could creep noiselessly along through the leafy green shadows and be chummy with the wild birds and animals, could absorb the beautiful autumn sunshine and the glorious October colors. Promptly on November 1st, use of the electric boat as well as all wandering through the woods must cease, because no one's life is safe during the gunning season. The human beings with lust for killing swarm out from cities and shoot at any moving object, often without making sure even that it is a wild animal and not another human being. The modern gunner is a remnant of the time when killing wild life was necessary for food; and only too often he manifests other degenerate tendencies when he runs wild over fields and forests, destroying property. He has exterminated the once plentiful wild pigeon, the ruffed grouse, the prairie grouse, the woodcock, the plover. The wild duck and goose are going the same way.

"In the Province of Pennsylvania, in the Realm of His Majesty, King George the Third," the old parchment deeds read. The mill stands partly in the waters of Swamp Creek, where they rush through a rocky gorge to pass under an old stone-arched bridge. The hillsides are covered with trees and ferns; beautiful half-century-old, gray-green lichens cover the rocks and cliffs. In this setting nestles the old mill. A date panel in the gable is inscribed 1765. The footing course of the massive walls is laid with huge stones resting on the outcropping strata. The rushing water of great floods has smoothly rounded the exposed edges, but the walls are as plumb, level, and true as on the day they were laid, a century and a half ago, a monument to the conscientious craftsmanship of men long since dead and otherwise unrecorded. The hands that so skillfully shaped, mortised, and pegged the massive beams and timbers are distintegrating no one knows where. The old hickory cog wheels with their oaken gear shifts were all tied together with strand upon strand of dust-laden cobwebs as though the generations of spiders had determined the huge wooden wheels should never turn again; efforts as futile as the attempts some of us make to arrest human progress. But when the water was turned into the penstock the old wheels went round and round, winding up the cobwebs on old pine shafts and starting reveries of the past. The dead and forgotten millwrights had carefully selected the hickory for the cogs and the gumwood for the wheels so that their work would give lasting service to the miller and turn his buhrstones that he might make the wholesome flour for his neighbors and feed for their cattle. How faithfully cog and man had done their duty was attested when the grain again ran through the chutes and the meal poured out from between the old millstones, as the water rushed through the race. The mill rumbles on, and one meditates on how almost all men and women have done the best they could to carry on faithfully the work they had to do. Shirkers and miscreants doubtless there were, and doubtless their misdeeds attracted attention out of all proportion to their numbers. Notorious evil doers doubtless then, as now, led the thoughtless to forget that almost all mankind is plodding along individually and collectively doing what is right.

For eighteen years I gladly made the seventy-eight-mile round trip between the mill and the bronchoscopic clinic in order to get completely away from the noise, dirt, smoke, and noxious fumes of the city. A few hours' rest in the quiet of the old mill farm was always a source of freshness and vigor with which to renew the attack on the duties and problems of the day at the clinic.

It is a misfortune that a smoke screen hangs over all cities, filtering out of the sunshine the particular rays most needed for health by human beings. One must go far beyond the suburbs to get unscreened sunlight, and, in many states, one does not go far before arriving in the suburbs of another town with its smoke screen.

A fireproof study was built, with concrete walls, floor and roof, to avoid all possibility of destruction of the irreplaceable case records; there were about thirty-five hundred cases of foreign bodies, and about as many of diseased conditions. Much of the later writings I did in this study with its high windows, abundance of sunlight, its succession of wild animals peeping in. In summer I did much writing in a boat on the mill pond.

Wood turning has been the hobby of a lifetime

On the way home
from the
Medical Congress
in Mexico, D.F.

(CHALK)

1932

FOREIGN BODY CASES AT OLD SUNRISE MILLS—THE INTRIGUE OF THE IMPOSSIBLE

Case 1: *"Aber nein. Das geht nicht.* You can't do dat. Imposseebla."

A rude interruption of my writing by thunderous sounds suggestive of the pounding to pieces of the old gristmill had brought me face to face with the old millwright. "He got a nail-spike in hees gitzard"—pointing to the corn-and-cob crusher.

"He got to come down."

"Can you not reach the spike from above?"

"Nein. Ich bin too short on one end. He gotta come down."

"There is no need of taking down the whole mill to get a spike out of the crusher."

"Gott verdammter foolishment. Imposseebla," said the millwright as he saw the lowering of a flashlight down into the "gizzard," of the mill, followed by a length of gas pipe with an improvised wire snare loop through the pipe. The loop encircled the spike and when tightened held it securely for withdrawal.

"Ach so-o-o-! Sehr gut. I learn somet'ing a'ready dis mornin' yet."

Case 2: "I qvit. I make finish. *Ich bin* millwright. *Ich bin nicht* boatwright. I qvit."

"Quit if you want to; but what is the trouble now?"

"Der verfluchte boat he umgerset und dump all mine tools in de vater. Fine tools vat I make mineself, all gone to der hell."

"Oh, they are not that far down."

"Aber nein. Seex feet vater, two feet mud. Imposseebla," he said as he saw a gang of iron-clearing magnets from the cleansing grain chute of the old gristmill lowered into the water on a rope tether. After plunging down in the bottom mud a few times the magnet gang came up bristling with the lost steel tools.

"Ach so-o-o!"

Epilogue: "Doctor Jackson, that old millwright is a great admirer of yours. Down at the store he said: 'Dot bronchoscoper is chust like me. I ain't got much eddication, but py Gott, I got prains!' "

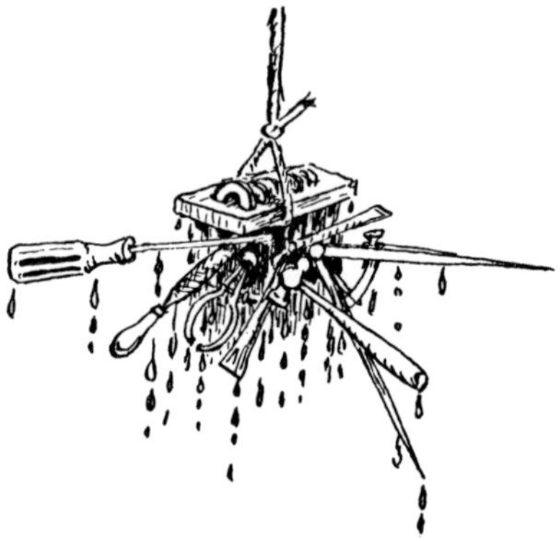

CHAPTER XXIX

MEDICAL LIFE IN PHILADELPHIA

(1917–1937)

Having recovered from the third attack of tuberculosis (1920) I settled down to complete my medical life's work in Philadelphia. All the laryngologists who had been doing bronchoscopy and esophagoscopy gave up the work and referred such cases to me. The rivalries of medical colleges and hospitals had been so keen that this was unheard-of, and notwithstanding Professor Hare's statement cited on a previous page I do not think it would have been possible in any city other than Philadelphia. The referred cases grew more and more numerous as time went on. Patients came in increasing numbers from all over the United States. Then they came from other countries. Although the percentage of charity cases was still high, there was a steadily increasing number of patients able to pay small fees; a few, moderate fees; and still fewer, abundantly able to pay what the work was really worth. Realizing at last my utter lack of financial ability—that is, utter inability to think of a patient in terms of dollars—I placed all financial matters in hands of a secretary whose duty it was to see that fees were collected from those able to pay; but she was to be sure that no hardship was inflicted on anyone. As a result of this arrangement I soon found great improvement in my financial condition. All bills could be paid promptly; no need for waiting to count the cost of any new instrument or appliance needed to help my poor little children in the ward; all the needs of my home and family were obtainable, though naturally our wants were few and simple.

At last I was in comfortable circumstances.

Medals came so thickly as almost to justify saying I was showered with them. Among the first of these was the Philadelphia Award. Mr. Edward W. Bok had created a foundation the purpose of which was to award each year a medal and a sum of money to a citizen who had rendered great service in the promotion of the best interests of Philadelphia.

In establishing bronchoscopic clinics in Philadelphia the thought that I was in any way contributing to the civic welfare or prestige had never occurred to me. In fact such a conception, if it had been mentioned by anyone at that time, would have seemed to me merely a pleasantry. Looking backward now, I can see that my work may have contributed a mite to the traditions of Philadelphia as one of the great medical centers of the world; but at that time my thoughts were only that I was indebted to Philadelphia for opportunities for wider spread of the gospel of safe bronchoscopy.

A few years after my arrival in Philadelphia I was besieged by my colleagues on the faculty and staff. Individually and collectively, they protested against my way of treating assistants. My views on this subject raised a storm of protest far beyond the institutions with which I was connected. Letters and interviews were numerous. Some of this material may be interesting:

Dear Doctor M——,

It would be a great pleasure to answer your letter about business arrangements with assistants; but I think my methods would probably be of little use to you. Your viewpoint is probably very different from mine. I have discovered in talking to many a great surgeon that when we spoke of an assistant he and I were not thinking about the same thing. He had in mind an aid; my thought was of a pupil. He was thinking of a helper in his work; I was thinking of helping a man to become a bronchoscopist. He wanted a man who for the longest possible time would be a helpful hanger-on at his clinic; I was thinking of teaching a man everything I know in the shortest possible time and setting him up as an independent unit at the earliest possible period of his life.

This attitude of mine is partly correlated with the objective of promulgating safe methods of bronchoscopy; but to an even greater extent it is the result of a feeling of the solemn obligation that rests on all of us to teach everything we know to the rising generation in order that they may carry on the work from where we are today, and especially to teach it so rapidly that the younger man will start out for himself before his aging arteries shorten his period of creative work.

A crusty old surgeon, the editor of a surgical magazine, asked for an article on "Training of Assistants" to form part of a symposium on "The Surgeon of the Future." In response to the request I sent in a manuscript. The editor wrote back: "Your MS. is returned herewith. I did not suppose you would send me a personal insult. You may think it a joke but I do not."

Assurances of serious intention were of no avail. Until his death he held his erroneous conviction of personal insult. That he should mistake it as intended for a joke is conceivable, but why he should regard it as a personal insult is incomprehensible.

It is always a blow to an author to have his effusion rejected by an editor; especially so when the article was written in response to a request from the same editor. There is a recondite joy when that same manuscript is elsewhere published. Here it is:

How to Train an Assistant

By Chevalier Jackson

Of course it may be wrong as to viewpoint, but my conviction is that a great mistake was made in the old way of browbeating an assistant and keeping him under until his initiative power was lost and his best creative years were past. It goes without saying that a man should not be turned loose on the community insufficiently trained; but to develop a man best fitted to carry on tradition he must be encouraged and brought along rapidly enough to enter the field for himself with all the energy of his younger years. This can be done. Here are the fundamentals that have been tested by many years' experience at the bronchoscopic clinic:

1. Elevate the ego. Encourage him. You cannot get any enthusiasm for work out of a man who has an inferiority complex as to either himself or his work.

2. Give him an easy case in which he can do full justice to the patient. Nothing will arouse his interest like the thrill of removing a foreign body, for example.

3. Encourage him to report the case before a medical society or staff meeting. Edit his case report. Supply him with lantern slides, drawings, the mounted specimen, half-tone blocks for illustration. Give him a bibliography, afford him access to reports of similar cases with which to broaden his paper and his knowledge. There are always new points to be developed on any subject: if he cannot see them show them to him. His paper will be a clinical fact with comments; all worth recording, and especially so if accompanied by a complete and accurate bibliography.

4. When the paper is read, be present yourself and tell the audience what good work the assistant is doing.

5. When the paper is published, buy him reprints and send a copy to all your professional friends and acquaintances.

6. In your own writings refer to his work, and do not be afraid to give him more credit than he deserves. Better still, add the names of two or three assistants as collaborators or co-authors. Even if they did not help you to write the article they helped you in the clinical work on which it was based. They will take just pride in listing the article as "in collaboration with" you in their future bibliographies. It will add enormously to the teamwork.

7. When you have done all this, your assistant is full of enthusiasm. He will work hard. He will rapidly acquire technical skill and powers of observation; he will know how to write; how to speak in meetings; how to devise instruments. Start him on some special line of research, in the laboratory, in literature, and in the clinic: a line that he can make all his own. Introduce him to all your friends and acquaintances. Keep on teaching him until he has nothing left to learn from you.

8. Do not let him think his services are not worth anything; pay him a good salary. Pay his expenses to medical meetings. Give him, as perquisites, secretarial service, nurse's service, operating room equipment, instruments, lantern slides, photographs, roentgenograms, copies of histories, charts, and other material concerning all his cases, and your own cases too. Load him up

with an abundant stock of clinical facts and of graphic evidence of those facts for future use.

9. Build up a following for the assistant among the profession and a clientele among the laity. To this end, put his name on your stationery.

10. In his early days do not permit him to take responsibility in difficult or potentially fatal cases. A fatal outcome would discourage him and would subtract from his growing reputation. Later, of course he needs such responsibilities to fit him for his life's work.

11. As soon as the assistant is fully developed, give him, or get for him, a teaching position where he can carry on tradition.

12. At the end of a few years, if you have done your job well, you have created a great surgeon, and he is young enough to do creative work: many years of it. He will have sufficient ego to think he has done it all himself. And that is just what he needs to go forth with confidence and carry on tradition, a power for good in this world. You have launched a great ship that will sail away an independent unit on the great sea of life.

The following group of letters from eminent physicians and surgeons have a bearing on this subject of treatment of assistants.

DEAR DOCTOR JACKSON:

I have always told you there are two kinds of gratitude, patient's gratitude and assistant's gratitude. Patient's gratitude is permanent. Assistant's gratitude is the most volatile thing in the world. You remember I warned you, when you were showering on ambitious young Doctor —— credit for discovering and accomplishing things you really did yourself, that he would "lick all the 'lasses off your bread and then call you nigger." Well, this evening I am dazed from listening to your assistant presenting ideas you have promulgated since before he studied medicine. I nearly exploded when I heard him tell how he had tried to convince you of his way of thinking! Is it any wonder that the knowing ones like —— the great surgeon never would have an assistant who was any good; or that —— the other great surgeon would never keep an assistant more than six months lest the younger man start to undermine him?

I repeat, assistant's gratitude is the most volatile thing in the world. You will find it out too late.

Now I suppose you will never forgive me for what I have written in this letter, but I feel I have done my duty toward one who has treated me better than I deserved.

Abstract from my answer:

Nothing that has come my way recently has given me as much joy as your letter about a certain assistant. He was the slowest man I ever had in the development of ego; it seemed he would never learn to stand on his own feet. Evidently, from your letter, he is ready to spread widely the gospel of safe bronchoscopy.

Dear Doctor Jackson:

You have the peculiar faculty of making assistants feel they did it, when anything worth while is done. When a problem comes up you think out a solution, make a drawing of the device, send assistant John Smith with the drawing to the instrument maker to explain it. If the instrument is a good one it becomes thereafter John Smith's instrument. After you have talked at a few meetings about the wonderful device of John Smith he really and truly believes himself he did it. You have not good sense; you need a guardian.

Abstract from my answer:

Thank you kindly for your frank letter. Can you not see that John Smith is, by the very fact you mention ("he really and truly believes himself he did it"), fully established as an independent unit? He is no longer merely traveling on the reputation of some one else. The more units there are, the more nuclei for new autonomous bronchoscopic growths.

Dear Doctor Jackson:

You are too good to your assistants. I know from bitter experience you will see the day when you will regret it. They will turn on you, and for all the good kindly acts (God knows how many hundreds) you have done for them they will do dirty tricks to you. I shall be dead by then. Keep this letter where you can get it out and think of me and of my prophecy.

Abstract from the answer sent:

Your kind letter is accepted in the spirit in which it was written.

My experience with assistants has been that nearly all are honest, trustworthy, fair, and grateful. A few turn out to be selfish, underhand, tricky, unworthy; but they are all human, and there is some good in all of them. It is my duty to teach them all I can. Let the world be their judge.

Dear Doctor Jackson:

Your statement that you are a provincial come to a big city emboldens me to make a few suggestions.

In the first place, your treatment of assistants will never do. I heard you today tell the audience what a wonderful ingenious instrument your assistant Dr. —— had devised. Now I happened to be near by when you made the drawings, drew up the specifications to the minutest detail, even of how the knots were to be tied and loops placed. I saw you give that drawing and those specifications to Dr. —— to take to the instrument maker. And here you are today giving all the credit to him who really was only a messenger boy in the matter. I know part of this magnanimity on your part is a desire to help along your assistant, part of it to build up in independent standing a group who will carry on your life-saving methods; but I believe a large part of it is moral cowardice. I believe you lack the moral courage to stand up and say, "I did it."

This is all wrong, and you will find it out. As Dorothy Dix said, "When one pays the poor widow's rent she does not chase her worthless sons and daughters to earn some money with which to pay one back, nor does she even goad them up to pay future rents; on the contrary she looks to the benefactor to keep on paying the rent and will abuse him for an old skinflint if he does not do so." Just so you will find your assistants will expect you always to write and keep on writing eulogistic lies about virtues they do not possess, genius they have not demonstrated and thoughts that never entered their heads until they heard you express them. This way of yours is an injustice to the men themselves; it engenders the wrong attitude.

Hoping you will accept this frank letter in the spirit in which it is written . . .

Abstract from my response:

Speaking of moral courage you had a lot of it when you wrote me your kindly letter of advice. I appreciate it more than I can tell you. You are exactly right from your point of view; but your point of view is not the same as mine. It has always seemed to me a solemn obligation resting on all of us to pass on to the next generation everything we know and to do everything we can to fit the coming men for carrying on our work when we shall have laid down the tools. It would be a crime to allow them to start where we started, to learn as we have learned by making over again the mistakes we have made. What difference will it make to the next generation whether it was Jackson, Johnson, Smith, or Jones who discovered bronchially lodged peanuts as potentially fatal to children? The important thing is for the disciples to expound the gospel of education of mothers as to the dangers of peanuts and nut candies to the baby without molars.

If I can so saturate the young man with an idea that he comes really to believe he originated the idea himself I feel I have done a good job.

My Dear Jackson:

For my own guidance please tell me how you remunerate your assistants. If the following questions are impertinent don't answer this letter at all. Just forget about it and I will do the same.

1. Do you pay assistants a salary? If so, approximately how much?

2. Do you remunerate them by giving them hospital positions?

3. If otherwise, what do you do for them?

Remember, dear Doctor Jackson, I shall not mind if you do not answer this letter at all.

Abstract from the answer:

It is a pleasure to answer your questions about what I do for my assistants.

1. Yes. About one fourth of the net profits.

2. I get and give them hospital and teaching positions, and professorships (five full chairs altogether to date) ; but I do not consider these positions remuneration, and neither do the assistants concerned. The object is to spread widely the gospel of safe bronchoscopy.

3. The enclosed rejected manuscript will give you an idea of what I have done and am doing for assistants; but these things are not remuneration: they are part of my life's work in developing men to help everywhere now and to carry on tradition when I am gone.

The manuscript mentioned as enclosed is the one printed near the beginning of this chapter.

Abstract of the reply received:

DEAR DOCTOR JACKSON:

Thank you for your letter. Pardon my saying so, but you are more different kinds of a fool than I thought you were. I quite agree with the editor who returned your manuscript. I also return it. You had better burn it before it does any more harm. If it ever got out assistants would be harder than ever to handle. I was tempted to burn it myself.

The following is from a laryngologist returned home after a course in bronchoscopy:

DEAR DOCTOR JACKSON:

You have done a wonderful and unique thing in the development of a special practice in the medical profession that stirs the imagination beyond expression. But you have done more than that. You have kept bound to you all those groups of splendid workers who have received their training at your hands, and together as a unit in Philadelphia your classes receive instruction from them all in the finest manifestation of coördinated action I have ever seen. I dare say there is not another similar situation anywhere. What a commentary on your personality and character!

The bronchoscopic clinic was founded and still depends on teamwork. My method of getting this teamwork seems to be regarded as unusual. For example, when a distinguished foreign visitor, a great surgeon, came to the clinic he was indignant at being ceremoniously and deferentially presented to the secretaries and nurses. The matter was afterward explained to him:

"These women are perfectly ladylike in their deportment, or they would not be part of our organization; and they deserve being treated accordingly. Moreover, nobody with me is ever allowed to develop an inferiority complex. Each is made to feel the importance of her or his part, and to take pride in it and in doing it well. One morning, after I got through saving a child's life in a particularly difficult case of bronchoscopy for foreign body, the colored woman who wheeled patients in and out of the operating room said, 'We did a good job this morning, didn't we, Doctor Jackson?' 'Yes, indeed, Hattie, and the courage you gave the little kiddie whispering in his ear when you wheeled him in helped a lot.' She, like every other one of the personnel, had always been made to feel that her work was an important part of the success of the bronchoscopic clinic, and she takes as much pride in the clinic as I do. You cannot get the best work out of an employee who thinks his job menial and unessential, a thing anybody can do, and to be got through with in any old way that may not entail reprimand. I repeat, no one here is ever allowed to get an inferiority complex about himself or his job."

This explanation was given to hundreds of nettled visitors.

The respective surgeons always admitted the soundness of the logic in the abstract, but probably on returning home, by irresistible force of habit, dropped back into the old routine of ordering, instructing, reproving, reprimanding, and scolding members of the personnel. And if the surgeon came from another country he probably dropped back into the old established, still prevalent foreign custom of regarding nurses as of an inferior class. It is said that this class distinction obtains even in the country of one of the greatest women who ever lived, the refined, cultured, educated Mother of all nurses, the angelic Florence Nightingale.

On my arrival in Philadelphia I was confronted with what to me was a very formidable problem. With the courtesy and hospitality for which the Quaker City is famous I was welcomed everywhere. The local honors, the decorations of foreign governments, and the social prominence of some members of the faculty opened widely the doors to social activities. Perhaps few men have sent regrets to a greater number of social invitations, many of them much coveted by persons with social ambitions. There was no end of luncheons, dinners, receptions, parties of all kinds, theatrical, musical, yachting; there were winter sports and summer gaieties.

My negative attitude in all these was not due to an unsociable nature, but simply that I felt I could not spare the time from the completion of a life's work, clinical and literary. There has been for many years a feeling that the grim reaper might take me away before the planned tasks were completed. I never had dread of death itself, only that life's work might be left unfinished. It was often said in effect, "But, Doctor Jackson, you must take time to eat dinner anyway, and a little relaxation by an evening among leading men would be beneficial to you." I never doubted the intellectual benefits, but there was always the feeling that an evening out subtracted from the energy needed for the next day's work. Early rising and especially early retiring habits rendered it a physical loss to stay up for a social evening.

Most of my pleasure all my life has been in daytime work, and a start early in the morning has seemed essential. It might be added that, unlike many men, I never in my life have been bored by an evening at home with the family; I could not understand how any man could say, "Oh, let's go some place." The arrival of a visitor, no matter who it might be, was always an intrusion, not resented as such, but carefully and politely concealed. As no call was ever returned, intrusions became fewer and fewer. Time-consuming social functions were entirely eliminated.

Since devising my first esophagoscope (1890—see Chapter XVII) I had been seeing many heartrending cases of lye burns of the esophagus in children. I had become convinced of the necessity for legislation as to labeling the packages with a warning, but had been advised by a practical politician (see page 109) that I should have a long and expensive way to travel to get such legislation enacted. Now that I was getting along better financially I resolved to undertake the work. During fifteen years I had been preparing by accumulating the convincing and appealing evidence.

I took the whole matter to the Section of Laryngology and Otology of the American Medical Association. They authorized me, as Chairman, to organize a Committee on Lye Legislation. I associated with me eventually a committee member from every state in the Union. It seems curious that so simple a piece of welfare legislation should take so great an expenditure of time and money. In all the states a campaign was undertaken by means of letters, photographs, interviews, lectures, talks, exhibitions, clinics, with two main objectives: to educate the people on the dangers of household lye, and to obtain state legislation requiring a poison label on this and similar caustics. In the aggregate, thousands of state senators and representatives were interviewed. Chairmen and members of hundreds of committees in state legislatures were informed of the necessity for the proposed legislature. Over and over again the bill died and was buried along with hundreds of other unenacted bills at the close of a legislative session. Two years would then elapse before the whole matter could be gone over again at the subsequent session. After more than twenty years of work, laws were enacted in twenty-four states.

In 1925 I noted two developments of importance. There were added to the local packers of household lye great corporations that were distributing millions of household packages of this poisonous substance through many states; the containers, in most instances, were inadequately, or misleadingly, labelled. The second development was the greatly increased and steadily increasing interest being taken by the Federal Government in the control of interstate commerce. Obviously Federal legislation would go a long way to protect children. The long struggle to obtain such legislation was similar to that in the various state legislatures.

Ninety-odd senators and nearly four hundred representatives had to be reached first through their constituents; then many had to be seen in Washington. This involved many trips and sojourns. With Doctor W. C. Woodward and Doctor Charles W. Richardson I went before the committees of the United States Senate and House of Representatives. These legislators I found very reasonable and very human; but they were so continuously besieged with self-seeking people that they could not understand why a physician would leave his practice and spend time and money in Washington unless he had an ax to grind. Evidently altruistic motives were rarely encountered. When I finally got before the Senate committee I presented hundreds of photographs of pitiable children almost dying of hunger and thirst, and along with each child's photograph a duplicate label showing no warning as to the poisonous nature of the contents. I called their attention to the resemblance of the contents to sugar. I told them that legislators probably never had seen a case of lye stricture; I had seen hundreds, and this made me feel it a duty to urge protective legislation. A committee member, Senator Copeland (a physician), said: "I have seen such cases. I will vouch for Doctor Jackson; he has no ax to grind; his appearance here is purely humanitarian." Senator Watson, the chairman of the committee, said: "Doctor Jackson, I cannot see from what source any objection could be raised to the enactment of such a law."

A model draft of a bill prepared by Doctor Woodward was left with the committee.

Then the same presentation was made before the Committee on Foreign and Interstate Commerce of the House of Representatives. The chairman and the members were soon convinced that

I had a humane and not a selfish or commercial interest in the matter. Their attitude became extremely cordial and even sympathetic.

I was afterward informed that the committees before whom I had appeared promptly and unanimously voted favorably. This was very encouraging, but I soon found there was a long way to go before final enactment.

It does seem strange, as implied in the comment of Senator Watson, how anyone could oppose such welfare legislation; yet no end of opposition was encountered, and from the most unexpected quarters. For example, the druggists, who themselves never questioned the justness of the law that compelled them to use poison labels, fought us bitterly. The explanation was that the grocers were already making heavy inroads on the druggists by selling medicines. The new law sanctioning the selling of poisons by grocers was regarded as an entering wedge, a harbinger of ruinous competition. Other opposing interests succeeded in attaching amendments that would have defeated passage. These amendments had to be defeated. The bill had to run the gantlet of various committees as one of hundreds of bills each of which had behind it interests urging passage. Attention was constantly diverted to these other bills. After over a year's work, during which I made many trips to Washington, we reached the stage at which we could get the consent of the president of the Senate, of the Rules Committee, and of the Committee on Foreign and Interstate Commerce to have the bill presented for action. It promptly passed. Then the same prolonged procedure was repeated in the House of Representatives.

After nearly two years' work the federal Caustic Act providing for a poison and antidote label was at last passed by Congress and signed by President Coolidge on the 2nd of March, 1927.

Besides the legislative work a campaign of education has been carried out for twenty-five years through all possible channels. There were no funds available for the work; each committee member himself bore the expense in his local activities. My own ex-

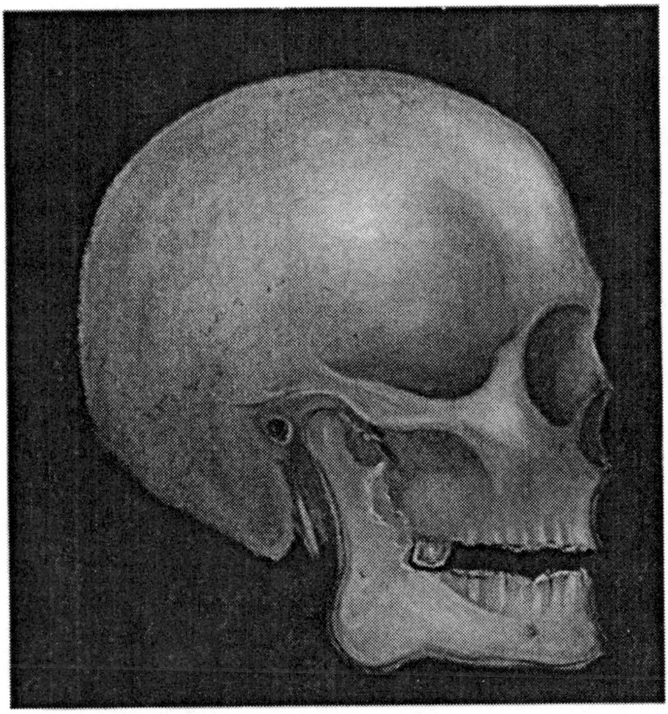

Skull hastily drawn with chalk for lecture purposes 1935

By Jere Wickwire 1935

penses as chairman were a steady drain for a quarter of a century; there seemed no end of printing, mimeographing, postal and secretarial expenditures. I should not have been able to carry on had not my income increased apace. All of my expenses in traveling to Washington in 1926 and 1927 were borne by myself. It is a great satisfaction to know that as the result of our work every can of lye or other caustic that goes into a house today (1937) has on it in large letters the warning POISON. And this has been the case since 1927. The Department of Agriculture is charged with the enforcement; and no misbranded caustic preparation gets very far commercially before the perpetrator of the misdemeanor is caught and convicted. The number of convictions every year demonstrates the necessity for the law. The need for this protection to children has been immensely increased in recent years by the enormous addition of all sorts of caustic substances, cleaners, drain-pipe cleansers, sanitary and laundry preparations, and the like. Notwithstanding the vast increase in the household use of caustics the cases of stricture of the esophagus are growing fewer and fewer each year as the result of the proper warning labels that go a long way toward keeping these preparations out of the reach of children.

The work of physicians in prevention equals their work in curing disease.

CHAPTER XXX

INTROSPECTION

(1930)

ONE DAY WHEN I was sixty-five years of age I received a request for an appointment from the editor of a leading magazine. I had saved him from death by a serious disease some years before, but he specified that the desired appointment was not professional.

When he came he requested permission to publish my biography. He wished me to supplement the data collected from various sources and particularly he wanted me to write for him my personal views on myself and my traits of character, so that he could work up a picture of personality.

I cited the well known lines of Burns:

O wad some Power the giftie gie us
To see oursels as ithers see us.

"But," he said, "Doctor Jackson, you seem always to have been so reticent, to use no stronger term, that no one knows very much about you personally. You never, so far as I have been able to discover, express yourself on your hobbies, recreations, or views on humanity, religion, politics, life in general. Now, what I wish you to do is to write out, under a list of heads that I shall give you, many things that the public want to know—indeed, have a right to know. If your modesty embarrasses you, just leave it to me."

This, at first, seemed a new thought to me, this looking at myself in the abstract. My feeling was that the lilting lines of Burns implied utter lack of the visual power necessary for any autobiographic appraisal. But on considering the matter further I became convinced that my habit of self-questioning and self-criticism present in boyhood and enormously developed in the practice of medicine had given me something in the way of an abstract viewpoint. But perhaps all autobiographers have thought the same thing, and the thought may be all egotism. However, at sixty-five years of age most of us have acquired, or think we have acquired, some judicial qualities of mind.

On still further consideration I was confronted with the fact that the thing was not a new thought anyway, inasmuch as I had for years been receiving in correspondence and otherwise inquiries on personal matters, and in later years I had even gone so far in some instances as to dictate answers to the questions—answers that were never sent. They were filed away with the thought that some day they might be useful to my biographer, if any.

Therefore the request of my editorial visitor was not new, after all. He died not long after his visit; but his list has been largely followed in the preparation of this chapter, in which are incorporated also the notes and answers to questions referred to above. He did not mention physical characteristics; probably he intended to supply such information from his own observations.

As a wholesome check on any egotistic tendencies a few cold-blooded opinions of "ithers" will be inserted.

Literary ambition in boyhood induced me to part with hard-earned money to the extent of twenty-five cents for a pamphlet entitled "How to Become a Writer." It started off with two pages on how to make ink. I did not acquire much literary knowledge, but I learned the importance of starting with the fundamentals. So here we shall start with physical characteristics.

The first impressions of Father and Grandmother as to physique, recorded at the beginning of this book, were about the same as anyone would get in any of the subsequent years; that is, slightly undersized but free from physical defect.

In stature about five feet eight inches, and broad in proportion, I was never physically robust; in fact most of my life has been a battle against impaired health. I never had much in the way of pains or aches or illness; but with more or less effort I plodded along with clinical work, writing, teaching, and other duties, but always seemingly under a disability rating.

Though I have never been what would be considered a strong man, I seem to have had great powers of endurance. Over and over again I have gone through a long, muscle-fatiguing series of séances in the fluoroscopic room or operating room, finishing without apparent fatigue while the personnel were exhausted, and this notwithstanding the load of the work, responsibility, and anxiety were of course on me as operator. Because of my sympathy with and love for children the ordeal was severe. What carried me through? It seemed to me chiefly faith, not physical endurance. Faith was based on the belief that what I was doing was best and would succeed in most if not all cases. I always felt that, whatever else I might lack, I could always depend upon having a clear eye and steady hand unimpaired by alcohol and tobacco. I was aware of one peculiar character of physique: my hand never trembled, no matter what the excitement or thrill might be. On the way to the clinic one day I was severely cut in an accident; ten stitches were required to close the wound. I went through with my clinic immediately after the dressing. A very observant, intelligent, and apprehensive patient among the number said: "I watched his hands. They did not tremble; if they had, I should have asked that his instrumental treatment [esophagoscopy] of me be done by his son."

I was very thin-skinned though not in the metaphoric sense. My skin has always been so thin the edge of the page of a book would cut it painfully. Sealing an envelope, opening a package, or turning the pages of a manuscript would cut deep enough to draw blood. Because of this, as well as to preserve delicacy of touch, I always wore gloves: in summer, thin gray silk to be taken off at meal time and for a change to rubber gloves for the operating room. There were rumors that the silk gloves were worn to hide Roentgen-ray burns. This was not the reason, though I had a few burns. Fortunately Father taught me always to wear gloves for all kinds of work, so that it became a habit; it was an especial boon when the rules of aseptic surgery required the wearing of gloves in operations. Although I never used my hands for severe or rough work, there seemed to be unusually great strength in the fingers. The touch, however, has always seemed gentle. Habitually I use a very soft pencil, and I never break a point writing. It has always been amusing to have a heavy-handed confrere crush the points of a number of my pencils in succession and then say, "What is the matter with these pencils, anyway?"

It has been borne in upon me that in some personal traits I am peculiar. Naturally I do not think so. The following is a restatement of the opinion of honest, frank, blunt Doctor John Boyce:

"Personally Chevalier Jackson has a very unusual, even peculiar, character. He never had an intimate friend, never a confidant. To say that he keeps his own counsel, is putting it too mildly. To say that he distrusts everyone, is not correct. He is very talkative on scientific matters; but when personalities are broached he promptly becomes silent and soon withdraws. Outside of scientific matters he is never free, frank, outspoken, and aboveboard with all he thinks and means. There is always a reserve that amounts to reticence. He seems always mild and gentle; but has a courage, a bulldog tenacity and stubbornness, out of all proportion to his frail physique. Though in his professional work his achievements have been in part, probably, due to these very characteristics, in other phases of life they are faults."

Professor McCrae, with Scottish candor, said: "Doctor Jackson is an unusual chap. He is generous to a fault, eager to help anybody out of difficulty at almost any sacrifice. We have been working together on all kinds of cases, all kinds of problems; he has done many kind things for me, during the past ten years, yet I feel I do not know him any better now than the day I first met him. If you ask him to dinner you feel him draw away from you and politely freeze. He is the warmest-hearted cold-blooded man I ever met."

Doctor James Stucky wrote: "I do not like you any the less for the way you treat me, but you are too darned stingy with your personality."

Personally, I do not concur in any of the foregoing opinions, but according to the implication of Robert Burns I am blind to my own shortcomings. In the abstract I agree with the great poet and observer and therefore suppress my own appraisal.

If we accept the opinions of "ithers" it becomes an abstract question how much of the traits of aloofness and stubborn tenacity were congenital and how much was due to the tortures and torments of early life at Greentree School. It is, of course, impossible to estimate accurately; but it seems not illogical to assume that they were in part the result of those bitter ordeals. Looking backward in cold blood on those pathetic early days when as a frail child I was struggling for an education against physical torture, I wonder why I did not become sullen and morose; I wonder how I escaped embitterment against mankind. Of course in later years analysis of the psychology of my tormenters enabled me abstractly to study them merely as interesting clinical problems; but I do not recall having, even in boyhood, any feelings akin to bitterness, resentment, or revenge.

There has often come to me a remark to the effect that one of my chief characteristics is abstemiousness. Though I am a small eater and usually leave the table hungry, the real basis for the remark, doubtless, is the fact that I do not use alcoholic beverages nor tobacco, though constantly associated with persons who do. It always seems absurd to regard as unsociable or impolite the simple, no-thank-you declining of these unquestionably poisonous and injurious substances when proffered. It becomes a hollow mockery when, as often happens, the host or hostess offers and partakes of the diluted poisons solely because of a feeling of obligation to do the proper thing. Though this may seem to refer especially to alcoholic beverages, it often applies even more forcibly to tobacco. Everyone knows that to learn the tobacco habit requires overcoming distaste and nausea. Why do it?

Entirely apart from injurious things self-denial always has seemed to me wholesome discipline for anyone. It is a platitude to say that modern parents who attempt to satisfy every whim of the child are laying the foundation for his future misery.

Be all this as it may, I know that, when I became fond of coffee, first cutting it out and then taking it abstemiously increased my self-respect to an extent affording more pleasure than indulgence. The same with tea. Likewise with any particular food.

Food has been incidentally referred to on other pages. It may be said that it has been habitual with me, after the 4:30 half-cup of creamless, sugarless coffee, to work until 8:30 or 9:00 and then to take tea, "postage-stamp" sandwiches, and a tomato or a little cooked fruit. The sandwich is a joke. It consists of paper-thin slices of bread with a leaf of lettuce between. This has to last until evening. Dinner is served on arrival home from the clinic, which may be at six, seven, or nine. It consists of vegetables, fruits, and buttermilk; no meat; sometimes oysters, rarely fish. It has been my lifelong habit to get up from the table, especially the breakfast table, hungry. It seems to me that better work can be done if one is not filled to repletion with nitrogenous food, as is the almost universal custom.

The habit of omitting luncheon developed in later years seems to suit me perfectly; but I would not advise others to follow my example. Probably a light luncheon, as in my earlier years, would be better for most persons.

Early morning scenic effects always have seemed the most beautiful, in any part of the world in which I have been. So much for the artistic viewpoint. Practically, Benjamin Franklin's dictum, "Early to bed and early to rise," always has had a strong appeal though the second of his three resultants never materialized. Mother said that as a baby "Chev would waken at four and would not go to sleep again; then he would fall asleep in the high chair at the dinner table; he would never waken when carried upstairs and put to bed." When somewhat older, I remember, I would fall asleep over attempted lessons at seven or eight o'clock in the evening. Then I would waken at four and do the real work on the studies. This habit has continued ever since. I never burned any midnight oil in literary or desk work. Care of patients, of course, often required night duty; but being thus kept awake late did not prevent early rising.

Clothing never seemed to fit me very well, probably because I insisted on a comfortable degree of oversize. In early life I discovered there was no use telling a tailor to make clothes a comfortable fit. The only effective remedy was to put on three suits of underwear when going to the tailor to be measured and fitted. By not wearing the extra underwear at other times I had clothes that were comfortable and not of bad fit, though probably a long way from perfect from a tailor's point of view. Linen collars must be two or three sizes too large; to prevent them from riding up on my neck, side collar buttons were worn. Perhaps they might be called "turtle collars," because of the way my head and neck protrude and move around in the collar opening. Shoes must be large to the point of sloppiness, their length requiring eternal vigilance lest I trip over my own feet.

Perhaps it was the economic instinct inherited from my thrifty Knickerbocker grandmother and French grandfather; or perhaps it was the impression made by early years of want; but certain it is that I could never throw anything away without a pang of regret. The result was that house, room, study, shop, garage, and other places have always been so cluttered up with possibly some day useful junk that disorder is inevitable. I realize this weakness. When John McLure Hamilton, the portrait artist, visited the mill and this was mentioned to him, he very politely said, "Well, this study has possibilities of disorder." One day, when thorough housecleaning demanded setting out of the entire contents of one of my dens, the helper before carrying in each object said, "Why, Doctor, you don't want this, do you?" If there has been any part of my life misspent it has been due to the tyranny of chattels.

These are favorite lines:

> Now is the winter of our discontent
> Made glorious summer by this sun of York.
>
> —SHAKESPEARE.

No sunshine even in the tropics was ever too hot for me. I never seem to feel the heat as others do. A delightful winter day can be appreciated in the abstract, but with a mental reservation as to paradox.

One of my greatest regrets is that the little kiddies in the clinic could not be in the country sunshine instead of in a city hospital with only occasional visits to the roof for a little of the pale, smoke-filtered sunshine available to city dwellers in the temperate zone.

Rightly or wrongly I was always a great believer in work as a powerful moral influence entirely apart from production. It is relatively seldom that a hard worker commits a crime. Most criminals are idlers. Of course, we cannot ignore heredity, alcohol, psychologic and other factors in idling as well as in crime; but most working people are honest people, and most honest people are workers. Truly,

> Satan finds some mischief still
> For idle hands to do.
>
> —WATTS.

If people would only stick to their work, and work hard, they would not get into politics and otherwise meddle in attempts to dominate other people. Most politicians and agitators are idlers who want to bedevil and live off workers.

Work with me was incessant. I do not remember a single day in the last thirty years getting up in the morning and asking myself: "Well, what shall I do today?" Never once have I been free to choose what I might want to do. Each morning there has been laid out a list of things I *must* do whether I wanted to or not. The only question was as to which must be done first, and even this, in later life, was usually decided for me by very efficient secretaries.

Though a great believer in the wholesomeness of work, I could not go so far as to advise others to carry it to the extreme herein indicated. On the other hand it is rather difficult to conceive of great success on the basis of a thirty-hour week.

The present political agitator's slogan of more abundant leisure means, I fear, more idle time to get into mischief.

Caution is natural and extreme with me. "Take a chance" has no appeal. I would not take a chance on anything. One day when I said so, Doctor Ellen J. Patterson added "nor anybody." It had often been said that I trusted no one, relied upon no one. This may be partly true. I feel one should drive a motor car on the principle that every other driver on the highway is deaf, dumb, drunk, or demented; one should never depend on the other driver's obeying the law or the rules of the road. I drove a car for thirty years, over 100,000 miles, equivalent to four times around the earth, without an accident, not even so much as a scratch on a fender. I never even slightly injured any living thing on the road. No speed laws were broken, likewise no records; but on the other hand there were no arrivals late because of accidents, when driving myself. It is true that during this time traffic conditions were not what they are today; but nevertheless safety first seems to have been part of my psychologic make-up long before it was adopted as a slogan by railway executives. In professional work it is often wise to leave things to nature, but never to mere chance. Even Nature is not to be trusted. A bronchoscopic aphorism is, "Nature helps, but she is no more interested in the survival of your patient than of the attacking microbes."

Caution is implied in other bronchoscopic aphorisms:

"Follow your judgment, never your impulse."

"Be sure you are right, and then look around to see what is wrong."

"Be sure you are right, but not too sure."

As indicated in a previous chapter, it is my firm conviction that what little I have been able to accomplish has been due to my home life more than to any other one thing. Since my earliest recollections my home has been a refuge. Always I could depend upon finding there sympathy, solace, security. Grandmother, grandfather, mother, father, wife, adopted sister, adopted mother, all had that happy faculty of making a serene and cheerful home. I do not see how, with my sympathetic, worrying disposition, I could have come through the continuous succession of ordeals involved in the care of suffering little children without the recuperative calm, quiet, restful atmosphere of my home life. Countless times I have arrived home so weak I did not believe I should live through the night, nor, if surviving, that I could return to work the next morning. But my home was always to me, metaphorically, what a charging plant is to a storage battery. I came home exhausted. The restful quiet and sympathy charged me with energy so that I could leave the next morning with stored power to get through the troubles, anxieties, and difficulties of the day at the clinic. But there came days when it was impossible to get home in the evening. Medical meetings, lectures, and official duties in other cities required travel. Those were the hard, sad days. As mentioned before, I have never traveled for pleasure; I would rather stay at home. I have done an enormous amount of traveling to meetings, to deliver lectures, to see patients in consultation. But I have always hurried back home as soon as possible. My idea of travel for pleasure is to go to bed at home at seven o'clock and read a book of travel until I get sleepy, about eight or nine o'clock usually, sometimes earlier. I do not care much for history. It is too full of what the kings, commanders, and politicians did. I should like to read history if it told us of daily home life of the common people, their craftsmanship, what they ate, how the sisters, wives, mothers worked and suffered; and they certainly did work and suffer, though history is mostly silent on the subject. Throughout all ages it has been the women at home who have suffered. But men wrote the histories. The future may see less one-sided records, as we get farther away from the "weaker-sex" arrogance and egotism of the cave man.

Another reason why I do not enjoy reading history is the record of many men unappreciated until after death. Comparison with my undeserved honors is embarrassing.

One of my greatest pleasures is to look out of the study window and see the songbirds, game birds, squirrels, and rabbits come and feed. Sister Jo, also a great lover of wild life, always sees to it that there is an attractive display of all kinds of suitable foods. No matter how busy writing I may be, I always can find a moment to look out of the window. I always get more pleasure out of one quail or pheasant or squirrel than any gunner possibly could. When he takes the life, all is ended; whereas the birds come back every day for me to watch them feeding. The squirrels run up the old apple tree, and while they eat they watch me as I watch them; sometimes they sit up on their haunches and look in the window at me. It is a sort of mutual admiration society, or at least I enjoy so regarding it.

About 95 per cent of the work of the bronchoscopic clinic was, and is, charity work. It is unknown and incomprehensible to laymen that the members of the clinical staff of hospitals are not paid by the institution. If a doctor has to stay at the hospital past a meal hour trying to save a charity patient's life, he must pay the hospital for his meal or go hungry. It is an age-old custom that the clinical staff doctor gets only reputation from the hospital; to get bread and butter for his wife and children, he must cash in his reputation by collecting money from such of his private patients as are able to pay.

My charity wards were always full, and the care of these patients was always a solemn obligation to me. The feeling that they were better housed and fed there than at home did not outweigh the fact that I alone was responsible for their care. Many of them were children. Here were added feelings of responsibility because their mothers had confided in me, had made sacrifices, and were longing for the day when the children could be again in their arms.

The following was sent as a reply to a letter of inquiry from a high-school student who was investigating the financial returns from different careers:

I have been on call at hospitals night and day for fifty years. No hospital has ever paid me one cent, nor even reimbursed me for the thousands of dollars I have been spending in serving hospitals. Even the instruments I used, I had to buy myself for many years. For nearly fifty years I have been teaching in medical colleges. Not one cent of salary has any medical school ever paid me for my work, nor has any reimbursed me for my expenditures. Many a time after saving a child's life I have given the parents money to pay their expenses home. Never once during this fifty years has any patient applying to me been refused treatment because of inability to pay.

In a recent case I took a nail out of the lung of a boy sent here from a distant foreign land. The fact that this was done without charge was heralded all over the world. The Department of State of the foreign government sent official thanks through official channels. Boys' clubs, Rotary clubs, and other organizations sent collective thanks. A few of the data of this episode are reprinted here from the Melbourne *Argus* because they illustrate a matter of which the general public seems to know nothing. Day in and day out, hospital physicians working without salary treat without fee all worthy patients brought to them. The only difference here was the long journey. The world-wide interest and the unique appreciation by the Australian people and their official representatives in this case are criteria of the lack of general appreciation of the daily routine work of unsalaried hospital physicians everywhere.

BOY WHO SWALLOWED NAIL PLANTS A TREE

Tribute to American Doctor

In the picturesque setting of the Melbourne Boys' High School grounds at Forrest Hill, South Yarra, Kelvin Rodgers, the child who achieved fame through the removal of a nail from his lung, planted a tree yesterday afternoon. His action was a tribute to Professor Chevalier Jackson who performed the operation in Philadelphia and to the American People whose generosity made it possible for his mother to take him to the United States for the operation.

A dais was constructed on the drive overlooking the school oval, on which 5,000 schoolboys from district schools were assembled. The ceremony was arranged by the League of Youth, an organisation formed several years ago for the protection of Australian fauna, following a suggestion by Mrs. Britomarte James of the Wattle League. Mrs. James presented to Kelvin's mother a basket of golden flowers, which included sprigs of wattle. Kelvin, notwithstanding his youth (three years of age), was not overawed by the occasion. He waved his hand cheerily in answer to the cheers of the boys. Then he sat on the grass and waited patiently for the tree planting ceremony.

All of this was very kind and is appreciated to the utmost; but it revealed that the general public has no conception of the fact that all physicians are doing these things all the time regardless of race, religion, or nationality, with no thought of remuneration, thanks, or gratitude.

It has always seemed a good thing that I got into a field of work where it was possible to get 98 per cent of the patients well. If I had specialized in the surgery of brain tumors or other work with high mortality I should probably have been dead long ago. No physician could take more profoundly to heart the death of a child. I find in a letter the following passage:

We do not expect to practice medicine with 100 per cent freedom from mortality; but the death of this child has hit us very hard. Personally I shall never get over the feeling of sadness. The nature of our work is such that we rarely have a death, so we are dreadfully depressed on the rare occasions when one occurs. I try to philosophize. I often repeat to myself the lines of Longfellow:

Toiling, rejoicing, sorrowing
Onward through life he goes.

I once hoped that as I got older I should get more hardened, or at least more philosophic; but the reverse has been the case.

One day I met a medical acquaintance on a street corner fuming and fussing because missing a car necessitated waiting five minutes. I said: "Why, that's no trouble. Listen to this letter I received this morning, and tell me what to do.

"Dear Doctor Jackson:

"I know how distressed you will be to learn that little Carl lost his mother. A letter came from him to her this morning; he did not know she was dead. He said you were so good to him and that all the nurses at the clinic tried to be like mother at home.

"Now, dear Doctor Jackson, what shall we do? Will you tell him, or would it be better for me just to write to him the same as his mother did? During her last illness I wrote letters for her anyway.

"Now, Doctor Blank, what shall I do?"

Before the discussion ended the next car was approaching.

"Some people don't know what trouble is."

"That's so."

From the time when the growing intelligence realized the meaning of the words "It cannot be done" I have always been fascinated by problems deemed insoluble. Reason has told me that there are impossibilities, but in things mechanical I have always felt a way could be found. This fundamental trait always has been paramount. The intrigue of the impossible apparently has been one of the greatest attractions in the fields of bronchoscopy, esophagoscopy, and gastroscopy, both in the technique of the procedures and in the problems of foreign body extraction. Perhaps the intrigue of the impossible was correlated with the dogged, stubborn determination to hang on in face of seemingly certain defeat that was developed, or at least paramount, in the days of persecution at Greentree School.

I have always been in favor of discussion but detested controversy; when altercation, acrimony, and vituperation have appeared I have always withdrawn unless bound to remain by reason of being chairman of the meeting. In such case, I have usually been able to bring things back to real and beneficial discussion by whimsical humor or parliamentary tact.

The same principle could often be applied to everyday life. One day an irate professor said to me, "Now, Doctor Jackson, I am going down there and tell that fellow just what I think of him," naming a thoughtless gossiping doctor of our mutual acquaintance.

"Don't! 'Back sass' yieldeth no profit."

The Professor did not go, and has often reminded me laughingly of what he called Jackson's proverb.

Lifelong experience has led me to believe that no end of human misery ranging from personal quarrels to feuds, murders, and national wars could be averted if there were a more general insistence on discussion rather than controversy in all cases of difference as to facts or opinions, personal or national. There come to mind hundreds of instances of lifelong feuds between two good physicians started by controversy over a case, or an opinion, or a misunderstanding so unimportant as to be absurdly out of proportion to the constantly recurring embarrassments and life-shortening worries so needlessly engendered.

No one, so far as I know, has ever accused me of lacking a sense of humor, even when the joke is on myself. Medical practice is filled with pathetic things; but there are many humorous incidents, and they help to lighten the load of woe. Indecent or even indelicate things have never seemed really humorous to me. Another kind of humor I could never appreciate is the so-called practical joke. I have often marveled at the strange psychology of the practical joker who finds joy for himself in the discomfort he has inflicted on others. This degenerate phase of mentality is seen in every school and college; it has become a tradition in the form of cruel hardship inflicted on freshmen by classmen who are ranked as "upper" but are mentally degenerate in that they get joy out of needless, cruel suffering inflicted on others. The psychology is similar to that of the cruel kind of sports characteristic of criminals, well known to criminologists. It has been claimed that hazing and hardships make a man of the freshman. I doubt it. Looking backward, I cannot realize wherein I was benefited by going hungry all day because my meager luncheon had been rendered inedible by the practical joker who sprinkled sand into the tiny bucket that my little freezing fingers had carried to school. Perhaps all this means I am deficient in a sense of humor. I do not know.

An archbishop in the Catholic Church who saw much of the bronchoscopic work with little children said to Doctor McCrae: "The things that have impressed me most about your colleague Doctor Jackson are his gentleness and endless patience with little children. His marvelous success in administering treatment that must be not only uncomfortable but painful seems to be based on patience, especially in doing painless things over and over again until the childish confidence is fully established. But oh, what endless, Christlike patience!" Doctor McCrae's comment was: "For a Catholic archbishop to acknowledge that any human being could be Christlike [he did not use the adjective Christian] is certainly a rare compliment." The archbishop had observed the most important of all factors in work at the bronchoscopic clinic, namely, patience; but to have this patience in this work one must be fond of children.

Though not a churchgoer I have always been a great believer in religion. Considered solely as a factor in human life and activity, religion is a great power for good. So long, however, as religion is to be administered by human beings it is essential that these administrators do not get much power over their fellow human beings. All the criticism, just and unjust, of Christian religion is applicable only to the human beings who have done things in the name of this beautiful faith. The trouble has been with the human beings who have honestly, dishonestly, or erroneously tried to apply Christ's teachings to the everyday life of themselves and others. It has always been a favorite method for rulers and other kinds of hypocrites to use religion as a cloak. The entourage of Ferdinand and Isabella could get rid of an enemy quickly by what the police now call "a frame-up," such as unjust conviction of heresy. The Salemite of two centuries ago could rid himself of an enemy with perfect safety for himself by a "frame-up" of witchcraft. These devilish things were done in the name of Christ; they were diametrically opposed to what he taught. His teachings are beautiful, gentle, and practical beyond criticism. History has not drawn as sharply as it should the distinction between the Christian religion and the things that have been done in the name of Christianity. Nowhere in His sayings nor teachings is there anything to justify infliction of reprisals or punishments on those who disagree with Him.

It may be permitted to quote here from an address to the graduating class of the Woman's Medical College:

And when your time comes, I hope you will have the consolation of *faith:* not only faith in yourself, faith in the scientific knowledge you have gained from your teachers and from your own efforts; not only faith in your remedial measures, but faith in human nature. I beseech you never to lose faith in human nature. It is frail, and it fails at times: but never lose faith in it. And now, over and above all these, I hope that when your time of trouble comes, you will have *religious* faith. Not necessarily of this denomination or of that, not necessarily Catholic, not necessarily

Protestant, not necessarily Jewish; but faith in a Supreme Being and a hereafter. And I hope you will belong to some sort of organization that will get together once a week to consider purely spiritual matters. That is sadly needed in this age of materialism.

Most of the people in the world, it seems to me, are doing what is right. Reading newspapers makes one think the world is going to the dogs. It is only a minute percentage that creates "news." What newspaper men call "news" is only too often murder, robbery, embezzlement, divorce, infidelity, misdemeanor, and crime. But it seems to me over 99 per cent of persons are plodding along, doing what is right each in his respective sphere. It is the occasional wrongdoers who are conspicuous out of all proportion to their relative numbers.

I have never faltered in my faith in human nature. If we look at the matter broadly enough we can see that the human race is improving. Wars, dictators, politicians, and rulers with lust for power have set us back; but if we take one century with another the progress is evident. It is true that no man or divinity under God today is better than or even as good as Christ. No individual has measured up to His teachings in nineteen hundred years. But the people as a whole have improved.

The Christian religion is good and beautiful; and we owe it to the Jews. They were preaching truthfulness, integrity, systems of morality, codes of equity, "Love thy neighbor as thyself," two thousand years ago. Then as now Rome was robbing foreign people of their land, killing them if they resisted. Julius Caesar says he found the Angles a race of savages painted with woad (blue mud). The Teutonic races, the Aryan races, were robbing, thieving, murdering, wild men with not a single ethic beyond "Kill or be killed." All of this at the time Christ and his Jewish Disciples were teaching the most beautiful code of morals and most kindly human relations the world has ever known. The whole world is and forever will be indebted to the Jew.

With physicians a patient is a patient; race, religion, color are considered only in so far as they may concern the scientific problems.

Broadly speaking, there are two great classes of people: (1) the producer, and (2) the politician with lust for power. The plodding producer is buried in his daily work; he follows along in other matters, accepting laws and rules of the powers that be. It is the political rulers with lust for power that make wars. One of their most powerful means is false education. Education beginning in childhood will be the salvation of the world. But it must not be a *false education.* The child of the headhunter is educated to collect heads of created enemies. For forty years the Prussian Monarchy falsely educated the German child in military conquest. Today dictatorship governments have indefinitely postponed proper education of all humanity because of the necessity of military education of all nations for defense. In addition dictatorships have revived the prehistoric principle of "Go and take it; if the rightful owner objects, kill him." So long as there are in this world nations with the same code of morals as a murdering thief, large armies, navies, and air forces for defense will be necessary.

What the people do not realize is that in dealing with any government we are really dealing with successive crops of politicians.

Strange as it may seem, the contracts made by the politicians of today in the name of the United States or any other government may be entirely repudiated by the crop of politicians in power when the time arrives for fulfillment of the contract. Legislation can then be rushed through Congress, or other parliamentary body, to prevent any redress. I have seen pathetic cases of human misery inflicted by repudiation of contract and legalized subterfuge done in the name of the Government of our beloved country.

Any life insurance company attempting to do business on such principles or lack of principles would be promptly put out of business by the courts and the people.

On the other hand, it would, of course, be unjust to imply that all politicians are unscrupulous. Like any other large group they include all kinds of men. It is an unfortunate fact that, as a result of rivalry, the vilification and vicious vindictiveness that the man in public life must endure have killed many a man and have deterred many honest men from accepting public office.

One of the most unhappy things in my life has been the constant hounding by the newspapers. I realize that a foreign-body accident is, like any other accident, a legitimate item of news to the publishing of which I have no right to object; but the exploitation of my name by the newspapers, I have always felt, was a needless injury to my reputation with professional brethren as well as a continually repeated galling of doubtless abnormally hypersensitive sensibilities. Statistical studies of hundreds of cases have taught me that more than 85 per cent of the foreign bodies in the air and food passages are there through carelessness, which is avoidable. For this reason newspaper publicity could be an enormous help in prevention; but to my sorrow I found that any promise of a newspaper to coöperate in such a welfare work ended only in personalities that were to the utmost degree offensive to me personally and injurious to my standing in the profession. I have been constantly and painfully aware of the endless suffering of little children that could be prevented if only parents knew of the avoidable dangers that surround every child in the land. Over and over again when a little baby came in with life in jeopardy from, for example, a safety-pin, I have said: "Why cannot such accidents be prevented? This baby could not have walked to get that pin; some one must have been so careless as to place it in his reach." Only too often the mother had actually taught the baby to put pins in his mouth by setting the bad example of putting a safety-pin in her own mouth and then leaving other pins in the reach of the baby. Babies learn everything by imitation, and they naturally think that is what safety-pins are for. Over and over again some listener has said, "Why don't you publish it in the newspapers?" I have tried that to my sorrow many times when newspaper men craved an interview. They would promise anything, and if they had had the power they would have fulfilled their promises; but when, after the manuscript had passed through the mill of the editor, the copy reader, and the "write-up" man, the article appeared, the babies were ignored; all the stuff was interpolated with nauseating references to "wizard," "inventor of the bronchoscope," and so on. There were few if any words about keeping pins out of the baby's reach.

And so it was also in publicity about prevention of lye accidents to children. The newspapers always wanted to exploit my name and personality, they had no enthusiasm for and little interest in warning mothers to keep lye, drain cleaners, and other caustics out of the reach of children.

The newspapers have only one ethic: "Get news—honestly if you can, but get it." The public is at the bottom of it all. The gossip-loving people want personalities, with name, age, and residence, even personal appearance; and they buy the paper that supplies such information. The right of privacy, the right to be let alone, is utterly unrecognized by news hawks because it is unrecognized by the readers of newspapers.

Another thing that dragged me out of my coveted seclusion was the publicity necessary to finance bronchoscopic clinics. The Honorable William Potter said to me: "Doctor Jackson, I must raise money to carry on the college and hospital work. Now, you cannot raise money directly from the doctors; it is necessary to raise it from the public. To raise it from the people, they must know about the work done in a hospital. If I should go to a wealthy man and ask him to give money for a bronchoscopic clinic, I would have a hard time getting a donation. If on the other hand he knows from the newspapers of the life-saving work done in a bronchoscopic clinic, he is easily persuaded to give freely. This is why it is necessary that you should sacrifice yourself to publicity in connection with particular cases in which the newspapers want to know about your life-saving work, especially the cases of children with foreign bodies. I know how distasteful it is to you, but it is necessary for the good of the clinic and its good work."

Unquestionably education should be promoted to the utmost degree. But eternal vigilance is necessary in order that improper kinds of education be minimized; to prevent them is impossible; insidiously they creep in and convert education into a curse. The public press is one of the greatest educational factors; yet all sorts of pernicious propaganda are insidiously inserted. The same is true of motion pictures, only more so. Over and over again, gross errors—political, governmental, and economic as well as moral—have permeated the entire rising generation before they were checked or even recognized. Even partial eradication of such errors requires years; many individuals retain the false education throughout life.

A believer in moderation in other things, I have been all my life a total abstainer as to alcohol. I have felt it a duty to the little children placed in my care, and to their tearful, trustful mothers, to have at all times confidence born of the knowledge that, whatever else I might lack, I had at least the clear eye and the steady hand that only total abstinence from alcohol could give me. My feeling is that the physician never knows at what moment he may be called upon in a desperate emergency to save human life. Humanity demands that he be at all times fit for duty, unbefogged by alcohol. Many researches have proven conclusively that the most moderate drinking lowers efficiency and at the same time exaggerates the ego, so that the drinker, while really doing inferior work, thinks he is doing better work than ever. This is a scientific fact. Obviously both skill and judgment are adversely affected. This is the scientific explanation of the great increase in serious automobile accidents. The maudlin drunk driver is not the greatest danger. One drink creates danger because while decreasing efficiency it exaggerates the ego so that the driver feels he can by consummate skill escape dangers; he takes chances that he would not have taken without the exhilarating drink.

Possibly my earliest decisions against alcohol were inspired by my grandfather Jean Morange. As a boy ten years of age (*circa* 1805), in the port of Bordeaux, France, he was bound by his mother in a navigational apprenticeship to a Yankee skipper, Captain Fairbanks of the *Kitty Clyde*. As cabin boy he was given the key to the locker where the ship's stock of liquor was kept because he did not drink. The worthiness of trust because of abstinence from liquor sank ineradicably into my youthful mind and fired me with an ambition for trustworthiness.

Apart from myself the reasons for my advocacy of total abstinence are logical, sympathetic, and medical, not religious. Since my boyhood every day has supplied examples of human misery due to drink. Part of my abhorrence of alcoholic beverages came from years of work in the dispensary prior to the days of prohibition. A large number of dispensary patients in those days were men whose downfall was due to drink. It was no uncommon thing to have a dozen such in an afternoon's work in the dispensary. The stale sour smell of beer and the fumes of whisky were mixed with the foul breath of decayed teeth and putrid remnants of food in a totally neglected mouth. Sometimes Limburger cheese of the free lunch counter had just been eaten, but it could make such a breath no worse. The associations of putridity, whisky, sour beer, depravity, and human degradation are indelible memories.

In this same dispensary experience were hundreds of instances of heartrending suffering of little children and their mothers due to drunkenness of fathers. In many instances the children were actually starving because the father spent the money the children begged or the mother earned. The mothers were often cruelly beaten, and the children flogged. In many other instances the children were suffering because of deficiency diseases that could easily have been avoided if proper food had been bought for them with the money the fathers spent for beer and whisky. Often the lacking vitamins were identically those wasted in producing the beverages.

Any unbiased observer at a free dispensary in the last few years before repeal could see the difference wrought by prohibition. Unquestionably there was less drunkenness, less depravity, less of all the ill effects of alcohol, immediate and remote. There were fewer starving rachitic children. There were fewer drunkards who had swallowed their false teeth. The down-and-out drunkard had disappeared. Any dispensary physician will corroborate this. These things are matters of statistics.

For a man who wishes to drink, one excuse is as good as another. It used to be such things as births, deaths, weddings, good or ill luck; then they said it was prohibition! The allure of forbidden fruits. The absurdity is obvious. It was the liquor interests that promulgated the idea that prohibition itself was an inducement to drink.

The prohibition amendment during the ten years of its enforcement made greater headway than any other method for dealing with the liquor problem. Any unbiased observer must admit that there was less drinking than ever before or since.

Then came the depression. The people listened to the harangue of the demagogue, and of the thousands of emissaries of the liquor interests; the people were convinced that prohibition not only was a failure but was a major cause of the depression! And the taxes to be raised from liquor and beer sales were going to balance the budget! There was a tremendous demand for repeal, not so much from people who wanted to drink alcohol as from those who wanted to sell it. Since repeal, one of the greatest arguments in its favor has been discovered; it prevented advertising of alcoholic beverages. Today almost every hotel and restaurant advertises its "cocktail room." Business men and society women, even welfare workers, are urged in flaming advertisements to make their various appointments at the cocktail hour. Every home in these United States is flooded with catchy advertisements that teach children to drink. Billions of dollars are paid annually to newspapers and magazines for attractive displays claiming wonderful qualities of beer and whisky. Worst of all, an enormous power for evil in politics is being developed in the billions of dollars flowing into the coffers of the liquor interests. These interests are well organized. All of these things were impossible under prohibition.

Again we shall see the down-and-out drunkard in our dispensaries. All the people will not become drunkards. Some people will not drink. Among those who do drink, all will not become hopelessly besotted. But general drinking will find the weak ones, and these weak ones will become drunkards beyond all hope of recovery. Then the parents who themselves drank moderately will reap their reward in humiliation and remorse. Everyone who drinks moderately sets an example that yields many drunkards among the weak. As a matter of fact I feel so strongly on the subject that I carry this matter of example much farther. I would not eat at any restaurant, nor stop at any hotel, where liquor is sold, if it were possible to avoid it. This is not fanaticism but simply the wish to avoid giving the false impression of approval that might be made upon the rising generation. In addition, I feel it a duty to patronize establishments that are trying to supply food without educating young folks to drink.

Introspection and retrospection have led me to believe that profound respect for woman is one of my traits of character.

Earliest recollections are of Mother's reading of Bible stories of angels, of the doings of Florence Nightingale, "the Angel with the Lamp." Then came the devout Mrs. Ward with more stories of angels. The earliest conceptions of budding mentality were of angels; these materialized in the conception that Mother was an angel; later Mrs. Ward, later still Miss Moore and Fanny Sheddon. After marriage my wife, her sister, and her mother became angelic to me.

Earliest conceptions were that angels were women and all women were more or less angelic. It seems to have been inconceivable that there could be such a thing as a man-angel. I always adored my father, whom I knew to be a good, honest, true, sympathetic, charitable man of good deeds, but the angelic conception was totally absent.

It is certain that the girls at Greentree School never manifested, as did the boys, the psychic phenomena of the inferiority complex and its defensive mechanism. Compared to the boys, very few had been kept at home to work, and these few probably had made good use of what educational opportunities they had had. Be this as it may have been, the fact remains that they took no part in the persecution and but rarely even knew of its occurrence. When anything did occur in their presence they always tried to restrain their brutal brothers. This attitude of the girl pupils probably added to the deeply rooted belief that girls and women are superior to men.

In my professional life many secretaries and nurses were part of my organization. They served the best interests of the patients and myself loyally. I always treated them with the utmost respect. Never a harsh word. I would no more think of speaking to them with my hat on than I would of thus addressing a queen. It seemed an instinctive respect for women, not an artificial politeness learned at dancing school; it is an unconscious part of my nature. In practice it was always the mother who had my utmost sympathy and solicitude. In fact this amounted at times to a fault. I seemed often to forget that the father of the little critically ill patient had feelings, too.

I am altogether at variance with the attitude man has taken and woman has accepted as to the existence of a "weaker sex." It is true that throughout the animal and vegetable kingdoms the female sex carries the heavier burden; but only man has arrogated to himself superiority. The lion overflowing with ego roars, proclaiming himself king of beasts, but he acknowledges the physical superiority of Mrs. Lion. He knows nothing about moral superiority, but he has no delusions as to a physically weaker sex. When he comes around and wants to kill the cubs or otherwise to display superiority she chases him out, and he stops not on the order of his going but goes. When we get down to the level of the cave man we find that he arrogated to himself the distinction of mighty warrior and hunter and relegated to woman an inferiority, physical, moral, and mental. She seems throughout the ages to have accepted the second rating. This must have been less a matter of judgment or of an inferiority complex, and more a matter of love and desire to please. It seems to me the time has come for man to recognize the fact that woman is his equal, intellectually, morally, and physically. Personally I am certain she is his superior; but, for the present, acknowledgment of equality would be sufficient; the future will see recognition of superiority.

The feeling that girls and women are superior never for a moment left me. At seventy years of age, when elected president of the Woman's Medical College of Pennsylvania, I retained all of the respect for womankind that grew out of my boyhood idealization of girls and women. It has been a solemn obligation all my professional life to help in every way possible every woman physician. The present generation knows little of the attitude of the profession and the laity toward the woman physician of fifty years ago. It is hoped that I contributed a little to bring about the breaking down of the old prejudice.

At the Fifth Anniversary Friendship Dinner, sponsored by the Soroptimist Club of Philadelphia, as President of the Woman's Medical College of Pennsylvania, I had occasion to say:

"It has always seemed remarkable to me that little or no consideration has been given to the medical education of women as an education. For some reason incomprehensible to me, the value of medical education for women is gauged on the basis of financial returns in the practice of medicine. Next in frequency to this viewpoint we encounter the statement, 'Oh, the chances are, after graduation she will get married anyway.' Both of these viewpoints are fallacies. The practice of medicine by woman or man never was and certainly is not today, considered on the basis of financial returns. If anyone wants to be wealthy, some field of work other than medicine should be chosen. Any qualified practitioner can make a living, but more than this is not to be expected. There are compensations in the practice of medicine that far outweigh the monetary returns, and which are entirely denied to persons engaged in commercial pursuits. As to the graduate getting married, she may or may not continue to practice. But I ask you, is there any education in this world that could better fit a woman for married life and motherhood than a medical education? Far be it from me to belittle the attainments of women who, for instance, go into the study of higher mathematics, differential calculus, trigonometry, and the like; every woman should be free to follow these studies if she so desires; but I am utterly unable to believe that such education would fit a woman for raising a family in the same way or to the same degree as would a medical education. It is absurd to regard a medically educated woman as a total loss if she does not practice."

The *Woman's Club Journal* carried on one of its covers a reproduction of one of my etchings, with the following editorial:

The charming dry-point etching which we are privileged to reproduce on the cover page of this issue of the JOURNAL is the work of Doctor Chevalier Jackson, President of the Woman's Medical College of Pennsylvania.

It is not often that a scientist of international reputation is also an artist, yet on reflection one may recognize the fact that the same dexterity and skill which enable Doctor Jackson to perform miracles in his operative field of bronchoscopy, lend themselves also to his artistic handling of the pen, brush and dry-point. The representation of the dignified colonial portico of the Woman's Medical College is entitled "Her Alma Mater," and was dedicated by the artist to the Class of 1935. A small "'35" will be found concealed in the shrubbery at the right. A staunch supporter of medical opportunity for women, his acceptance of the presidency of the Woman's Medical College of Pennsylvania in 1935 has given impetus to the program of expansion now in progress. The paragraphs from his own pen elsewhere on this page are significant of his belief in this program.

In my younger days the word "hobby" was used in a disparaging sense as being an obsession so benign in character that the possessor was not a monomaniac but certainly he lacked broad-minded interest in all things. Later, medical men saw the recuperative and recreative value and hobbies became quite fashionable. Later still my son, my secretaries and nurses have been besieged with inquiries as to my hobbies. This has led to introspection. I have found that I have had a few interests that could be called hobbies. With most men hobbies have a certain chronologic order ending up usually with golf in later life. Unfortunately "ending up" is often literally true. The unaccustomed strain on old arteries incidental to chasing around the links not infrequently hastens the end. Even if I had any interest in golf it would have been utterly out of the question for me because of the time required. It would have interfered with the race to complete life's work before death or disability should arrive. The race with the Reaper reminds one of a man hurrying to get through painting his house before his paint should give out.

Anyway, the few of my interests that might be regarded as hobbies had no chronologic sequence. The interests of youth never palled, and advancing years added none. Technique advanced from drawing to etching, but the fundamental fondness for drawing is the same. I can derive today as much pleasure as ever from shaping a piece of wood or metal in the lathe.

Evidently I inherited from Jean Morange, my French grandfather, a fondness for cooking. It was not merely the broiling of a steak or the melting of a rarebit, or the mixing of a salad, but the grand art of soups, entremets, rotis, hors d'œuvres, galantines, casseroles, salmis. With a battery of tinned French copperware and cooking crockery, most delicious things are turned out with much pleasure. I have not, myself, in later life, eaten the meat of my cookery, but I always partake of the vegetables, sauces, gravies, and salads. In boyhood on the few camping opportunities the agreement in the division of chores was that others should do the dish washing and I, as amateur chef, all the cooking. The cooking looked so easy that the dish washers sometimes demanded an exchange of jobs; but one burnt, uneatable meal promptly brought a protest from all campers and a demand for the reinstatement of the amateur chef. A parallel circumstance occurred on the fishing schooner out of Gloucester. Cooking is like drawing; it can be done well by anyone who wants to; but he must want to obsessively.

Love of trees was handed down from Father. It dates from my earliest recollections. It really seems to give me pain to see a tree cut down. In childhood it made me cry. What hurts me most is the ignorant, selfish farmer who considers undergrowth as weeds. Along with the briars and poison ivy he mows the little seedling trees a few feet high. If he would allow one to grow here and there, reforestation would be automatic, the future generation could have fine big trees, and he himself could have trees to cut all his life, in the way of thinnings. This morning's mail brought a circular letter requesting coöperation of Montgomery County citizens in planting dogwood trees along the roadsides—a very worthy and public-spirited movement. On my way home this evening I passed groups of farmers mowing off thousands of dogwoods, clearing fence rows.

"Why don't you leave one of those little dogwood seedlings here and there?"

"Them things? Them's jest bresh. Them ain't no good fer nawthin'."

The need of a campaign of education is obvious.

"The Doctor does love a piece of wood," was the remark of an observant workman. But the love of wood was always in conflict with the love of trees. It seems parallel to the cat at the goldfish tank. She loved the fish but refrained because she disliked wetting her paws. My collection of native wood represents trees dead on the stump or branches trimmed; a live tree was never sacrificed. It is a pleasure to know every native tree, even when leafless—especially to sketch it that way; it is a pleasure to know the wood of every tree by its grain, feel, and color. On entering a wood-working shop I know by its odor the wood going through each machine; and I love the odor. My work with sharp-edged tools began when I was four years of age. At seven I was doing Sorrento work, and at ten, beautiful inlaying. From then on I always had a wood-working as well as a metal-working lathe.

The members of the Section of Oto-Laryngology, College of Physicians, asked for some wood from an old easel or something of the kind from which to make a gavel for the Section. The following letter explains what was done about it:

> Some time ago you did me the honor to ask me for some wood from an old easel or something from which a gavel might be made for the Section of Laryngology of the College of Physicians.
>
> The easels that I have are not of suitable wood for the purpose. I have, therefore, made, myself, on the lathe in my workshop at the old water-mill, the gavel that I send herewith.
>
> The head I made from a piece of dogwood that I have kept ever since I was a boy. It came from my old home at Idlewood, Pennsylvania. The handle is of hickory. I turned it down from the handle of an old hammer with which I worked in my shop for years.
>
> The box is made from a Rambo apple tree planted by my grandfather, Jean Morange, in 1828, on his country place near Pittsburgh.
>
> It is from this grandfather that my parents thought I inherited the mechanical ability that, in their opinion, I possessed. Be this as it may, he was a wonderful mechanic for his time. He was a harbinger of the present mechanical age.

When President of the Pan American Medical Association I conceived the idea of a gavel and gavel box to be made of pieces of wood, one from each of the twenty-two nations on the Western Hemisphere, and I collected the wood for the purpose. This beautiful gavel and box were presented to the Association at Rio de Janeiro.

Unquestionably the aching void for making things was not limited to woodwork; but I was not fond of a piece of metal as I was of a piece of wood, although there is great pleasure to be derived from metal working. Probably the incentive and some ability since boyhood were inherited from my grandfather Jean Morange. I always had a little machine shop. When I became interested in esophagoscopy, direct laryngoscopy, and a little later bronchoscopy, the metal-working shop at home became a busy place. In it were worked out most of the mechanical problems of foreign body endoscopy. Sometimes the finished instrument was made. At other times only the models were made to demonstrate to the instrument maker the problem and the method of solution. This had the advantage that the instrument was ever afterward available to all physicians. No instrument that I devised was ever patented. It galled me in early days, when I devised my first bronchoscope, to find that a similar lamp arrangement had been patented by a mechanic for use on a urethroscope, and the mechanic insisted that the use of such an arrangement on a bronchoscope was covered. Caring nothing for humanity, the patentee threatened a lawsuit unless his patent right was recognized, during the few remaining years it had to run.

In attempts at art I have never taken myself very seriously because I realized that to accomplish anything really worth while, even if I had the ability, would require much more time than I should or could ever have to devote to it.

An intense fondness for nature, for looking at the landscape, was related to a fondness for sketching what was seen; but I soon discovered that, though one may sketch from nature, the interesting fact remains that nature and art are diametrically opposed to each other. There is a fascination in watching a white cottony cloud beyond a green tree top; but this fascination is not artistic appreciation, and art cannot produce the fascinating infinity of it.

Almost every man at some time in his life feels the urge to own a farm. The farmer as a fundamental element in human life is appreciated to the utmost; he should be encouraged and helped in every way. My own personal interest has been, not in the farm itself, but in the country, the sunshine, the sky, the stars and planets, the moonlight, the rocks and lichens, the vegetal and animal life.

All of my etching has been with the dry point. The messing around biting plates with acid, though necessary for some effects, damages the sense of touch by acid burning of the skin and is, moreover, a time-consuming process. Dry point on the contrary is of utmost simplicity. A copper plate and a scratching tool are all that are necessary; and they can be picked up or laid aside instantly if work is interrupted. The outline is scratched reversed from side to side. Then, with careful attention to the values and to the source of light, details are put in. With the heavy tool I devised heavy effects, and as strong lines can be obtained as with the acid-etched process: "Her Alma Mater," "Mother," and "A Bit of Old Blockley" show this way of working.

An editorial in the *New York Medical Record:*

The illustration on our front cover is a reproduction of a dry-point etching by Chevalier Jackson from one of his sketches made in 1925. It represents one of the then abandoned, quaint old wall gates within the enclosure. The prison-like building is one of the old insane departments, built in 1834, just a century ago. All these picturesque old structures have been destroyed and replaced by buildings and surroundings thoroughly in keeping with modern developments in sanitary engineering as well as in psychiatry. While no one will regret the fact that the indigent of the community now have in the commodious, clean and well equipped Philadelphia General Hospital, all that modern science can supply in the way of personal as well as medical care and management, the lovers of the picturesque and the historic cannot help feeling a pang of regret at the utter obliteration of quaint old Blockley. Fortunately, artistic pencils have preserved many of these "bits" for all time.

Chevalier Jackson is not only a leading man in the field of medicine, but is considered by critics an exceptionally fine artist.

What appeals most in sketching with chalk is the extreme simplicity of the means employed. Starting with a dark paper, all the drawing is of the lights; it is quite simple to pick out the strongest and drag the chalks over the paper in the proper place. To get some effects, dragging of two, three, or more colors may be used lightly, each showing through the other, and the underlying paper through all. The sketch is carried in a picture frame with heavy mat to keep the glass from touching. Turn buttons on the back with a cardboard keep the sketching paper in place. "Old Apple Trees," reproduced on a subsequent page, is an example of work with chalk.

Oil color appeals to me strongly, and it is rapid enough in its technique; but time is required in making ready and putting away. If the palette knife is used, there are no brushes to wash. Some effects in oil are obtainable in no other medium. It is best for illustrations of the interior of the larynx and bronchi as seen by artificial light.

My fondness for color, as color, and entirely apart from art, was always strong. Mother told me that as a baby before the talking age I would gather scraps of colored papers or fabrics and piece them together in crude attempts at patterns. In later life the colors of mucous membranes, especially of the bronchi as seen through the bronchoscope, in health and disease, have always been interesting to me, entirely apart from their medical significance.

Later boating experiences are not tinged with sadness, as are the memories of the *Fannie* and the *Katharine*. The more than two months' deep-sea experience on the fishing schooner out of Gloucester, notwithstanding the hardships and hard work, is a happy one in the retrospect. I have never been seasick in my life and am still very fond of the sea in rough weather, especially in small boats with prodigious motion; but this would bring great distress upon my family, whether they were with me or not, and so I go to sea on the mill pond, where I am not only not out of sight of land but not out of sight of the house! Quite parallel to simple Simon's fishing excursions. This form of boating has also the approval of manuscript-demanding editors of medical journals. The boat is a good place to write.

Codfishing on the Banks was brutal. This does not mean reprehensible or morally wrong, but it could not, by any stretch of imagination, be called sport. It was certainly satiating. In younger days the delicate skill of artificial-fly casting appealed strongly. I was given an outfit by the widow of an enthusiastic fly fisherman, but rarely could find time to use it. One evening a thrilling four-foot leap of a hooked black bass was found to have been due to the pain of the hook driven from the mouth out through the eye. That settled it. Hooks were cut off back of the barb. What little fly-casting I did after that was on the basis of winning if the fish could be fooled into rising and snapping at a tiny bunch of hookless, harmless feathers. This does not imply reproach to the fly fisherman; it means simply that the feeling of possibly again cruelly hooking a fish through the eye destroyed all my pleasure of fishing with a hook. With no thought of criticizing others I must admit total absence of pleasure in any sport involving suffering for any form of animal life. It seems inevitable that animals must be killed for food; but killing for so-called sport is evitable. The skill and dexterity of the bullfighter are admitted if not admired; but torturing and killing of bulls is no more sport to me than arriving in time to see the pack of hounds tear asunder, limb by limb, the living, hopelessly outnumbered fox. No arrogance of the Pharisee enters into this; I am trying simply to present my feelings as they seem to me. I would not think for a moment of attempting to dissuade anyone who feels differently.

Great pleasure is derived from achievement, considered entirely apart from the acclaim or glory, if any, and solely from the feeling that something worth while has been done. For example, there is an indescribable pleasure created by the removal of a foreign body, considered quite apart from all the collateral pleasures. If someone has said removal would be impossible, there is a criterion of achievement that enhances the pleasure. Greatest of all such pleasures is the feeling that a life has been saved. Then often, many years afterward, there comes a letter telling of graduation and perhaps accompanied by a photograph showing a young woman or a young man well started in life. Not only has a life been saved, but there is freedom from any handicap; the saved life is worth while. There can be no greater pleasure than to read the letter, look at the photograph, and picture in the retrospect what might have been.

It has afforded me great pleasure, on the few occasions when opportunity offered, to witness feats of strength and skill other than the pugilistic. Modern Olympics seem in every way praiseworthy; but never, even in boyhood, have I had either time or physical strength to participate in such activities.

A layman who smoked, drank, and talked all the time he was awake was filled with more or less righteous indignation when these things were forbidden as an essential part of the restoration of his laryngeal voice. His annoyance is ill concealed in the letter he wrote after returning home:

DEAR DOCTOR JACKSON:

I do not doubt the wisdom of your advice; but to settle an argument with Doctor —— will you please tell us what pleasure you have in life, if any? Doctor —— says that you do not smoke, drink, dine, dance, visit, hunt, fish, play bridge, golf, tennis or any other game, go out or receive socially, go to baseball or football games, movies, plays or concerts; that you never travel or take an auto trip for pleasure and that you do not take a vacation.

What in the world do you do with your spare time?

The following reply was sent:

My dear Mr. ——:

It is a great pleasure to answer your letter.

Your terminal question is easiest answered: I have no spare time.

The information given you by Doctor —— is correct; I do not do any of those things. But, except as to alcohol and tobacco, I do not disapprove of them, in the abstract. Concrete cases are always matters for decision by physicians; for example, tennis would be disapproved for a patient with valvular disease of the heart.

Your personal questions cannot be properly answered without much thought; for this they furnish food. Your letter will be filed at home, and data will be accumulated.

The data were accumulated; they are embodied in this book. If the inquirer be still living he will receive a copy of it.

CHAPTER XXXI

QUESTIONS OFTEN ASKED

THE MOST FREQUENTLY ASKED QUESTION: *What influenced you to study medicine?*

Undoubtedly the greatest factors were my mother and father. Yet neither of them, so far as I can remember, ever advised or expressed the wish that I study medicine. Mother thought prenatal influences were factors. Most medical men doubt the possibility of prenatal, maternal influence on the offspring. Doctor K. I. Sanes, a noted gynecologist and obstetrician, for many years co-tenant with me, when told Mother's belief said he fully concurred. Mother's belief was that the incentive to practice medicine came from her studies in medicine for years before and during the child-bearing period. Mother was a better physician than I ever was. I never considered myself as a medicine-giving doctor; I had utmost faith in what I could do with my eyes and fingers. I feel certain that my interest in medicine was aroused by my mother's medical knowledge and her application of it to my own ailments in early life. I am certain also that Father's constant reading and his talks and demonstrations of the scientific works—especially those of Darwin, Huxley, Tyndall, Spencer, Buckle, Faraday—aroused in me keen interest in biology and scientific research. Father obtained a microscope, and minute life—algae, diatoms, monads, rotifera—afforded no end of evening entertainment. It was thus, it seems, the foundation was laid.

What induced you to specialize in diseases of the larynx?

This frequently asked question is answered on a previous page (Chapter XII).

How did you come to take up the strange specialty of bronchoscopy?

Bronchoscopy does not seem to me a strange specialty; but perhaps that is because of familiarity with it. I am not sure I can answer the question accurately. Probably one factor was the call of the great beyond. That is to say, looking at the larynx thousands of times created a yearning to cross the border line into the mysterious, dimly visible, deeper air passages. But my inordinate dread of harming any patient who trusted me with his life prevented my crossing the threshold until Killian demonstrated the harmlessness of the procedure. Because of my twelve years of esophagoscopy supplemented by a few years of Kirstein's direct laryngoscopy, I was naturally filled with enthusiasm at the possibilities of bronchoscopy. Before I got very far, there developed many things that were considered beyond the range of possibility. This brought in the intrigue of the impossible elsewhere referred to herein. Then came the most powerful of all factors; I found my mechanical genius and training rendered it possible to save the lives of 98 per cent of the little children with potentially fatal foreign bodies in the bronchi. Going down after foreign bodies, I found the bronchoscope a great aid in the diagnosis and treatment of diseases of the bronchi and lungs. This enormously broadened the field of research with all its promise of great benefit to humanity. It was a great incentive to feel that each discovery was possibly a step toward that end.

Other factors were the never ending, new and awe-inspiring sights in the depths of the bronchi, surrounded by the throbbing heart and pulsating great vessels; the making of drawings depicting these revelations; the always changing panorama of beautiful colors, the pleasure of painting them, and of afterward demonstrating them with chalk.

How did you become ambidextrous? I heard you say at the meeting that you were not born so.

It is true I was not born ambidextrous; no one had a more

obstinate case of right-handedness. When a boy my paternal instructions were to educate the hands, especially the left. I sought every opportunity. When a board to be sawed did not require accurate sawing to the line I did it with the left hand. At the table I kept the fork in the left hand and fed myself with it, avoiding the natural inclination to lay down the knife and fork after cutting and take up the fork in the right hand for transferring food to the mouth. If I were a smoker I would handle the cigar with my left hand. It is these little everyday things that count in practice. To use both hands at the same time is easily learned by first using them together to do the same thing, as for example two parallel vertical lines on the blackboard. After this is done with facility the one is used to vary the line. To do this the faculty of divided attention must be developed. With a right-handed person the mind concentrates on control of the right hand; to be simultaneously ambidextrous each hand must be controlled. The boyhood feat of patting the top of the head with one hand while simultaneously stroking the chest with the other is easily learned by developing the control of the left hand separately. The most important factor, as in drawing, is eternal practice. Anyone can learn to draw, but he must obsessively want to draw.

Hoping I may be forgiven, I venture to paraphrase Matthew (VI, 3) and say that every child should be taught, "Let thy left hand know what thy right hand doeth and how to do it."

Is it true that good bronchoscopists are born, not made?

I do not think so.

Expert prize fighters and baseball players are. The fundamental element in their success is quick reaction time, and this is largely congenital. A blow must be seen and parried by reaction—there is not time to think. A ball deviates in less than a hundredth of a second before it reaches contact with the bat; to meet it the ball must be seen and the bat during the swing must be guided to meet it. Here again there is no time to think—all depends on reaction time. An individual born with a slow reaction time can quicken it somewhat by long practice, but can never catch up with the person born with exceedingly rapid reactions.

A bronchoscopist has no need of especially speedy reactions. He needs gentleness, an exquisite sense of touch, caution, orientation, mechanical ability, and patience. These can be acquired in a very remarkable degree by practice. It is true that emergencies occur, but they call for judgment and decision. Often there are only a few seconds for these, if the life is to be saved, but they require a mental process essentially different from the congenital, autonomic reactions needed for a successful pugilist or baseball player at the bat or catching behind it.

What is the best plan for success in medicine?

A successful career in *scientific medicine* requires a start with the broadest possible medical education followed by concentration of effort within the narrowest possible limits.

A successful career in the *practice of medicine* depends upon getting each individual patient's point of view.

CHAPTER XXXII

THE FIVE CHAIRS

How did it happen that you were simultaneously on the faculties of all five medical colleges of Philadelphia? Everyone knows, as Keen said, you have revolutionized a whole department of medicine, but that does not account for the revolution of collegiate tradition in Philadelphia. Tell us something about it.

Perhaps no other question has more frequently been asked.

Professor Hobart Amory Hare said in a public address: "Knowing as I do the temperament, character, training, rivalry, and ambitions of collegiate medical men, if asked beforehand I would have said it is impossible; and I still say it is impossible; but I must add that Chevalier Jackson has done the impossible. He tells us that it is all due to the atmosphere of the City of Brotherly Love. The atmosphere has been here a long time, yet nobody ever did this before. And I do not hesitate to say no one will again. No one anywhere in the world has ever before created, nor simultaneously filled, nor given away, five medical collegiate chairs. In Philadelphia as in other medical centers boards of trustees have deemed it for the best interests of their respective institutions to serve the ultimatum: 'You cannot work here and there too; you must give up one or the other. Take your choice.' Such an ultimatum was never served on Chevalier Jackson."

The unique condition resulted not from any desire on my part to occupy five collegiate chairs at once, but from the reluctance of each institution to accept the resignation I presented after the respective newly created chairs and clinics were established. The result was a period of overlap during which the respective boards and faculties were being gradually convinced that my continued presence was not essential. It should not be supposed that it cost me no regrets to move onward. On the contrary each separation meant sorrow and sacrifice; each time it was for me a pathetic breaking of home ties. But again became manifest that grim, stubborn, dogged determination that had carried me through so many ordeals in life. All of this was concealed under the cloak of unfailing courtesy. No harsh word was ever uttered.

The whole matter of the five overlapping chairs and clinics can perhaps be best understood by perusal of the following data.

Protests from boards of trustees and members of faculties in Philadelphia, at first, were as strong as when I left the University of Pittsburgh to go to Philadelphia. The Honorable William Potter, President of the Board of Trustees of Jefferson Medical College, said:

> You have established here a school of bronchoscopy; all the world is coming here. Why not just make this one clinic the World's School of Bronchoscopy? We'll give you everything you want. You can settle down and take life easy.

The following is an abstract from the reply sent:

> It is my duty to go; my duty to humanity, my duty to bronchoscopy, my duty to my mother. When a few years ago your offer of a chair came to me at Pittsburgh I took it to my mother, then over seventy years of age. She said:
>
> "Well, Chev, it will mean that you and I will not see each other many times before I die, but you must go; it is your duty to go. You will be able to spread much wider the knowledge of your life-saving methods of bronchoscopy. You and I will both pass away, but bronchoscopy as you have developed it will go on forever. We must think of the suffering little children whose lives can be saved. You must go."
>
> Now, Mr. Potter, you will know how I feel about duty to my mother's memory and about moving onward in the spread of knowledge of bronchoscopy. I know you would not subscribe to any such dictum as that students in need of knowledge of bronchoscopy shall come to Jefferson or go ignorant; nor that all patients in need of bronchoscopy shall come to Jefferson or die.

And I must move on now before age overtakes me and makes my hand tremble. Nothing could give me greater pleasure than to settle down to a life of cozy comfort among my friends here at Jefferson; but I feel like the Youth in "Excelsior" who could not linger where

> In happy homes he saw the light
> Of household fires gleam warm and bright.

Although the members of the respective faculties protested at the time, they later realized the broader aspects of the matter. Mr. Potter said: "Very well, Doctor Jackson. We understand your exceptional position. You can found as many clinics as you want; but don't talk of leaving Jefferson. You must retain your connection here." Mr. Alba B. Johnson said: "It is to be distinctly understood that your case is exceptional and does not establish a precedent. The rule against connection with another medical school applies to the membership of the Board of Trustees as well as of the Faculty."

John Chalmers Da Costa, the greatest surgical teacher of his time, while suffering pain from arthritic fixation of almost every joint in his body, dictated and signed with his crippled hands the following note:

> I cannot tell you with what pride and gratification I read of your decoration with the Cross of Officer of the Legion of Honor. I naturally felt gratification to see one for whom I have so much admiration justly honored and I naturally felt pride that American Medicine and Philadelphia should be brought by you into such distinction. I think your work in establishing a bronchoscopic clinic in practically every large city is the most extraordinary thing that I know of in medicine, and long years after you have passed away the achievement will be cited as an evidence of your greatness. I trust you will forgive me for intruding upon your valuable time with this letter. I am dictating in the midst of a storm of pain. I feel so much pride and gratification that they temporarily still the pain.

The following is an abstract from the answer sent:

I cannot tell you how deeply touched I am at receiving your letter of July 15; but I am much grieved to know that you are suffering so much pain. I shall always treasure your letter along with the decoration you mention. The promotion to Officer I appreciate because it indicates the feeling that the French government and my friends in France are not under the impression that they made a mistake when they gave the Cross of Chevalier.

The "work in establishing a bronchoscopic clinic in practically every large city" is an ideal; I am working along knowing full well that I shall be cut off long before I have lived a sufficient number of years to teach safe bronchoscopy in all new fields. I venture to hope, however, that I have created enough inspiration in others to build up in their respective home towns a satisfactory clinic.

I shall never forget how you used to send patients "against the current" out to the bronchoscopic clinic at Pittsburgh in the early stages of the work. It was this kind of support from the broad-minded men like yourself that made possible what little I have been able to accomplish.

The two following letters came from Professor W. W. Keen:

My dear Doctor Jackson:

I have just received your Bulletin from the University of Pennsylvania. I remember very well keeping tab on your work when you were in Pittsburgh. . . . The moment that ——'s Chair [Laryngology] became vacant by death, I got busy with the Trustees and secured your election. Of course, you have developed that department very greatly, but I am surprised to see that you have apparently gone over to the University of Pennsylvania to carry on very important work. Could you not have developed the same line at the Jefferson? I should hesitate much to criticize your work at the University, as well as the Jefferson, but it does seem to me that when you came to the Jefferson at my instance, that should have been the center and principal place for your work. If you chose to establish a branch at the University, I should not object, though it would be very unusual.

My dear Doctor Jackson:

I have received the three letters you sent me. The moment that our Professor of Laryngology at the Jefferson died, I began a campaign for your election to the vacancy. I saw every one of the Trustees; I explained to them what work you had been doing on a small scale in Pittsburgh and you came to the largest field of work in all the three Americas. You justified your choice by your genius in devising new methods, new instruments, and you became rightly the most famous man especially in what developed later into the removal of foreign bodies in the air passages which you extended also to the esophagus. You did your part splendidly and the Jefferson did its part. You could not have in any other place so great an audience which you added to by your many publications. Your ingenuity has been marvelous; your success unchallenged. Of course, you are at liberty to seek other and less famous places, if you desire to do so.

Dear Doctor Keen:

The enclosed copy of a letter to our mutual friend, Doctor Da Costa, and one to the Board of Trustees, cover an answer to your letter of April 18, 1929.

I might add that there are now more patients going to each of the Clinics that I have built and left than ever before. In a few short years I shall not be working anywhere, because, naturally, I shall be dead. In building up at each institution a clinic known all over the world; in making it permanent; in making each clinic stand on its own feet by leaving it—in doing these things I have done more for each institution than if I had remained in one for the few years I have to live; all would have ended at my death. Friends of each institution are too shortsighted to see this now; they will see it some day. They will see also that I have done better for Bronchoscopy and better for humanity than if I had insisted that every child in need of Bronchoscopy should come to the first clinic or die, and then had died myself leaving nothing. Bronchoscopy is too big a thing to be bottled up in one institution. I am only an evangelist; I must pitch a tent successively in various centers where there are heretics and doubters. It has taken the best years of my life thoroughly to convince the Faculty and Board of the place deserved by Bronchoscopy, Esophagoscopy, and Gastroscopy. It will not take that long *now,* in other places, because of the general realization that these procedures are worthy of consideration.

As I said in the letters I am primarily interested in Bronchoscopy and its allied branches. These great medical schools do not need me; Bronchoscopy does. Each school has strong friends to fight for it; Bronchoscopy has only me, a physically not very strong individual, and the few supporters I have rallied to the cause.

My dear old mother, my wife, and all my family have made untold sacrifices that I might complete my life's work. I will not falter now. I shall die fighting for the widest possible recognition of life-saving Bronchoscopy. Every last spark of energy I have and every dollar I can make will be spent in an effort to spread the gospel of safe Bronchoscopy as widely as I can spread it.

I take this occasion to say that one of the greatest aids to the recognition of Bronchoscopy has been the clear vision of Professor W. W. Keen. His prompt recognition of its possibilities and his support in its early days have done more than you have ever realized to obtain the large measure of recognition it now has.

The following letter came from Professor George E. de Schweinitz:

DEAR DOCTOR JACKSON:

With deep regret I have been informed that you have transmitted your resignation of your Professorship of Bronchoscopy and Esophagoscopy in the Graduate School of Medicine of the University. I am unfamiliar with the reasons which induced you to take this action. But it occurs to me that you may have been influenced in this request because of a recent ruling concerning the age-limit requirement, namely, sixty-five years.

But this does not apply to you, and your position is in no manner subject to this rule. Moreover, the rule is so framed that in any instance the Board of Medical Affairs, of which I am Chairman, has discretionary power.

Therefore, not only officially, but individually, I most earnestly request you to reconsider this resignation.

It is not necessary for me to point out how deeply we should regret discontinuance of your distinguished work in the Graduate School which adds so finely to the reputation of this and all other departments of University activities.

Once more, therefore, I beg you to withdraw this resignation and continue to hold the place you now occupy, and which you administer with such outstanding ability.

I add that should you assent to my request, it will in no wise interfere with any other commitments you may have made or have in contemplation.

With cordial regards and all good wishes.

The following letter was written in forcing the acceptance of my resignation from the Graduate School of Medicine of the University of Pennsylvania. Incidentally, it states clearly the plan of my life's work.

MY DEAR DOCTOR MEEKER:

Some matters arose in our conference a few days ago that seem to call for a clearer statement.

1. My objective in life is quite different from yours. You are interested only in the Graduate School of Medicine, which you, with the aid of those whom you have called to your assistance, have created. This is, of course, a great achievement, far broader in scope than anything I have attempted to do. My object in life is the creation of as many efficient bronchoscopic clinics as I can in my lifetime. Any particular institution is therefore secondary to what I deem my chief duty in life. . . . It is natural that you should feel that all children in need of bronchoscopy should go to the Graduate Hospital or die, and that all pupil physicians in need of instruction in bronchoscopy should go to the Graduate School of Medicine or remain uninstructed. I deem it my duty to create as many as possible of the centers for the teaching as well as for the clinical application of the life-saving methods to the development of which I have devoted my life.

2. Having built up for your Graduate School of Medicine an organization and a system of teaching worked out elaborately to the most minute details of principles and practice, the time has come when I can move on to the next station on the road of my life's work. As I have said before, I am only an evangelist; having spread the gospel of safe bronchoscopy in the Graduate School of Medicine and the Medical School of the University of Pennsylvania, it is necessary that I move on to where doubters and heretics abound. There shall be one more Clinic in Philadelphia, and later, one in another city if I last a few years longer. I am inspired by the responsibility to teach everything I know to everyone who will listen and learn.

My dear Doctor Jackson:

The Board of Managers [Hospital of the University of Pennsylvania] cannot let your retirement go by without writing a note of appreciation of the remarkable work you have done in connection with the years you have been connected with the University Hospital.

We want you to know that we regard your leaving us as a great loss, as you were responsible for creating at the University Hospital the first independent bronchoscopic clinic in the country.

Please let us take this opportunity of thanking you for your cordial coöperation with the Managers in the conduct of the Hospital, and with our best wishes for a great many full years of service, we are . . .

Reply to the foregoing letter:

My dear Mr. Curtin:

Words fail me with which to tell you how much I appreciate your kind letter of yesterday. Please assure the Board of Managers that the note of appreciation is very gratefully received. The busy days come and go and I am always concentrated on my objective, with little or no thought of any gratitude ever coming from anywhere except from patients and the parents of children whose life bronchoscopy has been able to save. In this busy life it comes as a bright spot to know that the Board of Managers deemed it worth while to send me the delightful note. I shall always retain it as a token. Please convey these thoughts to the Board.

Dear Doctor Jackson:

The Trustees of the University have asked me to say to you that they have learned with great regret of your resignation as Professor of Bronchoscopy and Esophagoscopy in the School of Medicine and the Graduate School of Medicine. The Trustees also have placed upon their record a minute concerning your resignation, a copy of which is enclosed.

MINUTE CONCERNING RESIGNATION OF DR. CHEVALIER JACKSON ADOPTED BY THE TRUSTEES OF THE UNIVERSITY OF PENNSYLVANIA

In accepting the resignation of Doctor Chevalier Jackson from the Chair of Bronchoscopy and Esophagoscopy in the Medical

School and the Graduate School of Medicine, the Trustees desire to spread upon the minutes their appreciation of his distinguished services to suffering humanity throughout the whole world, by his teaching, research and inventive genius. From a small beginning covering a limited field and practice by but a few pioneers, in the space of less than twenty-five years, peroral endoscopy has attained a major position in the science of medicine, with hundreds of exponents, largely through the instruction, clinical and didactic, of Doctor Jackson. No longer limited to the extraction of foreign bodies from the upper air and food tracts these procedures are now used for routine diagnosis and treatment of these cavities down to and below the diaphragm, and are an invaluable aid to the thoracic surgeon and the internist. The Chevalier Jackson Clinics are famous throughout the world and the name of Doctor Jackson is immortally connected with legislation designed to protect life and health by safeguarding the sale and use of caustics. This legislation originated in his wisdom and was obtained by his great untiring interest.

The Board of Trustees of the University of Pennsylvania then elected me an Emeritus Professor.

The other two of the simultaneously occupied chairs were at the Temple University and the Woman's Medical College of Pennsylvania, respectively. Cordial relations among the five clinics have been retained, and when my special courses in Bronchoscopy are given all clinics are represented.

The creation and giving away of five chairs was part of a definite plan to spread the gospel of "safe bronchoscopy." This was based on the premise that nothing so firmly establishes a new department of medicine as the establishment of a professorial chair to teach it. To lessen the teaching load, two chairs of Laryngology were also given away.

EPILOGUE

Retrospection reveals no feeling that any major decision should have been otherwise. This does not imply that no mistakes were made; but they all now seem trivial compared to the unregretted major decisions: the selection of a wife; total abstinence from alcoholic beverages and tobacco; the abandonment of art as a career; the study of medicine; specializing in laryngology; fundamental work in bronchoscopy and esophagoscopy; the move to Philadelphia; the resignation of seven college chairs in succession as part of the progress in the spreading of the gospel of bronchoscopy; the fight against tuberculosis by working in bed; and so on.

If I have made any momentous error it is the writing of this book.

It is impossible for me adequately to express my appreciation for the privilege to live in the era that has seen the development of the laboratory in industry, the utilization of electricity, the Roentgen ray, automobile, internal combustion motor, airplane, cinema, radio, radium, telephone, and thousands of other marvelous discoveries of the mechanical age.

I am even more grateful that my medical life has seen the end of one era of medical science and the establishment of another.

I am grateful to have lived in the dawn and daylight of the equally great new era of science, of medical science, of aseptic surgery, and especially of preventive medicine.

It is a privilege to have lived in the era of the building of the greatest monument of all time, the Panama Canal: a monument, not to the United States of America or its great executives, though these did their part and did it nobly, but to the science of preventive medicine.

I had just graduated in medicine when the world was shocked

by the cataclysmal downfall of Ferdinand de Lesseps and his associates. My teachers, the greatest medical men of their day, taught me all they could; but they did not know that the mosquito defeated De Lesseps; they did not know anything about preventive medicine; nobody did; with the exception of vaccination for smallpox it simply did not exist.

That period marked the end of the old era.

The new era started when Louis Pasteur inaugurated the fundamental principle of scientific research into the causes and prevention of disease. There quickly followed the development of the new science of bacteriology and, as one of its many practical applications, aseptic surgery, which means prevention of infection of wounds.

Early in this great era of preventive medicine physicians engaged in research discovered among other things the causes and means of prevention of typhoid fever, typhus fever, cholera, amoebic dysentery, and especially malaria and yellow fever, two diseases that had killed shipload after shipload of the workmen of De Lesseps and destroyed the morale of all his personnel. By the practical application of the newly found knowledge of preventive medicine the tropical Canal Zone had lower morbidity and mortality rates than any large city in the world.

De Lesseps unconsciously demonstrated that the greatest need of all humanity was prevention of disease. It is marvelous that within sixteen years physicians developed the science of preventive medicine. In the ten years of the building of the Canal the practical application of the new science was demonstrated.

I repeat, I am grateful for the privilege of having lived in an era that saw the birth of the science of preventive medicine and the building of its monument, the Panama Canal.

I am grateful that my humble lot should have fallen in the same profession as those who unselfishly founded the science of preventive medicine.

POSTSCRIPT

Like a hick'ry cog
In the old mill wheel
He did his part
As his turn came 'round.

CURRICULUM VITAE

1865 Born, November 4, at Pittsburgh, Pennsylvania.

1886 Degree of M.D. conferred by Jefferson Medical College.

1887 Began practice of medicine, specializing in laryngology.

1911 President American Laryngological, Rhinological, and Otological Society.

President Section on Laryngology, Otology, and Rhinology, American Medical Association.

1912 Elected Professor of Laryngology at the University of Pittsburgh.

1916 Elected Professor of Laryngology, Jefferson Medical College.

1917 President American Bronchoscopic Society.

Appointed Medical Advisory Board, State of Pennsylvania. Honorable discharge, March, 1919.

1919 Elected to fill the new Chair of Bronchoscopy and Esophagoscopy created and endowed for him by the Board of Trustees of the University of Pennsylvania, at the request of the Faculty of the Graduate School of Medicine.

1923 Degree of Doctor of Science conferred by the University of Pennsylvania.

1924 Professor of Bronchoscopy and Esophagoscopy, Chair created for him by Jefferson Medical College. At his request Doctor Fielding O. Lewis was elected to fill the vacated Chair of Laryngology.

Elected Professor of Bronchoscopy and Esophagoscopy, University of Pennsylvania (Chair established for him).

Appointed Lecturer (Lectureship created for him) on Bronchoscopy and Esophagoscopy, Temple University.

1925 Elected Lecturer on Bronchoscopy and Esophagoscopy, Woman's Medical College (Lectureship created for him).

American Medical Association Certificate of Honor for Exhibit of Bronchoscopic Work.

1926 President American Laryngological Association.

Recipient of the De Roaldes Award in Laryngology.

1927 Recipient of the Philadelphia (Bok) Award.

Chevalier de la Légion d'Honneur (France).

Chevalier de l'Ordre de Léopold (Belgium).

Degree of Doctor of Laws conferred by Ursinus College.

Passage of Federal Caustic Poison Law.

1928 Appointed William Potter Memorial Lecturer.

Recipient of the Henry Bigelow Medal, awarded by the Boston Surgical Society.

Bronchoscopic Clinic organized at the Graduate School of Medicine, University of Pennsylvania, constructed and equipped by donation of Mr. Frederick S. Bigelow and Doctor Alice H. Bigelow.

1929 Officier de la Légion d'Honneur (promotion).

Recipient of the Cresson Medal of the Franklin Institute.

1930 Degree of Doctor of Laws conferred by Temple University.

Elected Professor of Bronchoscopy and Esophagoscopy, Temple University School of Medicine (newly created chair).

Elected Professor Emeritus of Graduate School of Medicine, University of Pennsylvania.

1932 Recipient of the I. P. Strittmatter Award (for year 1927).

1933 Commendatore del Ordine della Corona d'Italia.

Recipient of the Gold Medal of the Radiological Society of North America.

1934 President Pan American Medical Association.

Elected Professor of Bronchoscopy and Esophagoscopy, Woman's Medical College of Pennsylvania (newly established chair).

Elected Visiting Professor of Bronchoscopy and Esophagoscopy, Louisiana State University Medical Center.

1935 President Woman's Medical College of Pennsylvania.
Grão-Mestre da Ordem Nacional do Cruzeiro do Sul (Southern Cross of Brazil).

1936 Tree planted in Forrest Hill, South Yarra, Melbourne, Australia, in commemoration, by Kelvin Rodgers.

1937 President American Therapeutic Society.
Degree of Doctor of Laws conferred by Pennsylvania Military College.

Fellow of the American College of Surgeons.
Life Member, American Academy of Ophthalmology and Otolaryngology.
Member of the American Medical Association.
Member of the Pan American Medical Association.
Member of the American Association for Thoracic Surgery.
Member of the Philadelphia Pediatric Society.
Member of the American Therapeutic Society.
Member of the College of Physicians of Philadelphia.
Member of the American Philosophical Society.
Member of the Philadelphia Laryngological Society.
Member of the American Association of History of Medicine.
Member of the Medical Advisory Board in America of the American Hospital of Paris.
Member of the American Gastroenterologic Society.
Membre de l'Association des Médecins de Langue Française de l'Amérique du Nord.
Honorary Member of the Allegheny County Medical Society.
Honorary Fellow of the Royal Society of Medicine, London.
Honorary Life Member of the Philadelphia Laryngological Society.
Honorary Member of the Scottish Society of Otology and Laryngology.
Honorary Member of the Polski Towarzystwo Otorhinolaryngologiczne.
Honorary Member of the Svenska Läkaresällskapet.

Honorary Member of the Società Italiana di Laringologia, Otologia e Rinologia.

Honorary Member of the Sociedad Otorinolaringologica Madrileña.

Honorary Member of the Societatae Romana de Oto-Rhino-Laryngologie.

Honorary Member of the Academia Nacional de Medicina de Mexico.

Honorary Member of the Sociedad Chilena de Oto-Rhino-Laringologia.

Honorary Foreign Member of the Brazilian College of Surgeons.

Honorary Member of the Academia Nacional de Medicina, Rio de Janeiro.

Honorary Member of the New York Academy of Medicine.

Honorary Member of the Medical Society of the District of Columbia.

Honorary Member of the Kansas City Society of Ophthalmology.

Membre d'Honneur de la Société Belge d'Oto-Rhino-Laryngologie.

Membre d'Honneur de la Société de Broncho-Œsophagoscopie de Langue Française.

Membre Correspondant de la Société de Laryngologie des Hôpitaux de Paris.

Membre Correspondant de la Société d'Oto-Rhino-Laryngologie de Lyon et de la Région.

Lauréat de l'Académie des Sciences, Paris in collaboration with Doctor Chevalier Lawrence Jackson.

Lauréat de l'Académie de Médecine, Paris.

INDEX

ILLUSTRATIONS

A four-year-old pupil at Mrs. Ward's School.

As a pupil at Greentree School; about ten years of age.

On graduation from medical college; twenty years of age.

In practice of medicine at twenty-one years of age.

A characteristic attitude studying a duplicate foreign body.
Fifty-three years of age.

At sixty-five years of age (Underwood & Underwood).

Grandmother Sarah Secor Morange, a Knickerbocker.

Grandfather Jean Morange, a mechanical genius. In 1805 as a boy of ten years, in the port of Bordeaux, France, he was bound in navigational apprenticeship to a Yankee skipper, Captain Fairbanks of the *Kitty Clyde*. The papers required that the boy should be taken back to his mother after four years. He remembered his mother kissed him good-bye; he never saw her again. Captain Fairbanks went ashore, retired, at Dedham, Mass., and bound out the boy as an apprentice in a machine shop.

Mother, Katharine Ann Morange Jackson.

Father, William Stanford Jackson, born in Lancaster County, Pennsylvania, shortly after the arrival of his parents from Holderness, Yorkshire, England.

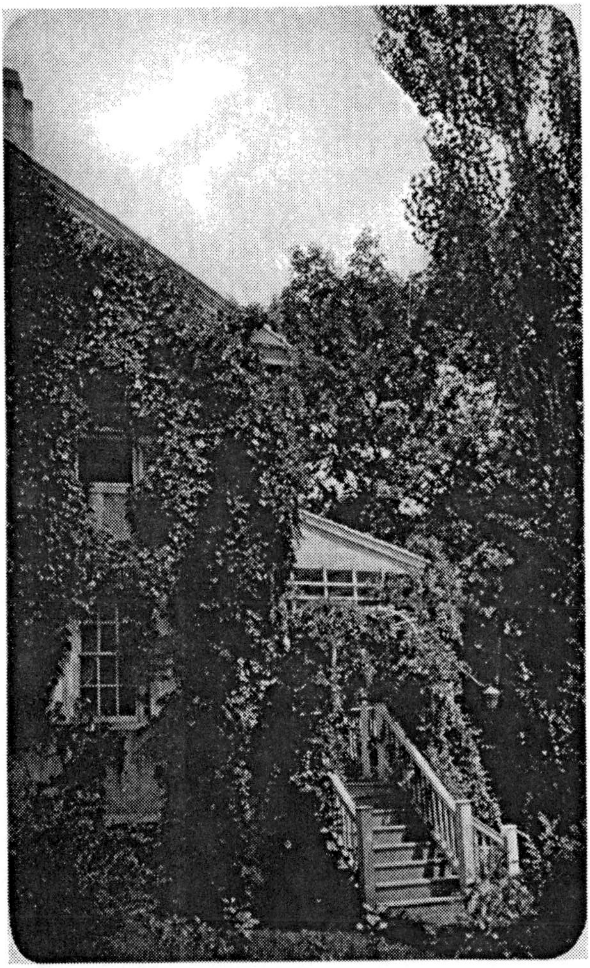

The vine-covered house at Old Sunrise Mills.

The clockcase was built of mahogany. One of many manifestations of an innate urge for making things. The oil painting over the cabinet was done on the Ohio River. Its frame was made in the home shop from weathered-gray, rough sawn cedar.

The mills and miller's house, about thirty-five miles from Philadelphia; for more than twenty years the residence of Chevalier Jackson.

Old Sunrise Gristmill. One of the older riparian deeds reads, "In the Province of Philadelphia, Realm of His Majesty, King George the Third." (Drypoint.)

Wooden machinery in the old gristmill. The two handles in the upper left-hand corner are the ends of gear-shift levers. When one was dropped, the hickory cogs on the corresponding vertical gear wheel meshed with those on the horizontal wheel. In the boxlike grain chute at the left is a gang of magnets for removing any bolts, nuts, nails or other bits of iron that might accidentally be present in grain. It was this gang of removable magnets that rescued the millwright's lost tools.

Wooden-cogged mortise wheel and iron pinion known as the "man-eaters." Arms, heads, or anything that got caught in the inmeshing side of the gears went through. All such dangerous machinery today must be guarded by screens or covers. The photograph was taken for use in emphasizing, by contrast, the lack of legislation to protect children from the dangers of lye.

Machine shop politely called "experimental laboratory" rigged in the old water mill. Bronchoscopes are on the table in the foreground.

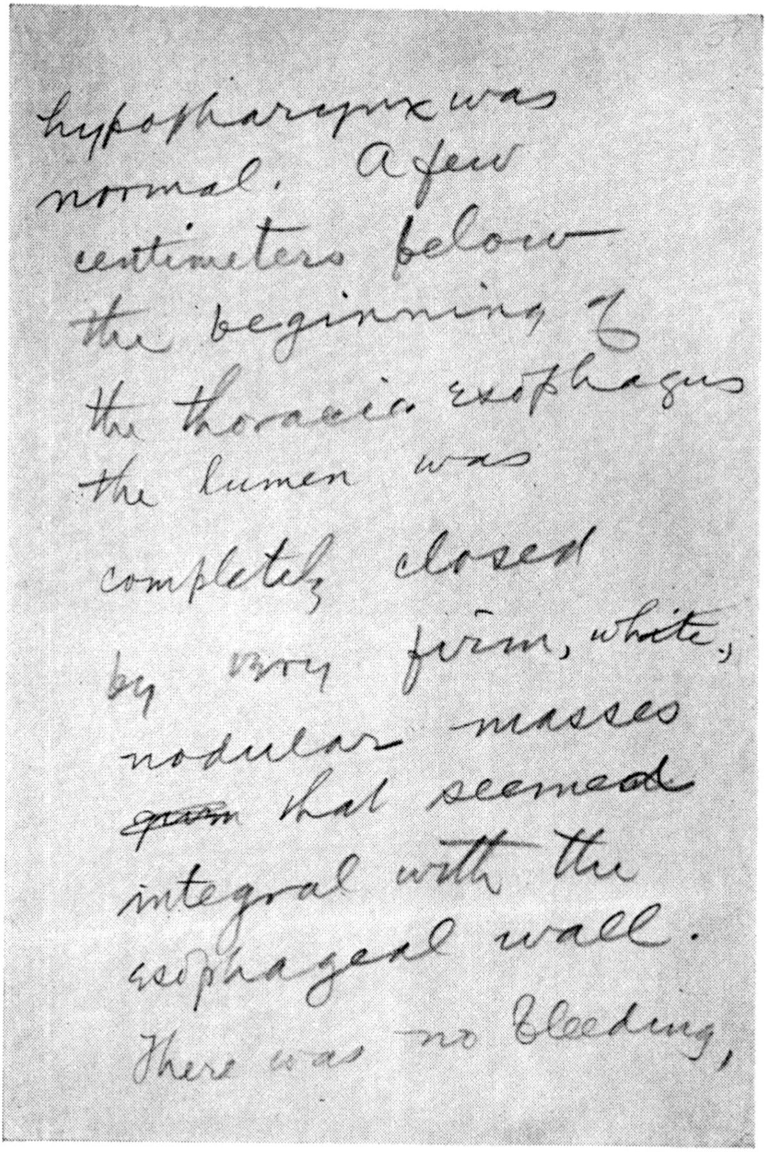

hypopharynx was
normal. A few
centimeters below
the beginning of
the thoracic esophagus
the lumen was
completely closed
by very firm, white,
nodular masses
~~gram~~ that seemed
integral with the
esophageal wall.
There was no bleeding,

A page of manuscript written with very soft pencil on manila paper. When writing outdoors green print-paper was used to diminish glare.

In the homemade writing chair with wide arms.

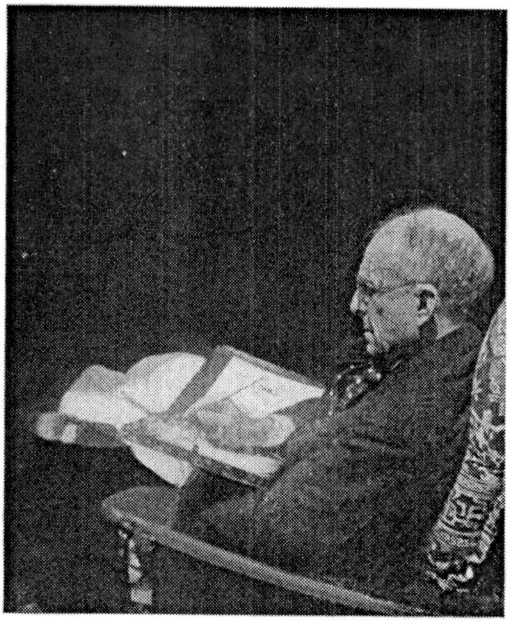

In the writing chair at the French window painting medical illustrations in oil colors.

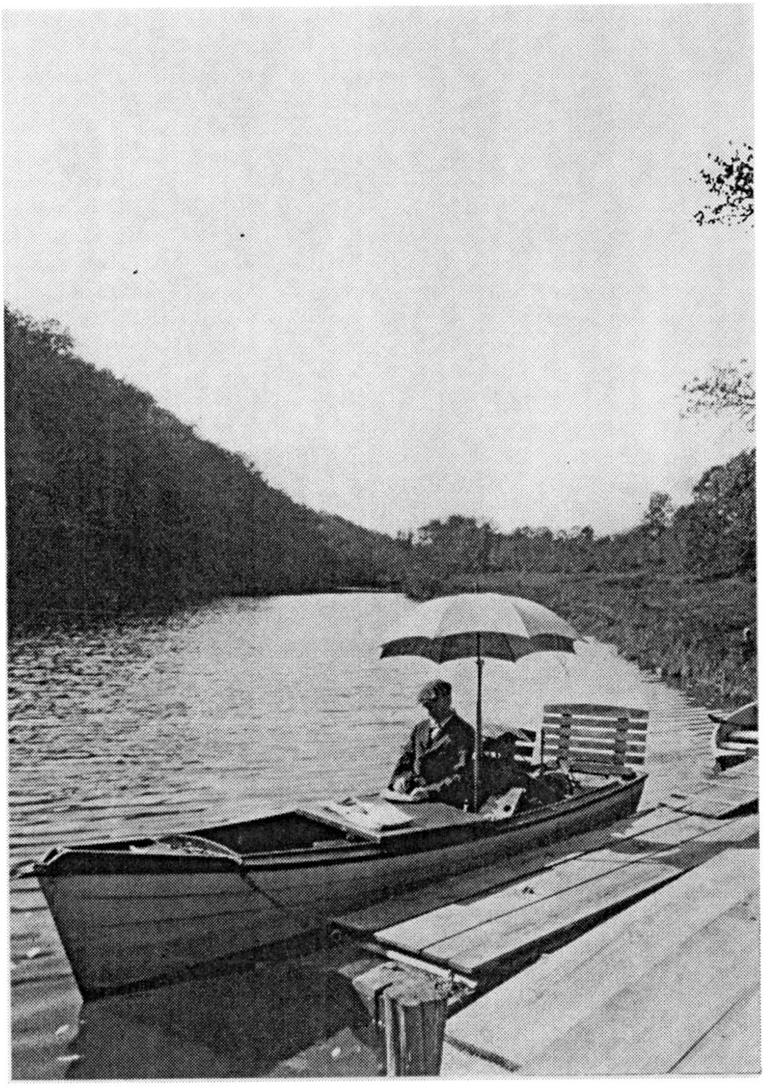

Sunday afternoon. Writing medical papers in the homemade electric boat.

Autumn evening on the old mill pond. Returning home after writing all Sunday afternoon in the rowboat.

A concrete fireproof study was built to protect irreplaceable case-records. In front of the French windows is a concrete piazza for feeding wild birds and other animals.

In winter the concrete piazza was shovelled clear of snow for a feeding station
There is a squirrel house in the old apple tree.

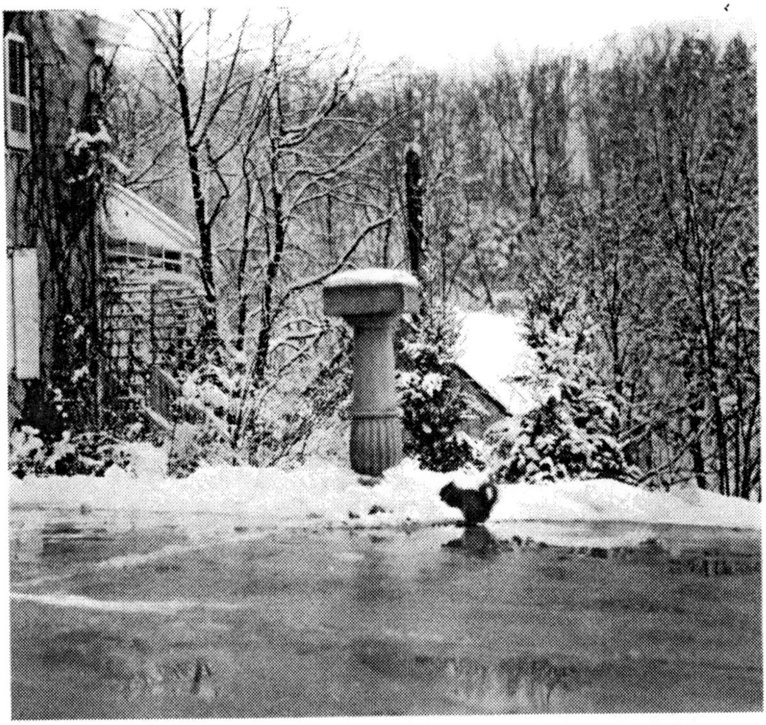

A regular winter companion. He lives on maize. When given walnuts he took them away and buried them to soften; but he failed to remember landmarks. A good crop of seedling walnut trees resulted.

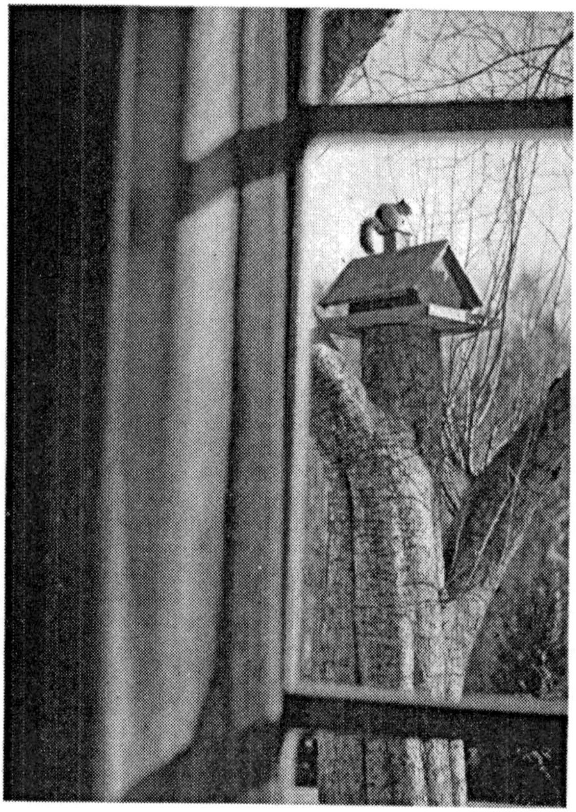

The squirrel is barking his protest at a companion on a limb beyond. Photographed through the window glass. In the spring baby squirrels scamper and play with one another like kittens around this house where they were born.

A cardinal grosbeak and a turtledove snapped through the window glass as they arrived at the feeding station early on a dark winter morning.

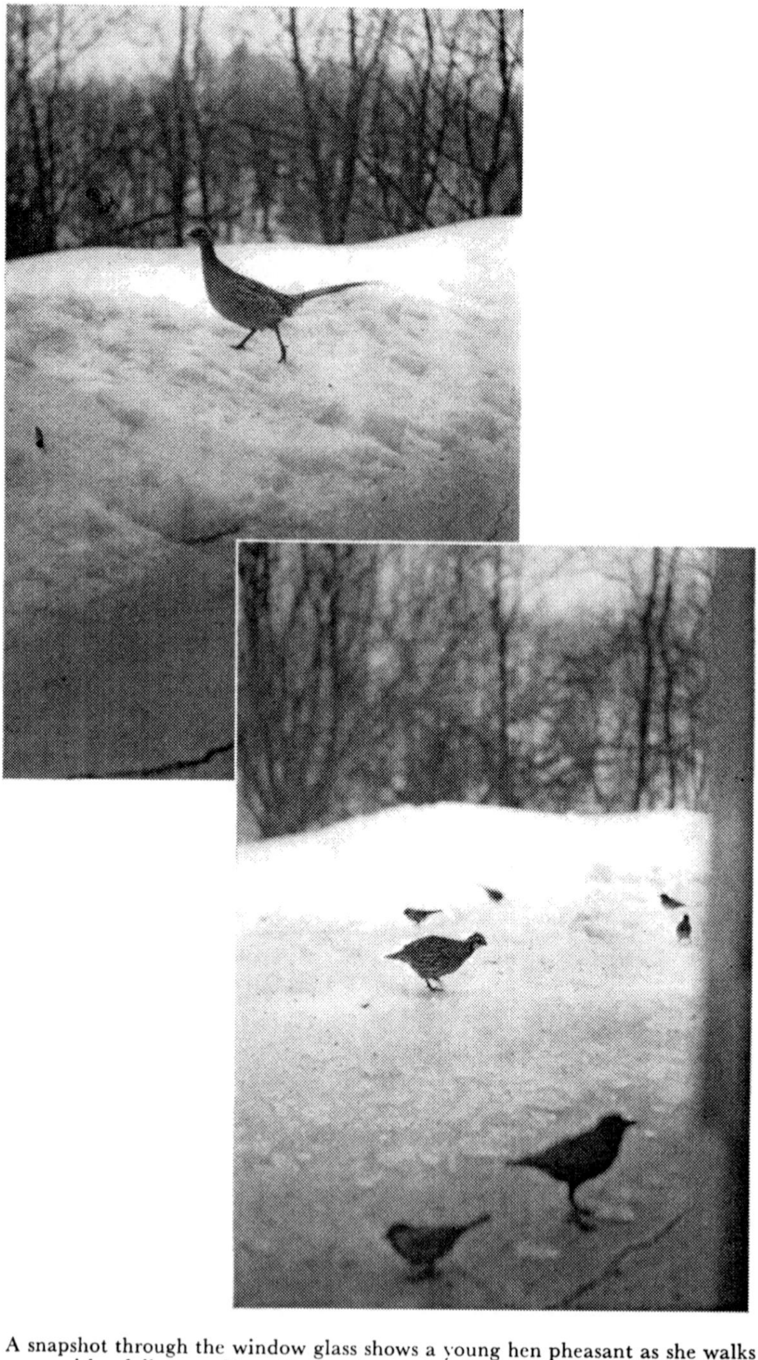

A snapshot through the window glass shows a young hen pheasant as she walks away with a full crop. She will come back when it is empty. A quail, a starling and some juncos come for afternoon feeding. Perhaps I am peculiar in thinking I get more pleasure from these constantly recurring visits than the gunner gets from killing. It seems to me that death ends all.

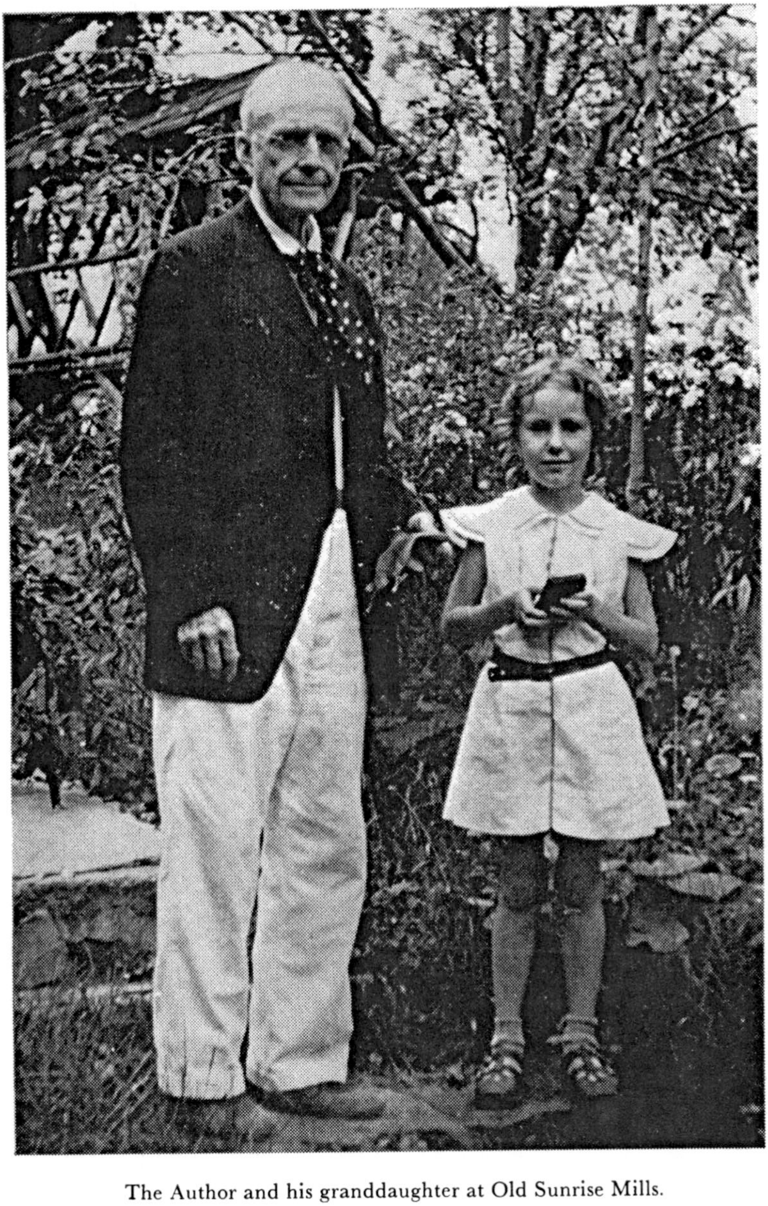

The Author and his granddaughter at Old Sunrise Mills.

Her Alma Mater. A dry-point etching dedicated to the class of 1935. The subject is the portico of the Woman's Medical College of Pennsylvania.

Ivied Walls. A dry-point. The subject is a corridor at the University of Pennsylvania. The walk is shifted because the cement pourer put it in an impossible place, artistically speaking.

A Bit of Old Blockley. A dry-point etching.

At the open window. She was always like mother to me.

The Bigelow Medal.

The Cassette of the Philadelphia Bok Award, containing the scroll and the medal. The medallion on the front of the pedestal is by R. Tait McKenzie. An alcove in the Mütter Museum of the College of Physicians of Philadelphia.

Presentation of the new gavel to the Pan American Medical Association of 1935, at the Theatro Municipal, Rio de Janeiro. The gavel is under the velvet cover on the table in front of the speaker.

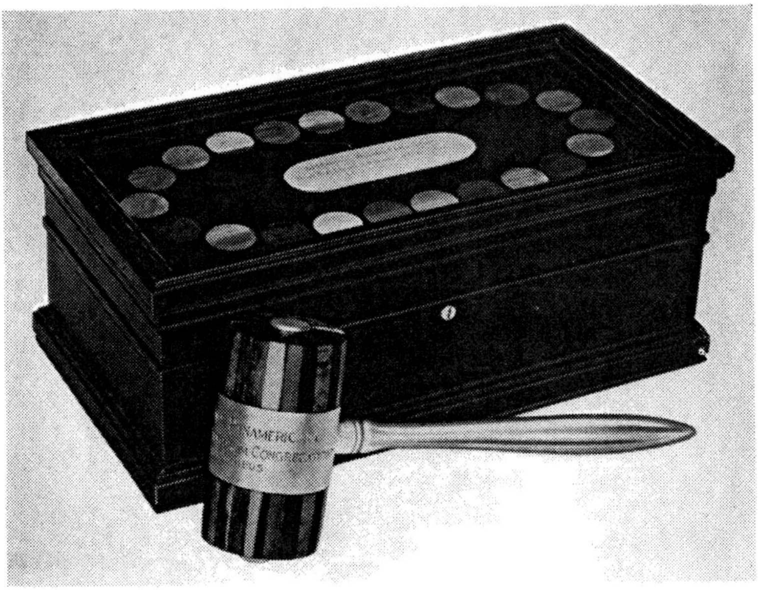

Gavel and gavel box presented to the Pan American Medical Association at its Sixth Congress by Chevalier Jackson, President, at Rio de Janeiro, July 14, 1935. The box is made of neutral wood, representing the neutrality of the Association; in the lid are inserted twenty-two discs of wood—one from each of the twenty-two nations of the Western Hemisphere. The gavel is made of twenty-two pieces of wood of similar origin. The separate pieces are bound together with a silver band, representing Medical Science binding together the Physicians of the several nations. On the band is a Latin inscription to the effect that "nothing but good can follow the forgathering of the medical men of twenty-two national flags under the single banner of scientific medicine." (Nihil nisi bonum in medicorum congregatione ex XXII nationibus.) The arrangement of the pieces of wood avoids precedence, and all are exactly the same size.

Sixth Pan American Medical Congress. Left to right, Dr. Leone Cottrell, New York City; Dr. Grace Ritchie-England, Montreal; Dr. Frances B. Tyson, Leonia, N.J.; Chevalier Jackson, President of the Woman's Medical College of Pennsylvania; Dr. Ellen J. Patterson, Pittsburgh, Pa.; Dr. Lydia A. DeVilbiss, Miami, Fla.; Dr. Virginia Van Meter, Denver, Colo.; Dr. Jeannette Cohen, Pittsburgh, Pa.

Discussions of clinical problems with foreign visitors were always delightful as well as mutually beneficial. From left to right, seated, Dr. Alfred Solacroup, laryngologist of Algiers; Dr. Maurice Philip, laryngologist of Bordeaux; Chevalier Jackson; Dr. Louis Levesque, Nantes. Standing, Mr. Maxwell Ellis of London, assistant at the bronchoscopic clinic; Chevalier L. Jackson, clinical Professor of Bronchoscopy; Dr. Jacques Vialle, bronchoscopist, of Nice.

Demonstrating methods of acquiring ambidexterity. At the right stands Mr. Frederick S. Bigelow, who with his sister, Doctor Alice H. Bigelow, founded the Bigelow Bronchoscopic Clinic for Chevalier Jackson. Mr. Bigelow was then on the editorial staff of the *Saturday Evening Post*.

At the International Conferences, Paris, 1925. From left to right, Chevalier Jackson; Professor G. H. Roger, Dean of the University of Paris; Professor Fernand Lemaître.

Opening the discussion on the problems of the tack by "chalk-talk" at Professor Lemaître's clinic, at the Hôpital Saint-Louis.

Inscription on the foregoing photograph. Souvenir of one of the international conferences.

We wish to express to Chevalier Jackson, M.D., D.Sc., F.A.C.S.,
our warmest gratitude and deepest appreciation.
His teaching, apostolic in design and brilliant in execution,
has opened to us the difficult road of peroral endoscopy,
and his infinite modesty, untiring patience, and
meticulous care will be a constant inspiration.

Leonard S. Nolan. Ian W. MacGregor Fred Stokes
Dr. P. Jims C. Gill Carey. Lindley Sewell.
V. Wan Caneghem. T. B. Jobson A. Soulas
A. Tapia H. Hutin E. Ducoin

UNIVERSITY OF PARIS

OTO-RHINO-LARYNGOLOGY,
FACIO-MAXILLARY SURGERY AND
BRONCHO-OESOPHAGOSCOPY
1925

Conferring of the decoration, Chevalier de la Légion d'Honneur, at the American Hospital in Paris.

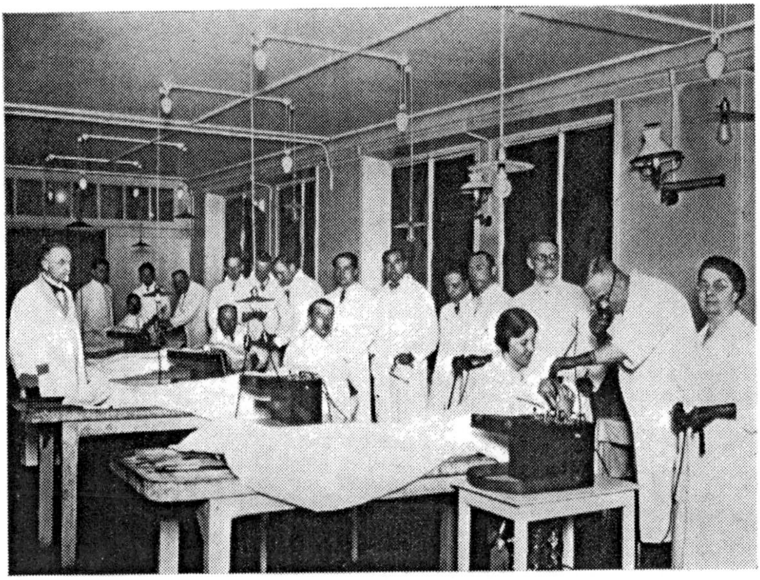

Working on the problems of bronchoscopy with an international group at the University of Paris, Department of Professor Lemaître.

One of the international groups forgathered at the University of Paris for the study of problems of bronchoscopy and esophagoscopy.

Christmas in the bronchoscopic clinic ward. Each longing mother at home always got a photograph at Christmas time. Encouraging letters were also sent at frequent intervals.

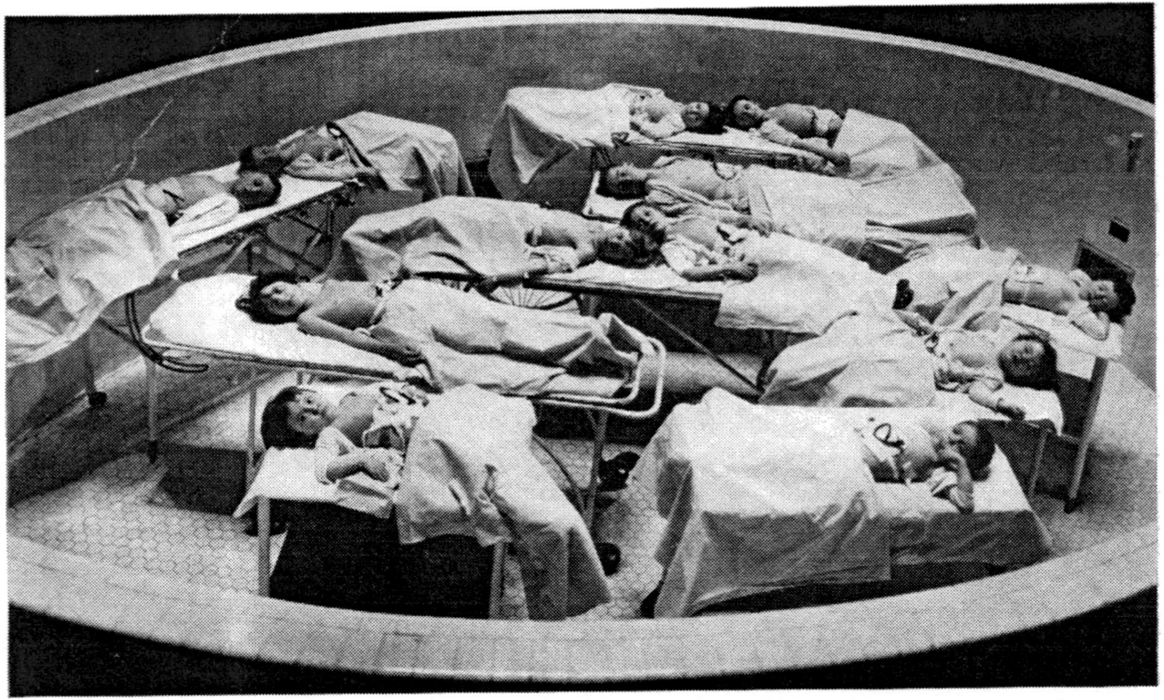

Before passage of the Federal Caustic Poison Act. Twelve children under treatment in the bronchoscopic clinic at one time. All had been unable to swallow food or water because of strictures from burns caused by swallowing household lye from containers that had no warning labels. They were safely over the emergency and had gained weight when this photograph was taken.

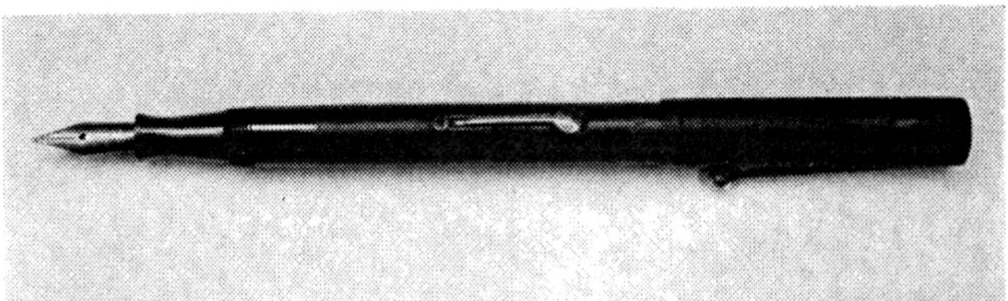

Pen with which President Coolidge signed the Federal Caustic Act. The pen was presented to Dr. Chevalier Jackson by Dr. Charles W. Richardson as a souvenir of the ultimate success of Dr. Jackson's prolonged efforts to obtain enactment of this piece of welfare legislation.

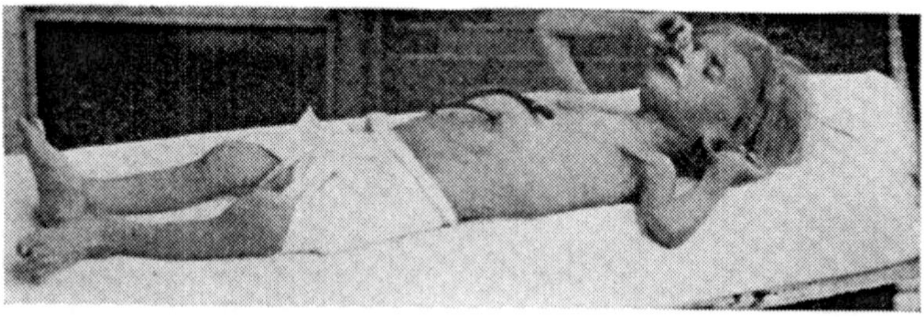

A boy burned by swallowing lye, before the passage of the Federal Caustic Poison Act, when household-lye containers had no warning label. A surgeon had prevented the child from dying of hunger and thirst by operative insertion of a rubber feeding tube, which also sustained life during the rather long period of treatment necessary to restore normal swallowing.

Bronchoscopic-clinic patients "playing doctor" at Temple University Hospital. All the dolls and toy animals have had tracheotomy done in imitation of the "surgeon" and "nurse" whose own larynges had been partly destroyed by diphtheria. Children imitate what they see. The boy has imitated even the pose of the hands of Chevalier Jackson.

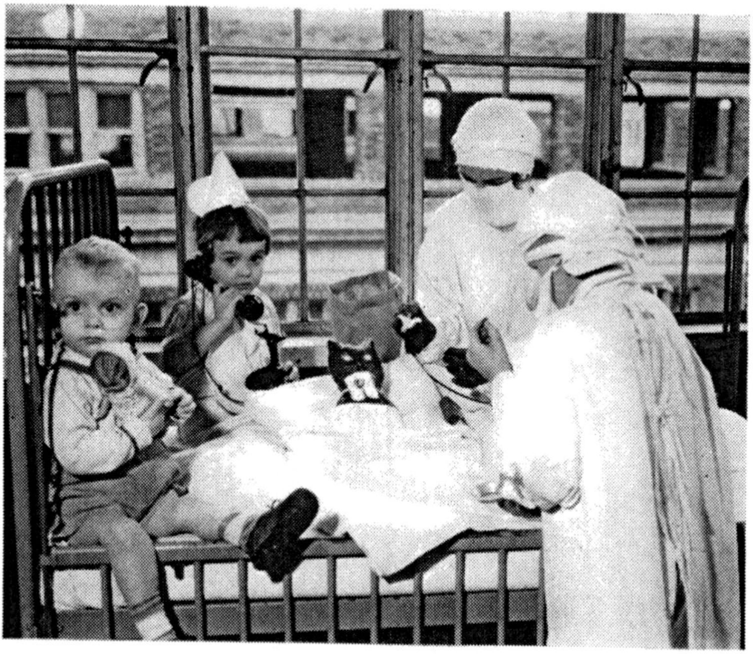

"Operation" (tracheotomy) on a toy cat by patients in the children's bronchoscopic ward at Temple University Hospital. Children imitate their elders. This and the preceding illustration were used in propaganda to prevent foreign-body accidents. Parents unconsciously, by bad example, teach children to put pins, coins and other potential foreign bodies into the mouth.

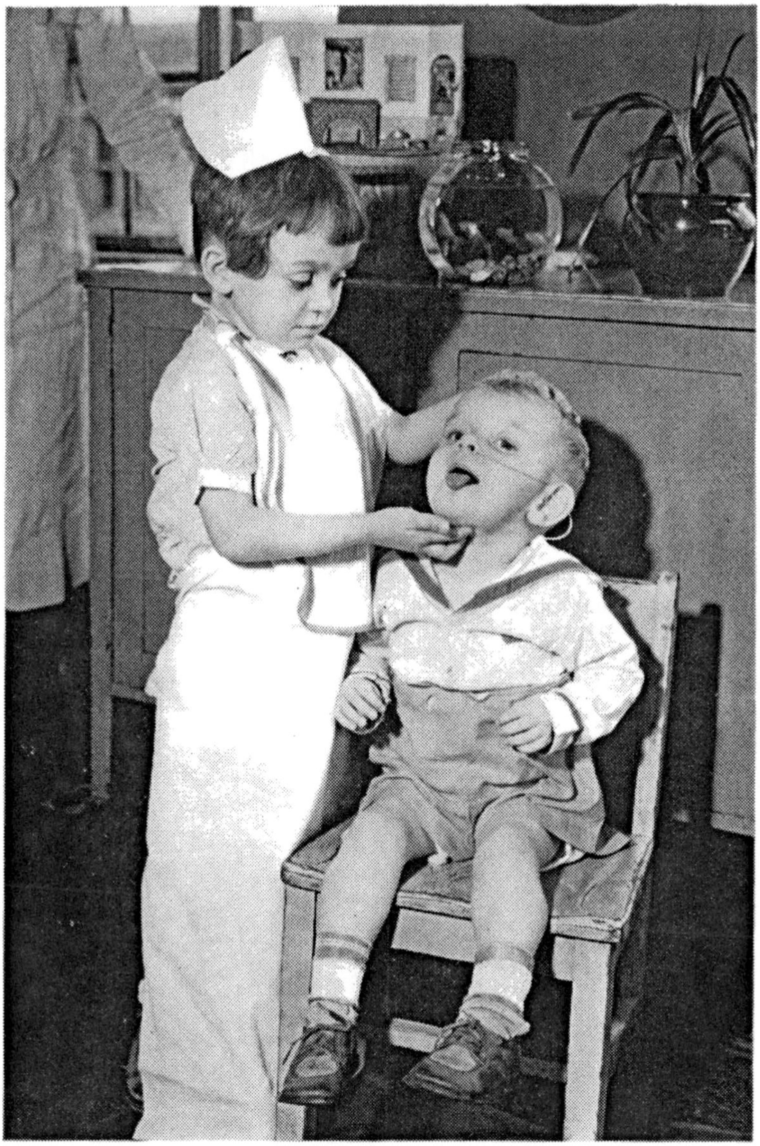

Playing doctor.

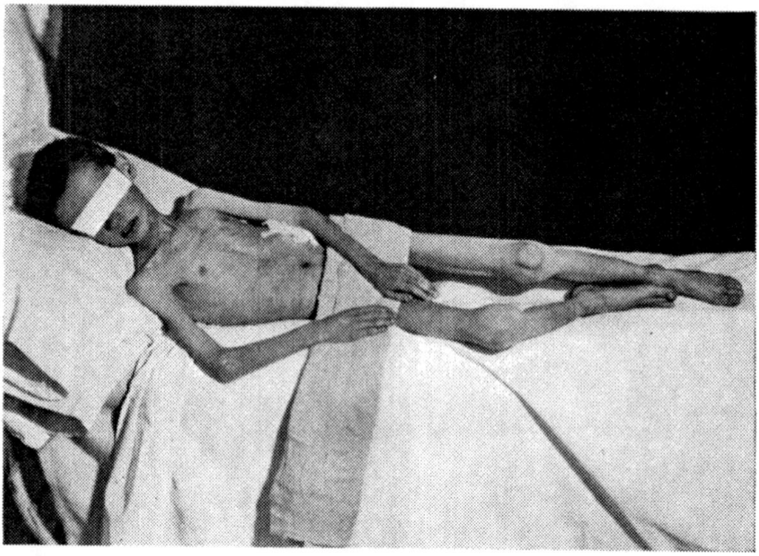

A boy nearly dead and emaciated almost to a skeleton from abscesses in his lung due to prolonged sojourn of a coin he had swallowed. Had he been taken to any hospital promptly, the abscesses could have been prevented by esophagoscopic removal of the coin. Better still, such an accident could have been avoided if the coin had not been put in the mouth.

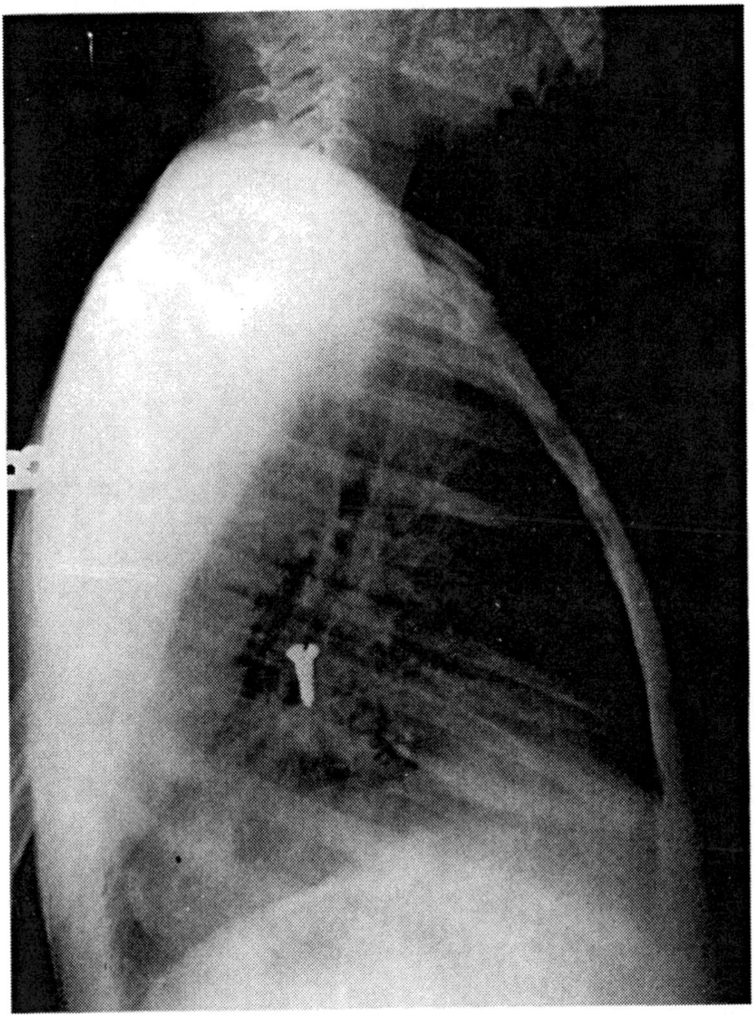

A screw in a bronchial tube of a child revealed by the X-ray. Life can be saved by the bronchoscope but such accidents are preventable.

Each specimen is evidence that a child's life is in danger when he plays with toys smaller than his fist. Teaching prevention of foreign-body accidents has been a lifetime's work of the author.

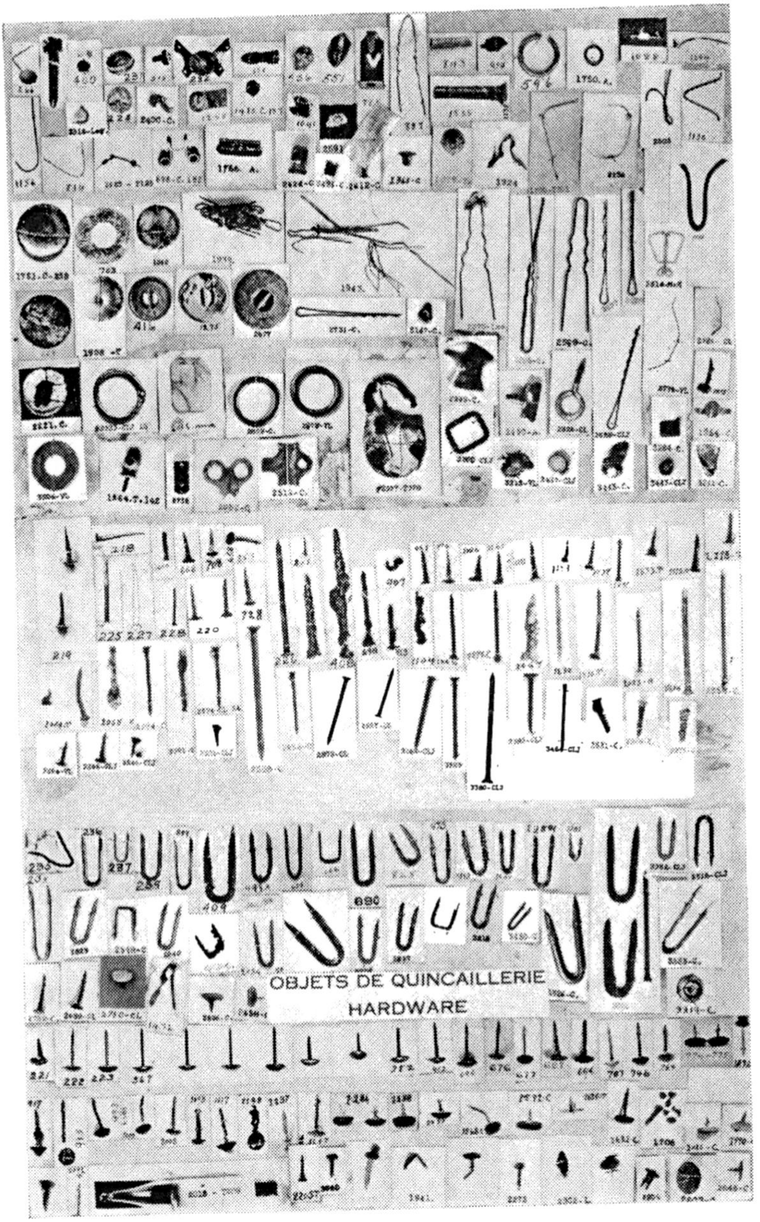

Carelessness is obvious when children are allowed to put hardware in the mouth. The need of preventive education is manifest.

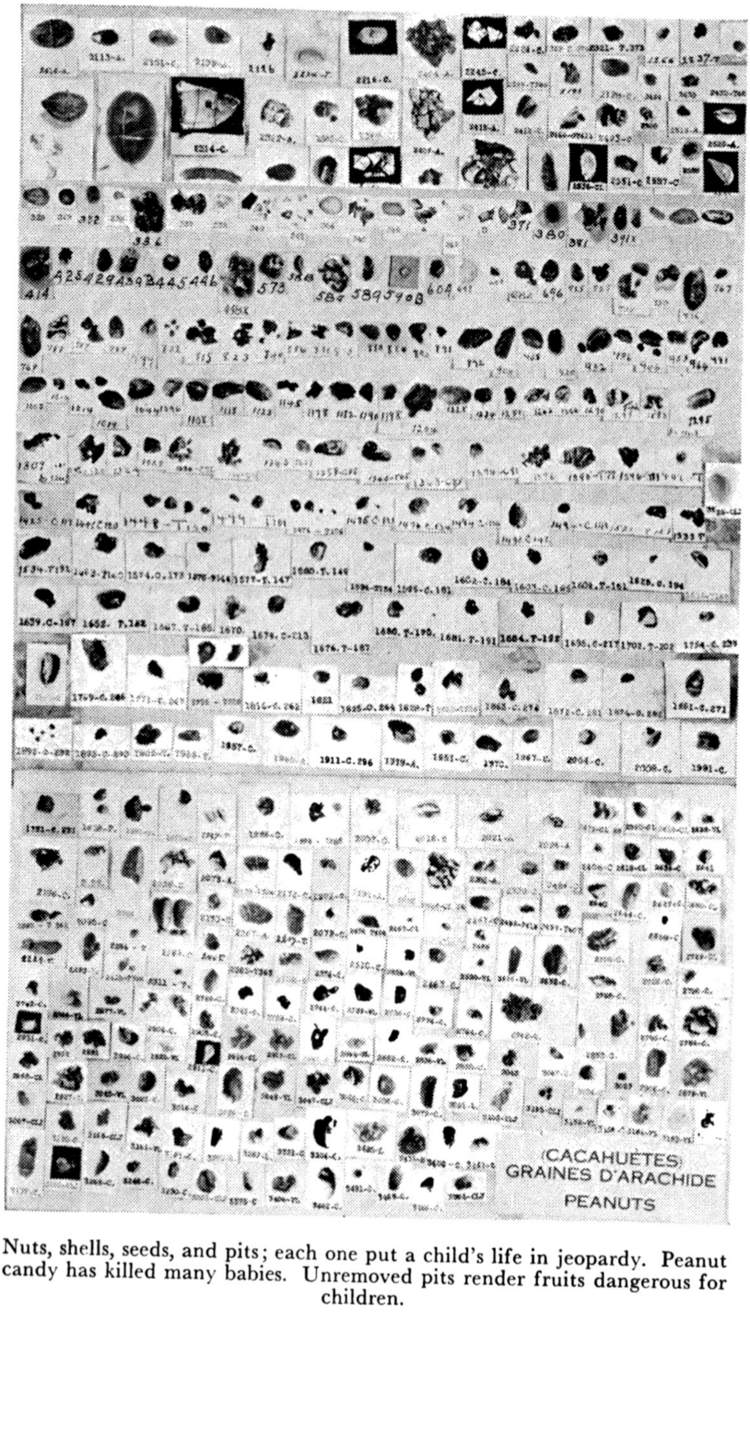

Nuts, shells, seeds, and pits; each one put a child's life in jeopardy. Peanut candy has killed many babies. Unremoved pits render fruits dangerous for children.

Evidence of the filthy and careless habit of putting coins in the mouth. A child's life was avoidably endangered by each coin. Such accidents are preventable by the simple expedient of keeping such things out of the mouth.

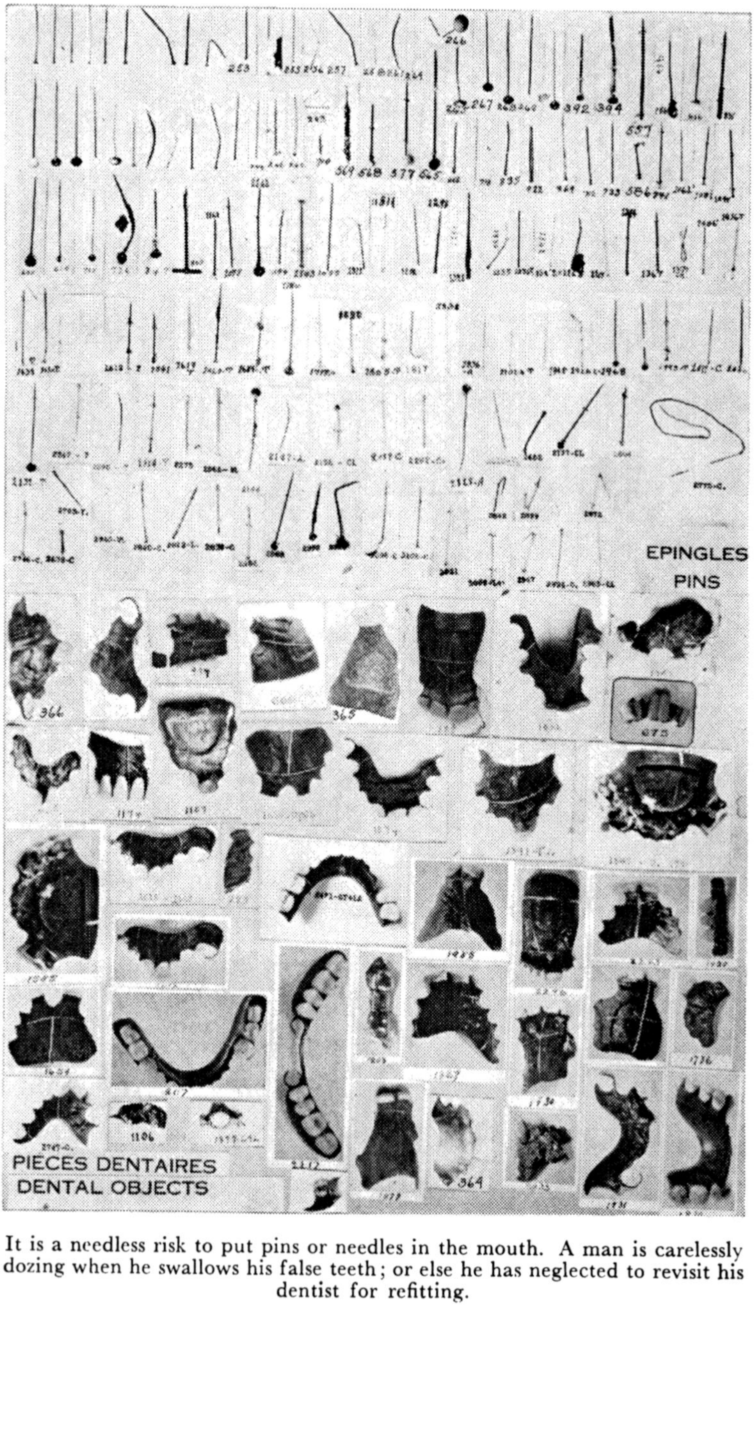

It is a needless risk to put pins or needles in the mouth. A man is carelessly dozing when he swallows his false teeth; or else he has neglected to revisit his dentist for refitting.

Specimens of bones that stuck in the throat. Each one is evidence of carelessness in eating or preparing food. Obviously prevention should be taught.

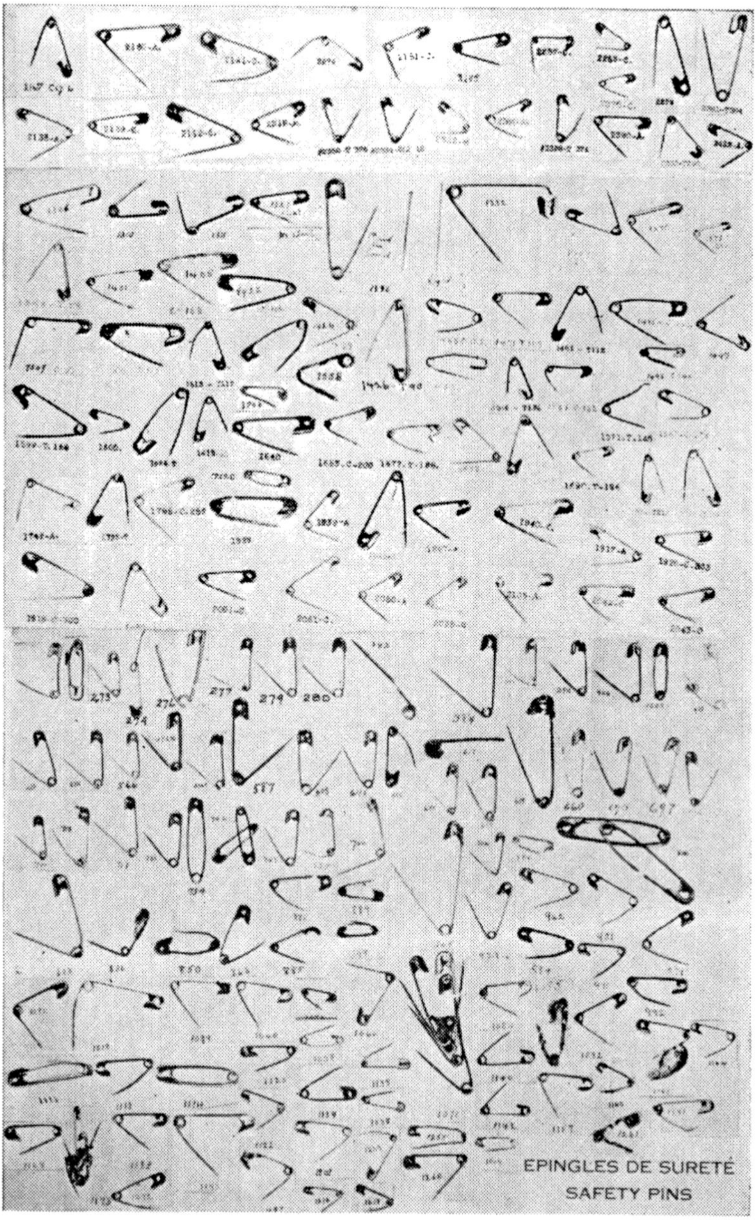

Each pin needlessly endangered the life of a child. Safety pins are really danger pins; they should be kept closed and out of the reach of children.

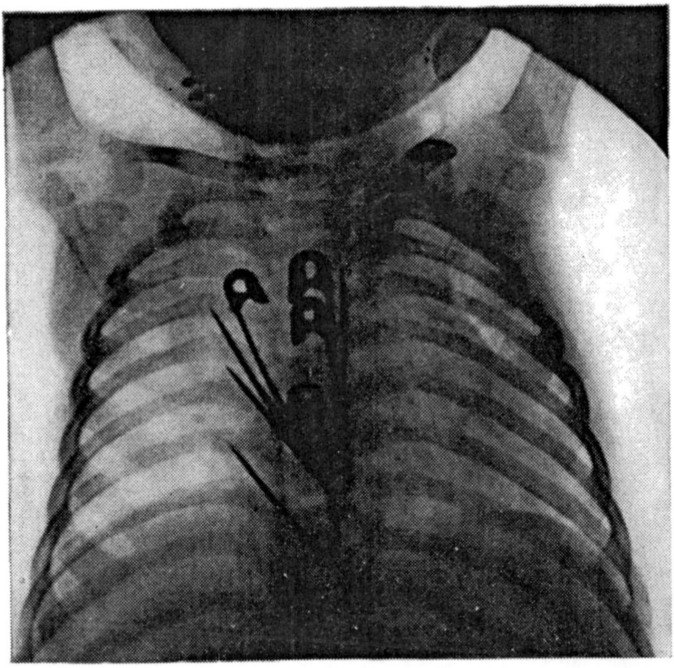

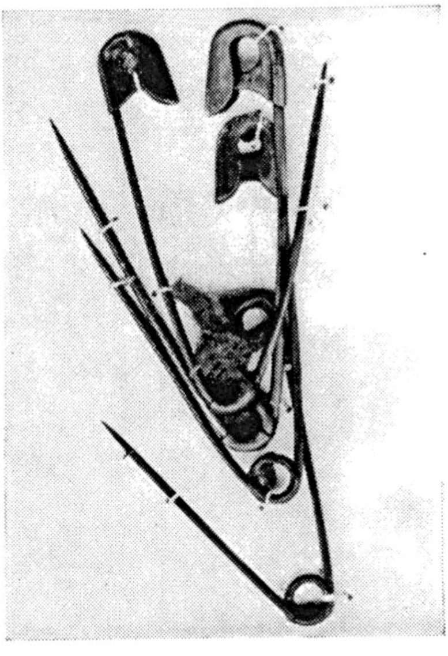

That the problem of the safe removal of this entangled mass of huge safety pins was solved does not alter the fact that when a nine-months-old baby gets an opportunity to swallow such objects, some one was careless. It is a platitude to say that prevention is better than cure.

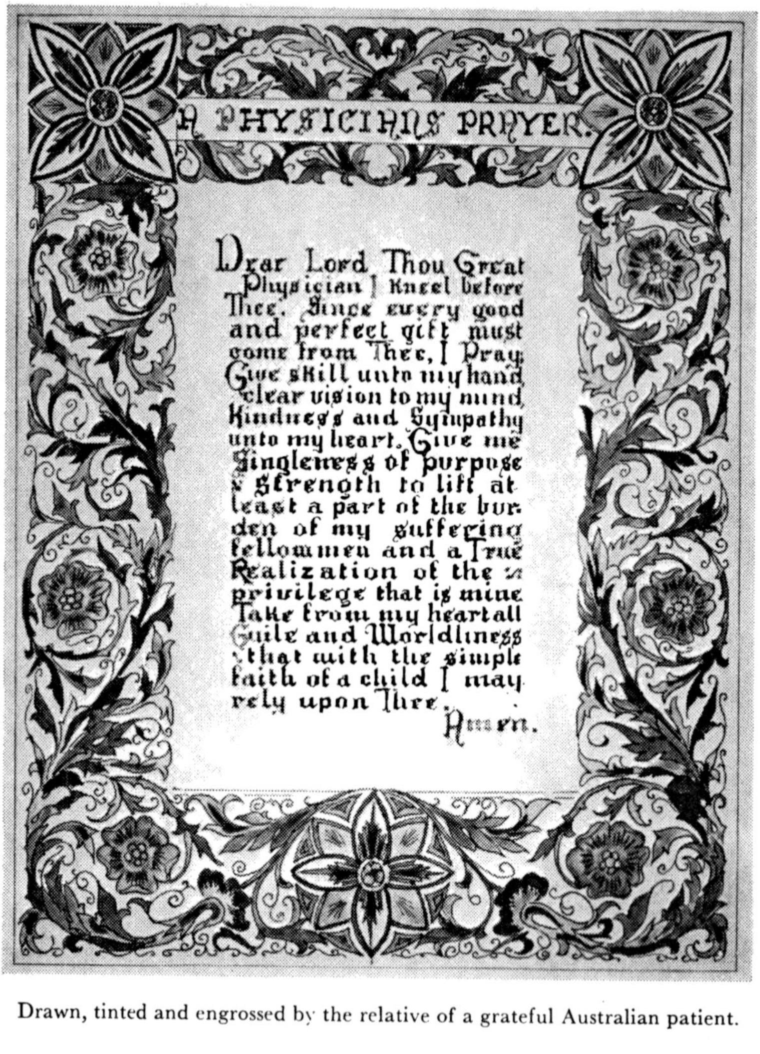

A PHYSICIANS PRAYER.
Dear Lord Thou Great
Physician I Kneel before
Thee. Since every good
and perfect gift must
come from Thee, I Pray:
Give skill unto my hand,
clear vision to my mind,
Kindness and Sympathy
unto my heart. Give me
Singleness of purpose
& strength to lift at
least a part of the bur-
den of my suffering
fellowmen and a True
Realization of the
privilege that is mine
Take from my heart all
Guile and Worldliness
that with the simple
faith of a child I may
rely upon Thee.
Amen.

Drawn, tinted and engrossed by the relative of a grateful Australian patient.

CPSIA information can be obtained at www.ICGtesting.com
Printed in the USA
BVOW012329280413

319346BV00017B/794/P